PRO TOOLS® 101

OFFICIAL COURSEWARE, VERSION 9.0

Avid Technology, Inc. | Frank D. Cook

Course Technology PTR

A part of Cengage Learning

COURSE TECHNOLOGY
CENGAGE Learning™

Australia, Brazil, Japan, Korea, Mexico, Singapore, Spain, United Kingdom, United States

COURSE TECHNOLOGY
CENGAGE Learning™

Pro Tools® 101 Official Courseware, Version 9.0
Avid Technology, Inc. and Frank D. Cook

Publisher and General Manager, Course Technology PTR:
Stacy L. Hiquet

Associate Director of Marketing:
Sarah Panella

Manager of Editorial Services:
Heather Talbot

Marketing Manager:
Mark Hughes

Executive Editor:
Mark Garvey

Project Editor/Copy Editor:
Cathleen D. Small

Interior Layout Tech:
Bill Hartman

Cover Designers:
Avid Technology and Mike Tanamachi

DVD-ROM Producers:
Avid Technology and Brandon Penticuff

Indexer:
Larry Sweazy

Proofreaders:
Ann Fisher and Michael Beady

Course Technology, a part of Cengage Learning
20 Channel Center Street
Boston, MA 02210
USA

For product information and technology assistance, contact us at
Cengage Learning Customer & Sales Support, 1-800-354-9706.

For permission to use material from this text or product,
submit all requests online at **cengage.com/permissions**.
Further permissions questions can be e-mailed to
permissionrequest@cengage.com.

PT101, Version 9.0

PN: 9900-65037-00

All product features, specifications, system requirements, and availability are subject to change without notice.

Library of Congress Control Number: 2010939135

ISBN-13: 978-1-4354-5880-2

ISBN-10: 1-4354-5880-X

Cengage Learning is a leading provider of customized learning solutions with office locations around the globe, including Singapore, the United Kingdom, Australia, Mexico, Brazil, and Japan. Locate your local office at: **international.cengage.com/region**.

Cengage Learning products are represented in Canada by Nelson Education, Ltd.

For your lifelong learning solutions, visit **courseptr.com**.

Visit our corporate Web site at **cengage.com**.

Printed in the United States of America
1 2 3 4 5 6 7 14 13 12 11 10

This book is dedicated to musicians, sound designers, audio editors, mixing engineers, and Pro Tools enthusiasts everywhere—industry leaders of the future.

Foreword

For more than 20 years, Avid has been developing Pro Tools training material and making it available for various audiences. Pro Tools training has been offered through venues such as Digidesign's formal Reseller Certification Programs, training sessions at tradeshow events and tours, and Avid's initial Pro Tools courses at Authorized Education Centers.

In 2001, Digidesign recognized the growing need for an official training program to serve the emerging education market in professional audio and post-production, as well as an industry need for Pro Tools certification. We began conducting research for the program, meeting with major audio engineering schools and audio industry leaders.

The result was the Digidesign Training & Education Program, which established comprehensive course and exam requirements for students with a choice of either a music production or a video post-production emphasis. Official training centers were established worldwide, offering two levels of certification for Pro Tools users within each emphasis: Operator certification and Expert certification. The Digidesign Training & Education Program first published the *Pro Tools 101* book in 2002 for Pro Tools version 5. Additional Operator- and Expert-level courseware was developed and published for use exclusively by Digidesign's Authorized Training Partners.

The Pro Tools courseware has since been continually updated, reflecting the features of various software updates.

In 2006, the training courseware was expanded, with the addition of a new Pro Tools 110 course and the later addition of the Pro Tools 310I course covering advanced ICON production techniques. Digidesign teamed with Thomson Course Technology PTR and Insource Writing Solutions to rework the *Pro Tools 101* book from the ground up and make it available through commercial distribution channels. For the first time, *Pro Tools 101* was made publicly available and offered through retail bookstores and outlets.

In 2008 and 2009, the VENUE 110V and 210V courses were added to the training curriculum, providing a certification option for live sound production. Also in 2009, we began research and development efforts toward a new course in the growing market of audio production for game development. Our Pro Tools 130 course, *Pro Tools for Game Audio*, became available in January 2010, and our Avid Authorized Training Partners quickly began implementation.

In this latest edition of the *Pro Tools 101* book, the content has been updated to reflect the exciting new world of Pro Tools 9, including support for high-definition sample rates and higher track counts, support for standalone operation and third-party interfaces, extensive new software features, and enhancements offered with the Complete Production Toolkit 2.

The book update also corresponds to changes to the larger training program. The Digidesign Training Partner Program has transitioned to become part of the new Avid Authorized Training Partner program. We also now offer a Pro Tools Certified User option associated with our 100-level Pro Tools courses.

With more than 300 training partners in over 30 different countries supporting more than 70,000 student enrollments to date, the Avid Worldwide Training program is the leading resource for training in Pro Tools software today. The Avid Certification Directory at www.avid.com offers a searchable database of more than 5,000 certified Pro Tools Operators and Experts. Avid continues to work with industry leaders in major audio production facilities to promote active recruiting of graduates trained in the curriculum. We are excited to be offering this updated book to complement the Pro Tools 9.0 release, and we encourage your participation in our program.

Andy Cook
Training Partner Program Manager
Avid Worldwide Training
November 2010

Acknowledgments

The following individuals have provided critical assistance, input, information, and material for this book and its many editions over the years.

Avid/Digidesign: Alex Steinhart, Andy Cook, Andy Hagerman, Anthony Gordon, Chandra Lynn, Cheryl Panepinto, Chris Now, Christopher Woodland, Dave Lebolt, Don Falcone, Eric Kuehnl, Greg Robles, Jim Metzendorf, John Given, Ken Johnson, Mark Altin, Mark Jeffery, Paul Foeckler, Rachelle McKenzie, Scott Church, Simon Sherbourne, Tim Carroll, Tim Mynett, Tom Dambly

Amanda Goodroe, DDB San Francisco

Frank Brooks, DDB San Francisco

Joe Kay, Independent Pro Tools Consultant

Joel Krantz, Independent Pro Tools Consultant

Mark Garvey at Course Technology PTR

Mark Hughes at Course Technology PTR

Rob Campbell at Encompass Audio

Special Thanks
Special thanks to Cathleen Small for diligently editing the manuscript and to William Hartman for providing continuous updates to the layout.

Extra-Special Thanks
Kudos and extra-special thanks to all Avid Authorized Training Partners and certified instructors, who have tirelessly worked with us to help shape this program and who have generously provided their valuable feedback for our courseware.

About the Authors

The courseware for this book was developed by Avid Worldwide Training, with contributions from numerous Avid staff and independent contractors. **Frank D. Cook** serves as the primary author, through an ongoing partnership between Insource Writing Solutions and Avid Technology, Inc.

Frank is a bass guitarist and longtime Pro Tools user. The owner of Insource Writing Solutions and NextPoint Training, Frank has worked in the technical publications and education industries for more than 15 years. As a writer, editor, technical publications manager, and business owner, Frank has authored and contributed to hundreds of guides, manuals, reports, and other publications for clients in a wide variety of industries. His writing and consulting company, Insource Writing Solutions, specializes in documentation for the digital audio industry. His new venture, NextPoint Training, focuses on advanced training in Pro Tools, VENUE, digital media, and related products and technologies.

Frank teaches Pro Tools courses as an Adjunct Professor at American River College in Sacramento, California.

Contents

Part I: Background Information

Part II: Working with Sessions

Chapter 7: Selecting and Navigating 129

Part III: Hands-On Projects

Part IV: Course Completion

Preface

Welcome to Pro Tools 101

Congratulations on entering the official Avid Worldwide Training program. This book represents the first step on your journey toward mastery of your Pro Tools system. The information and projects you will find here apply to all Pro Tools 9 systems. Whether you are interested only in self study or you would like to pursue formal certification through an Avid Authorized Training Partner, this book will develop your core skills and introduce you to the awesome power of Pro Tools. Avid's award-winning Pro Tools technology is embraced by audio production professionals around the world. Get ready to join their ranks as you unleash the creative power and technology of Pro Tools!

About This Book

We wrote this book for the audio enthusiast with relatively little Pro Tools experience. While *Pro Tools 101* can be completed through self study, Avid recommends obtaining hands-on experience through an instructor-led class offered by one of our authorized training partners. For more information on the classes offered through the Avid Worldwide Training program, visit www.avid.com, click on Support & Services, and then click on a Training link, or go directly to www.avid.com/training.

Pro Tools 9.0 Edition

This edition of *Pro Tools 101* has been updated and improved for Pro Tools 9.0. The material is focused to cover the basic principles you need to understand in order to complete a Pro Tools project, from initial setup to final mixdown. Whether your project involves recording live instruments, preparing MIDI sequences for virtual instruments, looping and beat-matching audio files, or editing notation and preparing scores, *Pro Tools 101* will teach you the steps required to succeed.

The DVD at the Back of the Book

Included at the back of this book is a DVD-ROM containing *Pro Tools 101* hands-on project files, introductory Pro Tools videos and video tutorials from the Pro Tools Accelerated series, and PDF files providing additional Pro Tools documentation.

Hands-On Projects

The Hands-On Projects folder on the DVD provides content for two projects included in Part III of this book. The Music Hands-On Project folder includes a session template file and associated media for Project 1, and the Post Hands-On Project folder includes a session template file and associated media for Project 2. These project folders will need to be copied to your hard drive for use with Pro Tools.

Video Extras

The Video Extras folder on the DVD includes various Pro Tools video files providing an introduction to the software and some of its features.

Also included in this folder is a collection of Pro Tools Accelerated tutorial videos covering popular virtual instruments, Elastic Audio features, and production techniques.

These video files are provided in a high-resolution format (1280×720). For best playback results, you should copy the files to a local hard drive prior to viewing them.

Documentation Extras

The Documentation Extras folder includes PDF files that provide additional information on Pro Tools 9 shortcuts and preference settings:

- Pro Tools Shortcuts
- Pro Tools Preferences Primer

Course Prerequisites

Most Pro Tools enthusiasts today have at least a passing familiarity with operating a computer. If you consider yourself a computer novice, however, you should review some basics before beginning this course. You will need to know how to complete such tasks as:

- Starting up the computer
- Using the mouse, standard menus, and keyboard commands for standard operating system commands
- Locating, moving, and renaming files and folders
- Opening, saving, and closing files

This course focuses on using Pro Tools in a digital audio recording and production environment. The work requires a basic understanding of recording techniques, processes, and equipment, such as the following:

- Miking techniques
- Mixer signal flow
- Audio monitoring equipment
- MIDI devices

If you are a beginner in the field of audio production, you can supplement this text with independently available literature on audio recording tools and techniques. Visit your local bookstore, library, or community college to research available study materials and courses.

Course Organization and Sequence

This course has been designed to familiarize you with the practices and processes you will use to complete a recording project. The material is organized into four parts. Part I provides background information that will help you understand the material that is presented later and put it into context. Part II presents specific processes and techniques that you would use to complete a project, from creating a new session to completing a final mixdown. Part III provides tutorial-style walkthroughs of various tasks required to complete two hands-on projects (included on the enclosed DVD). Part IV, to be completed at any Avid Authorized Training Partner location, includes information on additional projects and course completion options.

Part I: Background Information

Part I focuses primarily on background information relevant to Pro Tools and audio production. This part builds a foundation for using Pro Tools by introducing concepts of digital audio, Pro Tools hardware configurations, Pro Tools session file structures, and the Pro Tools user interface and tool set.

Part II: Working with Sessions

Part II provides information and instructions for working with Pro Tools sessions to accomplish common audio production tasks. In this part, we discuss creating sessions, creating audio and MIDI recordings, navigating within audio and MIDI recordings, and editing and mixing using Pro Tools.

Part III: Hands-On Projects

Part III is designed to provide you with experience applying the concepts of Part II. Two projects have been selected to represent typical scenarios and workflows encountered in music and post-production environments. The project tutorials follow roughly the same progression as the chapters in Part II. The tutorials are written to allow students to complete the projects without having first completed Part II, enabling a hands-on learning experience that draws on Part II as a reference.

Part IV: Course Completion

Part IV of the Pro Tools 101 course can be completed in an instructor-led environment at an authorized Pro Tools training center. In this part of the course, students have the opportunity to work on additional projects using a variety of Pro Tools hardware components.

Conventions and Symbols Used in This Book

Following are some of the conventions and symbols we use in this book. We've tried to use familiar conventions and symbols whose meanings are self-evident.

Menu and Key Commands

Menu choices and keyboard commands are typically capitalized. Hierarchy is shown using the greater than symbol (>), keystroke combinations are indicated using the plus sign (+), and mouse-click operations are indicated by hyphenated strings, where needed. Brackets ([ ]) are used to indicate key presses on the numeric keypad.

Convention	Action
File > Save Session	Choose Save Session from the File menu.
Ctrl+N	Hold down the Ctrl key and press the N key.
Command-click (Mac OS)	Hold down the Command key and click the mouse button.
Right-click	Click with the right mouse button.
Press [1]	Press 1 on the numeric keypad

Icons

The following icons are used to call attention to tips, important notices, shortcuts, cross-references, and examples.

 Tips provide helpful hints, related steps, or alternative methods of working.

 Important notices provide alerts to operations that may affect audio, system performance, or Pro Tools session data or may otherwise require caution.

 Shortcuts show useful keyboard, mouse, or control surface shortcuts that can help you work more efficiently.

 Cross-references alert you to another section, book, or Pro Tools guide that provides additional information on the current topic.

 Examples provide descriptions of typical situations in which a concept is applied.

Introduction to Pro Tools

Pro Tools—the most widely used application for music and post-production in the world today—is a Digital Audio Workstation (DAW) that uses the power of the personal computer to integrate hard disk audio recording, graphical audio editing, MIDI sequencing, notation, digital signal processing (DSP), and mixing into a fast and intuitive application for personal and professional projects. Other features, such as desktop video integration and support for Open Media Framework (OMF) and Advanced Authoring Format (AAF) files, allow Pro Tools to fill almost any role in post-production—from home DV movie projects to feature film productions.

Creation

With the increasing availability of software-based virtual instruments, synthesizers, and samplers, more people than ever are using Pro Tools as a creative tool for writing and developing their projects. In the early stages of a project, Pro Tools provides a natural environment for experimentation and sound design, and its flexibility allows you to extend your creativity to every stage of a project.

Recording

Disk-based recording opens the door to an entirely new world of audio production. As the cost of hard disk storage continues to decline, the quality and flexibility afforded by digital audio recording continually improves with advancements in technology. Removing the restrictions of tape has changed the audio industry forever.

Editing

The impact of non-destructive editing on audio production is similar to that of the word processor on writing or of computer-aided design on architecture. Pro Tools provides straightforward audio editing features designed for efficiency, freeing up more time for you to put into the creative aspects of a project.

Mixing

Over the years, Pro Tools has emerged as the hub of the mixing process. Multitudes of professional-quality plug-ins are included standard with Pro Tools 9. Combined with a growing array of third-party plug-ins, these tools provide options to suit all tastes, needs, and individual preferences. Mix automation in Pro Tools takes your mix to a whole new level, with incredibly powerful, yet remarkably simple automation tools.

Mastering

While mastering will always be an art unto itself, the benefits of Pro Tools—the highest sound quality and the ultimate in digital processing—lend themselves to the mastering process. From surround sound DVD encoding, to high-quality stereo mixes for CD, to encoding for MP3 files, Pro Tools is ideal for final preparation and delivery in a variety of formats.

The Avid Authorized Training Program

Pro Tools 101 has been written to serve as a textbook for learning Pro Tools. In addition to being an off-the-shelf guide for consumers, this book is also the official text for the first course in the Pro Tools certification program. By completing the coursework in this text, you are taking an important step toward certification. And consider this: Having a certification from Avid just might help you land that next gig, find others with similar skills and interests, or even obtain your dream job in the industry.

To become certified in Pro Tools, you must enroll in a program at an Avid Authorized Training Partner location, where you can complete additional Pro Tools coursework and take one of Avid's Certification Exams. Detailed information on current requirements is available at avid.com/training.

Curriculum and Certification Levels

Avid offers three levels of certification associated with Pro Tools Training: Pro Tools Certified User, Pro Tools HD Operator, and Pro Tools HD Expert. The 100-, 200-, and 300-level Pro Tools courses are designed to prepare candidates for each of these certification levels, respectively.

User Certification

The User certification program prepares individuals to operate a Pro Tools system in an independent production environment. Courses associated with User certification include Pro Tools 101, *Introduction to Pro Tools*, and Pro Tools 110, *Pro Tools Production I*. These core courses can be complemented with Pro Tools 130, *Pro Tools for Game Audio*.

Operator Certification

The Operator certification program prepares engineers and editors to competently operate a Pro Tools|HD system in a professional environment. Candidates can specialize in Music Production, Post-Production, or both.

Courses associated with Operator certification include Pro Tools 201, *Pro Tools Production II*, Pro Tools 210M, *Music Production Techniques*, and Pro Tools 210P, *Post Production Techniques*. Control surface certification options and a live sound certification option are also available at the Operator level.

Expert Certification

The Expert curriculum offers professionals the highest level of proficiency with individual or networked Pro Tools|HD systems operating in a professional, fast-paced environment. Candidates can specialize in Music Production, Post-Production, and/or ICON worksurface techniques.

Courses associated with Expert certification include Pro Tools 310M, *Advanced Music Production Techniques*, Pro Tools 310P, *Advanced Post Production Techniques*, and Pro Tools 310I, *Advanced ICON Techniques*.

Courses Offered in the Training Program

Avid Authorized Training Partners offer three levels of coursework to help you become proficient using Pro Tools: 100-level, 200-level, and 300-level.

- 100-level Pro Tools courses provide the foundational skills needed to learn and function within the Pro Tools environment at a basic level. The goal of the courses at this level is to help individuals start working on their own projects in Pro Tools.

  The 100-level VENUE coursework covers essential skills for operating a VENUE system in a live sound environment.

- 200-level courses build the fundamental skills needed to competently operate a Pro Tools|HD system, control surface, or VENUE system in a professional environment. Pro Tools coursework at this level involves a study of production essentials and post-production, music production, or control surface techniques.

    VENUE coursework at the 200-level involves comprehensive hands-on training on a VENUE system, including system hardware and software configuration.

- 300-level courses focus on advanced operation of Pro Tools|HD systems for music or post-production. Coursework involves working in real-world scenarios through example exercises from advanced music production projects (Music Production track), TV and film production projects (Post-Production track), or direct hands-on worksurface techniques (ICON worksurface track).

Training Program Course Configuration

The coursework for the Training Program has evolved and expanded over the years. Avid uses a version-specific approach to course design, enabling our training partners to teach classes based on products and software versions that meet their particular needs and training environments.

Audio Curriculum

Avid's audio coursework includes programs supporting certification in dedicated focus areas, including Pro Tools, Worksurface operation, and Live Sound. Available certification paths are illustrated below. Course components are designed to be completed individually and in sequence. However, individual training partners may offer the same content through slightly different class configurations.

Descriptions of each of the courses offered through the Avid Training Program are available on the Avid website. (Go to www.avid.com/US/support/training/curriculum.)

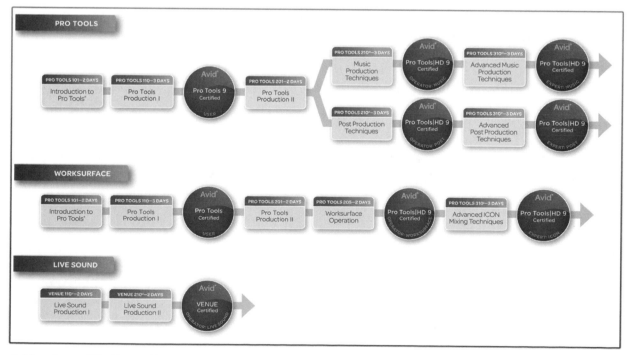

Avid audio certification options

Pro Tools User Certification

Pro Tools 101 is the first course of study in the training curriculum targeting User Certification. The User Certification training material (100-level coursework) prepares students to operate a Pro Tools system in an independent production environment. Following completion of the User Certification coursework and certification exam, students can proceed to the 200-level courses to pursue Operator Certification.

Pro Tools User Certification path

How Can I Learn More?

If you want to learn more about the Avid Training Program, please check out our official online resource by going to www.avid.com/training. There you will find information about our training partners, specifics on the various certification options available, and detailed course descriptions for each course offered through the program.

DVD-ROM Downloads

If you purchased an ebook version of this book, and the book had a companion DVD-ROM, you may download the contents from www.courseptr.com/downloads.

If your book has a DVD-ROM, please check our website for any updates or errata files. You may download files from www.courseptr.com/downloads.

PART I

Background Information

Components

- Chapter 1, "Getting to Know Pro Tools"
- Chapter 2, "Getting Inside Pro Tools"

Overview

Part I focuses on background information relevant to Pro Tools and audio production. This part builds a foundation for using Pro Tools by introducing Pro Tools' capabilities in audio, MIDI, notation, mixing, and video post-production; providing a brief history of Pro Tools systems; introducing concepts of digital audio; and providing an overview of available Pro Tools configurations. Chapter 2 introduces basic Pro Tools operations and functions, reviews the Pro Tools session file structure, and provides an overview of the Pro Tools user interface, tool set, and modes of operation.

Chapter 1

Getting to Know Pro Tools

This chapter introduces you to Pro Tools' capabilities in audio, MIDI, mixing, and video post-production. You will learn about the evolution of Pro Tools technology and get an introduction to factors that affect digital audio and analog-to-digital conversion. You will also get a glimpse of what's new in Pro Tools 9.0 and learn about the different Pro Tools configurations available today.

Objectives

After you complete this chapter, you will be able to:

- Identify the advantages of recording and editing in the digital realm
- Recognize the contributions of historical developments in sampling and sound editing, MIDI technology, computer I/O, and recording technology to today's digital audio workstation
- Describe the relationship between sample rate and frequency response in digital audio
- Describe the relationship between bit depth and dynamic range in digital audio
- Recognize components and features of various Pro Tools systems

What Is Pro Tools?

Pro Tools is the most widely used application for music and post-production (sound for film, video, and multimedia) in the world today, integrating capabilities in audio and MIDI recording, composition, editing, and mixing, as well as support for desktop video. As such, Pro Tools software empowers both music and post-production professionals to easily achieve all of their production tasks within one easy-to-use interface.

At its core, Pro Tools is a multi-track software-based digital recording and editing system. It uses the power of the personal computer to combine hard-disk audio recording, graphical audio editing, MIDI sequencing, digital signal processing (DSP), and mixing into an integrated system. With the ability to incorporate QuickTime and Avid video files, Pro Tools has also established itself as an industry choice for post-production video editing and mixing to picture.

Audio

Pro Tools works with audio that is stored electronically in digital format. The software records audio and stores it as files on your hard drive. Like a digital camera that stores a photograph as a collection of discrete pixels, Pro Tools stores recorded audio as a collection of discrete samples. Pro Tools supports audio formats with resolutions up to 24 bits and sample rates up to 192 kHz.

Just as you can use an image editor to modify, enhance, and otherwise alter your digital photographs in creative ways, so too can you use Pro Tools to take your digital audio in new directions. Working in the digital realm makes it easy to copy, paste, move, delete, modify, and otherwise manipulate your recordings. Pro Tools lets you trim waveforms, reprocess regions of audio, pitch-correct a compromised performance, replace drum sounds, rearrange song sections, and more. With Elastic Audio, you have the power to manipulate the speed of your audio clips in real time, allowing you to freely experiment with tempo. You can even quantize audio for quick rhythmic fixes or creative exploration.

MIDI

Using built-in sequencing technology, Pro Tools also enables you to record and edit MIDI data in the same work environment as your audio recordings. MIDI recordings differ from their digital counterparts in that they capture performance event data rather than sound samples. You can record MIDI signals from a keyboard or other device through a MIDI or USB interface and then edit the data using Pro Tools' intuitive graphical display. Pro Tools' MIDI Editor windows provide a platform for detailed MIDI editing on one track or on multiple superimposed tracks.

A Pro Tools 9.0 session can have up to 512 MIDI tracks in addition to its Audio tracks. Available features include MIDI Time Stamping, Groove Quantize, Restore Performance, native ReWire support, tick-based and sample-based timelines, and a growing array of plug-in virtual instruments. Pro Tools 9.0 includes several great-sounding virtual instrument plug-ins from Avid's Advanced Instrument Research group.

Notation

Pro Tools supports standard music notation display for MIDI notes. MIDI Editor windows provide a Notation view, in which each MIDI and Instrument track is represented on a separate staff. Additionally, Pro Tools includes a dedicated Score Editor window, allowing you to view, edit, arrange, and print MIDI data from your session as music notation.

The notation features and Editor windows in Pro Tools provide productivity and workflow enhancements for composers, songwriters, and others. With a focus on speed and usability, the Notation view and Score Editor window provide additional ways to display and work with your music, utilizing Sibelius-quality music notation and printing capabilities.

Mixing

Beyond recording, editing, and arranging, Pro Tools offers a software-based mixing environment that provides control over signal routing, effects processing, signal levels, panning, and more. The mixing operations in Pro Tools can be automated and stored with your session, enabling you to recall, edit, and refine your mixes over time. When you save a session, all routing, automation, mixing, and effects settings remain exactly as you've left them.

Additionally, Pro Tools software can be combined with Avid and third-party hardware in various configurations to provide multiple channels of simultaneous input and output for your Pro Tools sessions. Massive sessions including up to 192 simultaneous Audio tracks can be managed without audio degradation. Pro Tools systems can range from very simple to extremely advanced and powerful.

Post-Production

Pro Tools also provides a powerful platform for audio post-production tasks. You can import QuickTime movies, Avid video files, or Windows Media (VC-1 AP) clips (Windows systems only) and use Pro Tools' fast, random-access visual reference as you "sweeten" the audio by adding and modifying sound effects, music, Foley, and dialog. With support for QuickTime HD, multiple Video tracks, and video editing, you can now perform non-destructive editing and arranging of video files and scenes like never before. When completed, your finished movie file can be exported with the final audio mix embedded.

The Story of Pro Tools

The art of manipulating digital audio has evolved with, and been dramatically influenced by, the evolution of Pro Tools. Introduced in 1991 by Digidesign, Pro Tools helped pioneer the concept of multi-track digital audio recording and is recognized for having revolutionized the audio recording industry. While Pro Tools 9.0 introduces a unified software platform and loads of new capabilities for native systems, the core functionality of Pro Tools traces its roots to humble beginnings and the experimental work of the company's founders, Peter Gotcher and Evan Brooks.

In the Beginning

In the early 1980s, Peter Gotcher and Evan Brooks were college band-mates searching for a new sound. In their quest, the two devised a process for recording drum and percussion sounds onto computer EPROM chips.

Recognizing a growing market in electronic music, Peter and Evan began offering their chips for retail. Soon they were producing multiple chip sets, including Rock Drums, Electronic Drums, Latin Percussion, Sound Effects, and more.

Early drum-sound chip sets

In 1984, Peter and Evan formed Digidrums and found themselves selling their drum chips by the tens of thousands. With this success, they forged ahead into other types of software and hardware design.

Among their software projects was a product named Sound Designer, which enabled users to edit sounds captured by a sampling keyboard. Sound Designer was the first commercial product to combine waveform editing with a front panel emulation/editor.

The original Sound Designer package

Evolving into Digidesign

In 1985, the company changed its name to Digidesign. Over the next few years, Digidesign began developing products for working with MIDI and synthesis on Macintosh computers.

By 1987, Digidesign began prototyping a mono sample playback card for digital audio, and the following year, the company released Sound Accelerator, a CD-quality two-channel output card for the Mac II. This proved to be the first step toward enabling computer systems to provide professional-quality audio output.

Digidesign continued to develop software products for sampling and synthesis. At the same time, the company began work on products designed for digital recording. In 1989, Digidesign released Sound Tools, a two-track hard-disk recorder. Billed as the world's first "tapeless recording studio," Sound Tools consisted of Sound Designer II software, a Sound Accelerator card, and a hardware box called the AD-In that provided two analog-to-digital converters.

Components of the Sound Tools system

In 1990, the first AudioMedia card was created and marketed toward musicians, consumers, and independent studios. Its low cost helped drive the "democratization" of music and the recording industry, making hard-disk audio recording accessible to the masses.

The Birth of Pro Tools

The first-generation Pro Tools system was released in 1991, supporting four tracks of audio. Eventually, using additional cards and interfaces, these Pro Tools systems expanded to support up to 16 tracks of simultaneous recording and playback.

In 1992, Session 8 was released as the first Windows-based version of Pro Tools. Two years later, Digidesign introduced Pro Tools TDM, opening the door for real-time effects plug-ins as we now know them.

The Pro Tools TDM system utilized Time Division Multiplexing (TDM) technology to reliably route multiple streams of digital audio data between system components. TDM technology paved the way for rapid expansion among third-party applications and plug-in developers.

By March 1995, Pro Tools was recognized as having dramatically changed the economics of the recording industry, providing the same capabilities found in million-dollar studios at prices that small studios could afford. That year, Digidesign merged with its biggest customer, Avid Technology.

Early Pro Tools system

The Session 8 system for Windows NT

Pro Tools Matures

In 1997, Pro Tools|24 was released, offering 24-bit audio capabilities. These systems included the 888|24 I/O audio interface, new cards called DSP Farms, an increased number of inputs and outputs, and higher track counts than ever before.

The first Pro Tools TDM system for Windows was released in 1998. The following year, Pro Tools LE was introduced, providing host-based audio processing.

As Pro Tools systems evolved, so did the need for compatible mixing consoles and control surfaces. Operating as a division of Avid, Digidesign soon began offering a line of dedicated control surfaces for Pro Tools, starting with the ProControl console in 1998 and followed by Control|24 in 2001. These consoles provided touch-sensitive control of mixing, automation, and plug-in parameters.

ProControl integrated control surface for Pro Tools TDM systems

The Control|24 integrated front end for Pro Tools LE and TDM systems

The influence of Pro Tools continued to spread, and in 2001, Digidesign received a Technical GRAMMY® Award from the National Academy of Recording Arts and Sciences®, for "breaking the boundaries of digital recording and revolutionizing the way music is produced."

In 2002, Pro Tools|HD systems were unveiled as successors to Pro Tools TDM and Pro Tools|24. These systems provided support for higher sample rates and very large mixing topologies, addressing the needs of high-end music and post-production studios.

On the opposite side of the spectrum, the first Mbox was introduced as a portable "studio in a box" for the hobbyist and small project studio markets. The Digi 002 and Digi 002 Rack audio interface options followed, extending the capabilities of Pro Tools LE.

Growth of Avid Audio

In August 2004, Avid acquired M-Audio, a leading provider of computer audio peripherals, keyboard controllers, and related music and recording gear. The subsequent release of Pro Tools M-Powered software provided compatibility with a vast array of existing M-Audio devices and interfaces.

One year later, Avid acquired Wizoo Sound Design, a pioneering developer of virtual instruments, sample libraries, and real-time effects. The Wizoo R&D team formed what is now Avid's Advanced Instrument Research (A.I.R.) group. The A.I.R. group has since developed a host of innovative plug-ins for Pro Tools, including all of the virtual instruments and effects in the Creative Collection (included with Pro Tools 9), as well as the Hybrid, Strike, Velvet, Structure, and Transfuser virtual instruments for Pro Tools.

In 2006, Sibelius Software Ltd. joined the Avid Audio family. Under Avid, Sibelius continues to develop and market its own line of software, including its well-known professional music notation package. Today, Pro Tools incorporates notation capabilities directly and can export MIDI data as a score for Sibelius software.

ICON Integrated Console Environment

The ICON integrated console environment debuted in 2004. ICON systems feature either the flagship D-Control worksurface or the medium-format D-Command worksurface. Both ICON options employ a modular architecture, allowing facilities to scale their system as needs dictate.

The ICON integrated console for Pro Tools

Expandable to 80 physical faders, D-Control provides a central mixing environment for facilities with larger rooms. D-Control includes a comprehensive array of touch-sensitive controls and provides operators with extensive hands-on control over their Pro Tools projects.

The more compact D-Command worksurface is expandable up to 40 physical faders, providing a similar feature set configured for single-operator facilities. D-Command offers hands-on control of Pro Tools in a smaller package.

ICON D-Control worksurface with 32 faders (expandable to 80 faders)

ICON D-Command ES worksurface with 24 faders (expandable to 40 faders)

VENUE Live Sound Environment

Digidesign introduced VENUE in 2005 as a purpose-built solution for live sound. VENUE is a state-of-the-art live sound mixing and production environment. VENUE systems seamlessly integrate with Pro Tools for direct recording and playback of multi-track live performances.

A VENUE system is built around one of three consoles: the flagship VENUE D-Show mixing console, the smaller VENUE Profile, or the compact and fully integrated VENUE SC48.

The VENUE D-Show mixing console (expandable to 56 faders)

VENUE Profile (24 bankable input faders)

VENUE SC48 (16 bankable input faders)

Where We Are Today

Recently, Avid began an effort to consolidate operations and unite its various products under the Avid brand. Avid continues to develop its audio hardware and software offerings alongside its video editing, broadcast, and newsroom systems. Avid audio systems address all segments of the music creation and video post-production markets, from home recording enthusiasts to large-scale motion picture sound designers and mixers. The addition of the Euphonix series of control surfaces and mixing systems to the Avid family provides an exciting new dimension for music and post-production workflows. Recent audio-specific releases include the new Pro Tools Mbox family of audio interfaces, new HD-series interfaces, the HD-Native platform, and the all-new Pro Tools 9 software.

Pro Tools 9 software represents a radical change for Pro Tools users. Pro Tools 9.0 provides a single, unified installer for all versions of Pro Tools. On systems with Pro Tools|HD or Pro Tools|HD Native hardware (and a valid license), launching Pro Tools 9.0 will run Pro Tools HD software. Launching Pro Tools 9.0 with any other hardware (and a valid license) will run standard Pro Tools software. Standard Pro Tools software (known simply as *Pro Tools*) replaces the former Pro Tools M-Powered and Pro Tools LE platforms and is compatible with any current Pro Tools M-Powered or Pro Tools LE audio interface, as well as any Core Audio or ASIO audio interface with supported drivers. This means that, for the first time ever, Pro Tools software can be run with third-party hardware, providing a wealth of new I/O choices for Pro Tools users. In addition, Pro Tools 9.0 provides an Aggregate I/O option for using the built-in audio on a Mac, meaning the software can be run with *no* connected interface, allowing Pro Tools to record and play back through the computer's onboard audio ports.

 Although Pro Tools M-Powered and Pro Tools LE are no longer being developed, users can upgrade from lower versions of Pro Tools M-Powered or Pro Tools LE to Pro Tools 9.0 for use with their existing hardware.

This release sees numerous improvements for standard Pro Tools systems, including increased Audio track counts (up to 96 simultaneous mono or stereo tracks), increased MIDI track counts (up to 512 tracks), increased I/O capabilities (up to 32 channels), and increased internal mix busses (up to 256). Pro Tools 9.0 also brings Automatic Delay Compensation (ADC) to host-based Pro Tools systems for the first time. The Complete Production Toolkit 2 provides expandability options for Pro Tools systems, including surround mixing capabilities, further increased track counts, and a variety of advanced features otherwise available only with Pro Tools|HD or Pro Tools|HD Native systems.

Pro Tools 9.0 puts unprecedented capabilities at your fingertips. However, to make the most of your experience and to optimize your results using the software, it is helpful to understand some of the technology behind Pro Tools.

Basics of Digital Audio

Today's Pro Tools systems give you the power to capture the subtlest details of a sound or performance and to work on digital audio with absolute precision. The sample rates and bit depths supported by Pro Tools 9.0 provide the frequency response and dynamic range required for truly professional results. Becoming acquainted with the fundamentals of sound and digital audio will help you to maximize the power of Pro Tools and the capabilities of your system. This section describes some of the factors that affect sound and influence the accuracy of digital audio.

 The following information provides an overview of the concepts of digital audio theory. Although you do not need to be an expert in this material, gaining exposure to these principles now will enrich your understanding of many of the processes discussed later in the book.

Basic Parameters of Sound: Waveform, Frequency, and Amplitude

To work effectively with sound, it is helpful to understand a bit about what sound actually is and what gives a sound its character. When we hear a sound, what we actually experience is variations in the air pressure around us. These variations result from vibrations in material objects—whether a tabletop, a car engine, or a guitar string. When a vibrating object moves through one complete back-and-forth motion (one cycle), the variation in air pressure that it produces becomes an auditory event. If the object is vibrating at a frequency that falls within the range of human hearing, we perceive it as a sound. The nature of the sound we hear is determined by the waveform, frequency, and amplitude of the vibration.

 The range of human hearing is between 20 and 20,000 cycles per second.

Waveform

The waveform of the sound pressure variations that reaches our ears creates our perception of the sound's source, be it a knock on a table, a running car engine, or a plucked guitar string. The waveform is the "shape" of the sound—or, more accurately, the shape of the vibration that produced the sound. As a vibrating object moves through its back-and-forth motions, its path is not smooth and continuous. Instead, the cycles of vibration are typically complex and jagged, influenced by factors such as the physical material that the object is composed of and the resonance induced by the object's surroundings. Each object vibrates differently; the waveform of the vibration gives the sound its unique character and tone.

Frequency

The frequency of the sound pressure variations that reaches our ears creates our perception of the pitch of the sound. We measure this frequency in *cycles per second* (CPS), also commonly denoted as *Hertz* (Hz). These two terms are synonymous—15,000 CPS is the same as 15,000 Hz. Multiples of 1,000 Hz are often denoted as kilohertz (kHz). Therefore, 15,000 Hz is also written as 15 kHz.

As the frequency of vibration increases, the pitch of the sound goes up—numerically higher frequencies produce higher pitches, while numerically lower frequencies produce lower pitches. Each time the frequency doubles, the pitch raises by one octave. By way of example, the A string on a guitar vibrates at 110 Hz in standard tuning. Playing the A note on the 12th fret produces vibrations at 220 Hz (one octave higher).

Amplitude

The intensity or amplitude of the sound pressure variations that reaches our ears creates our perception of the loudness of the sound. We measure amplitude in *decibels* (dB). The decibel scale is defined by the dynamic range of human hearing, with the threshold of hearing defined as 0 dB and the threshold of sensation or pain reached at approximately 120 dB. The dB is a logarithmic unit that is used to describe a ratio of sound pressure; as such, it does not have a linear relation to our perception of loudness.

As the amplitude of pressure variations increases, the sound becomes louder. Doubling the intensity of sound-pressure variations creates a gain of 3 dB; however, we do not perceive this change as doubling the sound's loudness. An increase of approximately 10 dB is required to produce a perceived doubling of loudness. By way of example, the amplitude of ordinary conversation is around 60 dB. Increasing the amplitude to 70 dB would essentially double the loudness; increasing amplitude to 80 dB would double it again, quadrupling the original loudness.

Recording and Playing Back Analog Audio

The task of a recording microphone is to respond to changes in air pressure—the waveforms, frequencies, and amplitudes that make up a sound—and translate them into an electronic output that can be captured or recorded. The continuous electrical signal produced by a microphone is an alternating current with a waveform, frequency, and amplitude that directly corresponds to, or is analogous to, the original acoustic information. Hence the term *analog audio*.

If this continuous analog signal is captured on traditional recording media, such as magnetic tape, it can be played back by directly translating the electrical waveform, frequency, and amplitude back into analogous variations in air pressure through the means of an amplifier and loudspeaker.

Analog-to-Digital Conversion

Before you can record or edit with Pro Tools, the analog audio signals relayed by a microphone, guitar pickup, or other input device must be digitized, or translated into digital (binary) numerical information that can be stored, read, and subsequently manipulated by a computer. This process is referred to as *analog-to-digital conversion*, commonly abbreviated as *A/D conversion*. Two essential factors affect the A/D process: *sample rate* and *bit depth*.

How Sample Rate Affects Frequency Resolution

Sampling is the process of taking discrete readings of a signal at various moments in time. Each reading, or sample, is a digital "snapshot" of the signal at that particular instant. Played back in succession, these samples approximate the original signal, much like a series of photographs played back in succession approximates movement in a film or video.

The sample rate is the frequency with which these digital snapshots are collected. The sample rate required for digital audio is driven by a fundamental law of analog-to-digital conversion, referred to as the *Sampling Theorem* or the *Nyquist Theorem*.

The Nyquist Theorem states that in order to produce an accurate representation of a given frequency of sound, each cycle of the sound's vibration must be sampled a minimum of two times. If the sample rate is any lower, the system will read the incoming frequencies inaccurately and produce the wrong tones. (In concept, this is much like the effect seen in early motion pictures, where a wagon wheel will appear to rotate backward due to the low frame rates being used.) In digital audio, the false tones produced by this type of frequency distortion are known as *alias tones*.

Because the range of human hearing is generally accepted to be 20 Hz to 20 kHz, this law indicates that a sampling rate of at least 40 kHz (twice the upper range of human hearing) is required to capture full-frequency audio. Most professional digital recording devices today offer sampling rates of 44.1 kHz and 48 kHz or higher. The digital information on an audio CD is stored at a standard sample rate of 44.1 kHz.

How Bit Depth Affects Amplitude Resolution

The useful dynamic range of speech and music is generally considered to be from 40 to 105 dB. To capture this range, an A/D converter must be able to accurately represent differences in amplitude of at least 65 dB; stated another way, it must have a minimum 65-dB dynamic range. The relative amplitude (or loudness) of a sample is captured through a process known as *quantization*. This simply means that each sample is quantified (assigned) to the closest available amplitude value.

Computers use binary digits called *bits* (0s or 1s) to quantify each sample that is taken. The number of bits used to define a value is referred to as the *binary word length*. The range of values represented by a binary word is defined by the binary word length and is equal to 2 to the *n*th power (2^n), where *n* is the number of bits in the binary word.

 The binary word length is also commonly referred to as the bit depth.

A 4-bit binary word is able to represent 16 different numeric values (2^4); used by an A/D converter to capture amplitude, this 4-bit binary word would record the amplitude continuum using 16 discrete amplitude levels. By contrast, a 16-bit digital word could define 65,536 discrete amplitude levels (2^{16}), and a 24-bit digital word could define 16,777,216 discrete amplitude levels (2^{24}).

As such, larger binary words are able to quantify variations in amplitude with much greater accuracy. Therefore, a 24-bit audio file will always more accurately reflect the dynamic range of the original sound than its 16-bit counterpart.

A very general rule of thumb can be used to calculate the dynamic range capability of an A/D system. By multiplying the word size by six, you can estimate the useful dynamic range of the system. For example, a system with an 8-bit binary word (or 8-bit quantization) would produce a dynamic range of about 48 dB, while a 16-bit system would accommodate a 96-dB dynamic range. A 24-bit system would have a theoretical dynamic range of 144 dB.

 In theoretical terms, the dynamic range (or signal-to-quantization noise ratio) increases by approximately 6 dB for each bit added to the binary word length.

A consequence of larger binary words is the higher storage capacity required to record them. Each minute of 16-bit/48-kHz stereo audio occupies about 11.4 MB of hard-drive storage space. In contrast, each minute of 24-bit/48-kHz stereo audio occupies about 17 MB of hard-drive storage space.

Recording in Digital Format

When you are recording into Pro Tools using audio that is already in a digital form (on DAT or CD, for example), you don't need to translate the audio before bringing it into the system. The process of converting from digital to analog and back to digital can introduce distortion and degrade the original signal. Therefore, unnecessary conversions should be avoided. If the audio information remains in the digital domain while being transferred between machines, it will retain its sonic integrity with no discernible signal degradation.

On the rear panel of many Pro Tools audio interfaces are two types of connections for accomplishing digital transfers. One is labeled *S/PDIF*, which has RCA jacks (sometimes called *coaxial jacks*), and the other is *AES/EBU*, which uses XLR-type connectors. S/PDIF is the *Sony/Philips Digital Interface* standard, a consumer format, and AES/EBU is the *Audio Engineering Society/European Broadcast*

Union digital interface standard, a professional format. Although both formats are nearly identical in audio quality (it's virtually impossible to hear the difference), if given the choice, you should always use the AES/EBU format over the S/PDIF format because the professional format is technically more stable and filters out any copy protection encoded in the digital audio stream. Almost all digital recording or storage devices will support one or both of these formats.

Pro Tools System Configurations

The requirements for your digital audio recording projects will determine the type of Pro Tools system that you will need to use. Pro Tools 9.0 is supported in three types of systems: Pro Tools, Pro Tools Core Audio/ASIO, and Pro Tools HD. All three options are available for both Mac OS X (Snow Leopard or later) and Windows 7 operating systems, and all deliver the same core technology. The primary difference between the options is the hardware that each Pro Tools software option works with.

Pro Tools systems are host-based, meaning they use the processing power of the host computer to carry out real-time routing, mixing, and processing of audio signals. These systems use Pro Tools 9.0 software with an audio interface from the 003 or Digi 002 family, the Eleven Rack interface, a Pro Tools Mbox or Digidesign Mbox 2 family audio interface, or M-Audio hardware to provide input and output (I/O) to the Pro Tools software.

Pro Tools Core Audio/ASIO systems are also host-based and use Pro Tools 9.0 software with third-party audio interfaces with supported Core Audio (Mac) or ASIO (Windows) drivers, including the built-in audio available on Mac computers (Core Audio).

Pro Tools HD software is supported with Pro Tools|HD or Pro Tools|HD Native hardware. Pro Tools|HD Native uses one or more Pro Tools HD-series interfaces combined with a Pro Tools|HD Native PCIe card and host-based processing. By contrast, Pro Tools|HD systems use one or more Pro Tools HD-series interfaces combined with one or more HD-series PCI/PCIe cards, providing dedicated digital signal processing (DSP) power for mixing and real-time processing operations.

PRO TOOLS VS. PRO TOOLS HD

Throughout this book, we will use the term **Pro Tools** to refer to software running on any system with a supported Pro Tools or M-Audio interface, any supported third-party audio interface (using Core Audio or ASIO device drivers), or the built-in audio on a Mac computer (via Core Audio). We will use the term **Pro Tools HD** to refer to software running on a system with either Pro Tools|HD or Pro Tools|HD Native hardware.

All Pro Tools options use the same software installer, which also installs a variety of included software plug-ins, providing additional functionality. All systems share the same file format, with full cross-compatibility between Macs and PCs, providing seamless interchange between Pro Tools systems.

Pro Tools 9.0 Software

Pro Tools 9.0 effectively replaces all lower versions of Pro Tools LE and Pro Tools M-Powered software. This new release provides sampling rates of up to 192 kHz, with bit depths up to 24 bits. It will power up to 96 simultaneous mono or stereo Audio tracks (up to 128 total voiceable tracks) and up to 512 simultaneous MIDI tracks.

The Complete Production Toolkit 2 increases the Pro Tools track count, providing up to 192 simultaneous voices, with up to 512 total voiceable tracks. See the "Complete Production Toolkit 2" section later in this chapter for more details.

A variety of PCI, FireWire, and USB peripherals are available, providing a multitude of interface options, for up to 32 channels of I/O to the system. Many of these peripherals can be powered by the computer's FireWire or USB bus, enabling laptop systems to function as completely portable Pro Tools workstations.

Supported M-Audio peripherals include FireWire family interfaces, such as the ProFire 2626; USB interfaces, such as the Fast Track series and the ultra-compact Transit; and PCI audio interfaces, such as the Audiophile and Delta series.

M-Audio ProFire 2626 audio interface

M-Audio Transit audio interface

M-Audio Delta 44 audio interface

All current Pro Tools LE audio interfaces also work with Pro Tools 9.0, including the Pro Tools Mbox (third generation) and Digidesign Mbox 2 family audio interfaces, Eleven Rack, and the 003 and Digi 002 family audio interfaces.

 The original Mbox hardware (first generation) is not supported in Pro Tools 9.0. Support for this product ended with Pro Tools 8.0.3.

The Pro Tools Mbox Family

The third-generation Pro Tools Mbox family includes the high-performance Mbox personal studio, the compact Mbox Mini, and the high-definition Mbox Pro desktop studio. The Mbox family interfaces are designed to provide ease of use and portability while maintaining professional sound quality at an affordable price.

The Mbox and Mbox Mini feature powered USB connectivity. The Mbox Mini supports up to 24-bit/48-kHz audio resolution. It includes a single XLR mic/line combo input and 2×2 simultaneous channels of I/O. The larger Mbox provides supports up to 24 bits at sample rates up to 96 kHz and features two XLR mic/line combo inputs, 4×4 simultaneous channels of I/O, and MIDI connectivity.

Pro Tools Mbox and Mbox Mini audio interfaces

The Mbox Pro is a FireWire-powered interface that provides high-definition audio and MIDI in a portable package. It features support for audio resolutions up to 24 bits at sample rates up to 192 kHz. The Mbox Pro includes four XLR mic inputs, four ¼-inch TRS line inputs, six ¼-inch TRS balanced line outputs, two channels of S/PDIF digital I/O, and MIDI input and output.

Pro Tools Mbox Pro audio interface

Eleven Rack

Eleven Rack is a guitar recording and effects processing system designed to serve as an audio interface for Pro Tools as well as a standalone amp tone and effects signal processor for guitar. When used as a Pro Tools interface, Eleven Rack provides up to eight simultaneous channels of recording at bit depths of up to 24 bits and sample rates up to 96 kHz. The unit provides stereo balanced XLR outputs as well as dedicated ¼-inch outputs. Also included are a mic input, two ¼-inch line-level inputs, AES/EBU and S/PDIF digital I/O, and MIDI I/O. Eleven Rack communicates with Pro Tools via a high-speed USB 2.0 connection.

Eleven Rack audio interface

The 003 Family

The 003 family consists of the 003, the 003 Rack, and the 003 Rack+ FireWire-enabled interfaces. All three units provide up to 18 channels of simultaneous I/O. The 003 provides I/O by way of an integrated control surface with eight motorized, touch-sensitive faders in a portable 8×4×2 digital mixer. The 003 Rack and 003 Rack+ each provide the same I/O functionality in a rack-mounted unit, with the 003 Rack+ providing additional mic preamps built into the interface. All units provide 24-bit, 96-kHz audio and include the following I/O features:

- Eight analog inputs
- Eight ¼-inch analog outputs
- Professional mic preamps (four on the 003 and 003 Rack; eight on the 003 Rack+) with gain controls and high-pass filter switches
- Stereo ¼-inch TRS monitor outputs with level control
- Eight channels of 24-bit ADAT optical I/O
- Two channels of 24-bit S/PDIF digital I/O
- MIDI input and output ports
- Dual headphone outputs with individual level controls

003 audio interface

003 Rack audio interface

003 Rack+ audio interface

Pro Tools HD 9.0 Software

A Pro Tools HD 9.0 authorization lets you run Pro Tools HD 9.0 on a supported Mac or Windows computer with Pro Tools|HD or Pro Tools|HD Native hardware. A Pro Tools HD 9.0 authorization also authorizes Pro Tools with Complete Production Toolkit 2 functionality on supported Mac or Windows systems without Pro Tools|HD or Pro Tools|HD Native hardware. This allows Pro Tools HD users to run Pro Tools HD software in the studio and to run a Pro Tools laptop system with Complete Production Toolkit 2 for on-the-go editing and mixing, using the same authorization.

Pro Tools|HD and Pro Tools|HD Native audio interfaces provide sampling rates of up to 192 kHz, with bit depths up to 24 bits. Pro Tools HD 9.0 software supports up to 192 simultaneous Audio tracks (record and playback), up to 512 voiceable tracks, and up to 512 simultaneous MIDI tracks.

Pro Tools|HD Native provides up to 64 channels of I/O, while Pro Tools|HD provides up to 160 channels of I/O. Pro Tools|HD systems provide the most robust Pro Tools option, utilizing dedicated DSP hardware and TDM II technology to carry out real-time routing, mixing, and processing of multiple audio signals. The TDM II bus architecture design provides support for extremely large mixing configurations.

Pro Tools HD 9.0 software requires at least one HD-series interface to be connected in order to run. All Pro Tools|HD-series interfaces can be used for either Pro Tools|HD or Pro Tools|HD Native systems.

HD OMNI

HD OMNI provides two premium mic/DI inputs with built-in preamps, four line inputs, and eight line outputs in a compact, single space rack-mountable chassis. It also provides digital I/O, including eight channels of ADAT I/O with S/MUX II and IV support, 2×8 channels of AES/EBU I/O, and two channels of S/PDIF I/O.

Avid HD OMNI audio interface

HD I/O

HD I/O is available in one of three configurations, providing differing analog and digital I/O options. The standard 8×8×8 configuration provides eight analog inputs, eight analog outputs, and eight channels of AES/EBU digital I/O, in addition to two channels of AES/EBU digital I/O provided on the chassis in all configurations. The 16×16 analog configuration provides 16 channels of analog input along with 16 channels of analog output, plus the two channels of AES/EBU digital I/O on the chassis. Similarly, the 16×16 digital configuration provides 16 channels of digital input and 16 channels of digital output, plus the two channels of AES/EBU digital I/O on the chassis.

Avid HD I/O audio interface

MADI I/O

MADI I/O is a 64-channel MADI interface for Pro Tools HD. This single rack space unit provides coaxial and optical connectors for sending and receiving digital audio streams between Pro Tools and other MADI devices. The MADI protocol enables up to 32 channels of digital audio to be transmitted across distances of up to 2 kilometers via a single connection. The HD MADI interface provides bidirectional sample-rate conversion on both inputs and outputs, enabling easy integration into complex mixed sample-rate environments.

Avid HD MADI audio interface

Included Plug-Ins and Extras

Plug-ins are special-purpose software components that provide additional signal processing and other functionality to Pro Tools. Pro Tools plug-ins come in three varieties: Real-Time AudioSuite (RTAS) plug-ins, which process audio in real time using the host computer's processing power; TDM plug-ins (Pro Tools|HD only), which utilize DSP chips for real-time processing; and AudioSuite plug-ins, which provide non-real-time, file-based processing.

Pro Tools 9 includes a number of RTAS, TDM, and AudioSuite plug-ins that are installed with the Pro Tools software. Plug-ins installed with Pro Tools include the DigiRack plug-in collection, the TL Utilities plug-ins, and the Pro Tools Creative Collection suite of instruments and effects.

DigiRack Plug-Ins

The DigiRack collection is comprised of plug-ins that are installed with Pro Tools. DigiRack plug-ins provide digital signal processing effects, such as EQ, dynamics, delay, and more. More than 30 separate plug-ins are included in the DigiRack collection, many in RTAS, TDM, and AudioSuite formats. The plug-ins included in the DigiRack collection are listed in Appendix A, "DigiRack Plug-Ins."

TL Utilities

The TL Utilities plug-ins provide professional metering, metronome, and instrument tuning for Pro Tools. TL Utilities include the following plug-ins:

- **TL Metro.** A versatile metronome used for quickly and easily creating a click track.
- **TL InTune.** A professional tuner providing the performance of a rack-mounted digital tuner in a convenient plug-in format.
- **TL MasterMeter.** The first oversampling meter for Pro Tools, designed for critical mixing and mastering applications.

Pro Tools Creative Collection

Pro Tools Creative Collection is a set of Real-Time AudioSuite (RTAS) effects and instrument plug-ins included with all Pro Tools systems. The Creative Collection includes twenty A.I.R. effects plug-ins and six A.I.R. virtual instruments. These plug-ins are all installed automatically with Pro Tools 9. A list of the Creative Collection plug-ins is provided in Appendix B, "Creative Collection Plug-Ins."

Complete Production Toolkit 2

The Complete Production Toolkit 2 for Pro Tools 9.0 enables numerous Pro Tools feature enhancements and plug-ins for non-HD systems. This software add-on provides full surround mixing in Pro Tools 9.0 and enables up to 512 voiceable tracks for greater session interchange with Pro Tools|HD systems. The Complete Production Toolkit 2 provides multi-channel surround tracks, QuickPunch support on up to 64 tracks, up to 160 Auxiliary Input tracks, and up to 128 Instrument tracks. It also provides VCA tracks, AutoFades, advanced automation features, advanced video features and video editing capabilities, and other functions that are otherwise available only with Pro Tools HD software.

Mixing and Automation Features

The Complete Production Toolkit 2 supports multi-channel formats up to 7.1 surround with an appropriate audio interface:

- Surround mixing up to 7.1 with a compatible audio interface
- Snapshot automation for writing or trimming automation data
- Glide Automation commands
- Trim Automation modes

Video Features

The Complete Production Toolkit 2 provides the following advanced features for working with digital video:

- Multiple Video tracks in the Timeline (only one can be played back at a time)
- Multiple QuickTime movies on an individual Video track
- Multiple playlists for Video tracks
- Ability to store video files in the Region List
- General video editing capabilities, including non-destructive editing; multiple undos; selecting and editing across multiple tracks; capturing, separating, and healing regions; region looping; and more
- Video region groups

Cross-Platform Issues

Each Pro Tools configuration is available for both Mac and Windows systems. Most Pro Tools controls, tools, procedures, and menus are similar on both systems. There are, however, some differences in keyboard commands and file-naming conventions that can impact your work when moving between different platforms.

Keyboard Commands

Many keyboard commands in Pro Tools use *modifier keys*, which are keys pressed in combination with other keys or with a mouse action. In addition, other equivalent keys have different names on each platform. The following table summarizes equivalent keys on Mac and Windows:

Mac	Windows
Command key (⌘)	Ctrl (Control) key
Option key	Alt key
Control key	Start (Win) key
Return key	Enter key on main (not numeric) keypad
Delete key	Backspace key

File-Naming Conventions

A few differences exist in the way files are named and recognized by Mac and Windows.

File Name Extensions

For cross-platform compatibility, all Pro Tools files in a session must have a three-letter file extension added to the file name. Current Pro Tools session files use the extension ".ptf." Sessions created in versions of Pro Tools older than 7.0 may use the extension ".pts" or ".pt5." WAV files have the ".wav" file extension, and AIFF files have the ".aif" file extension.

Incompatible ASCII Characters

Pro Tools file names cannot use ASCII characters that are incompatible with a supported operating system. The following characters should be avoided in order to maintain cross-platform compatibility:

/ (slash)	" (quotation marks)
\ (backslash)	' (apostrophe)
: (colon)	< (less-than symbol)
* (asterisk)	> (greater-than symbol)
? (question mark)	| (vertical line or pipe)

You should also avoid any character typed with the Command key on the Macintosh.

Chapter 2

Getting Inside Pro Tools

This chapter covers basic Pro Tools operations and functions. It introduces the user interface as well as common tools and modes of operation.

Objectives

After you complete this chapter, you will be able to:

- Explain the basic Pro Tools session file structure
- Power up a Pro Tools system
- Navigate the Pro Tools menu system to locate common commands
- Recognize and work in the main Pro Tools windows
- Understand the Edit tools and Edit modes
- Work with Time Scales, Timebase Rulers, and MIDI controls

Introduction

This chapter presents an overview of basic Pro Tools operations and functions. You will be introduced to the filing structure that Pro Tools uses for its sessions and backups, the steps required to start up a Pro Tools system, the primary elements of the Pro Tools interface, and some of the common tools and modes you will use to work in Pro Tools.

Target Systems

Although most of the concepts discussed in this book are applicable to all Pro Tools systems, the book is specifically targeted at users running Pro Tools 9 with a qualified Pro Tools or M-Audio interface. While Pro Tools 9 can be used with many third-party audio interfaces, certain menus, commands, and functions may differ slightly. Pro Tools HD users and users with the Complete Production Toolkit 2 will also have access to additional features.

New features introduced in Pro Tools 9 are generally identified as such in the text. All descriptions are based on the user interface in Pro Tools 9 systems, unless otherwise noted. Screenshots represent Pro Tools version 9.0 running on Windows 7 with an Mbox 2 interface, unless otherwise noted.

Pro Tools File Structure

Before you create or edit a recording project, or *session*, in Pro Tools, it is helpful to understand how the software works with the various files that are related to a project. Rather than storing a session as a single file, Pro Tools stores various session components separately and maintains a roadmap to the files it uses in a session file. All of the files used for a project are grouped together in a *session folder*.

File Organization

When you create a Pro Tools session, the system sets up a standard hierarchy for the session and its associated files by automatically creating a top-level session folder containing the session file as well as subfolders for various types of supplemental files used for the session. When you record, convert on import, or edit material, specific files will appear in each of these subfolders.

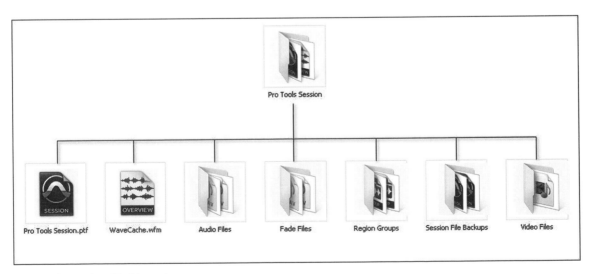

Pro Tools session file hierarchy

Pro Tools keeps related files together in this hierarchy to facilitate backups of sessions and transfers between Pro Tools systems.

File Types

The types of files that Pro Tools generates and stores in each folder in the hierarchy are described in the following sections. Many of these files are created by Pro Tools automatically as you work on a project, although some are generated by export operations only.

Pro Tools Session File

A *session file* is the document that Pro Tools creates when you start a new project. Pro Tools creates this file (along with various subfolders) inside a session folder by the same name. Pro Tools session files are recognizable by their *.ptf* extensions.

The session file contains a map of all the tracks, audio and video files, settings, and edits associated with your project. Session documents can be saved and reopened, recalling a given project with all of its edit information, input/output assignments, and links to the associated audio files. You can easily copy and rename session documents, allowing you to save alternate versions of a project without changing the source audio.

WaveCache File

Each Pro Tools session you create will also have an associated *WaveCache.wfm* file created inside the session folder. This file stores all of the waveform display data for any audio in the session and enables the session to open more quickly. The WaveCache file can be included whenever a session is transferred to another Pro Tools system.

Pro Tools also maintains a distinct WaveCache file inside the Digidesign Databases folder on the system drive, which retains waveform data for all files used on the system.

 WaveCache files can be deleted without harming the session or your system. If the WaveCache is missing, Pro Tools will recalculate the session waveform data; however, the session may open more slowly.

Audio Files

When audio is recorded into a Pro Tools session, each take of the audio recording is stored as a separate file inside the corresponding session's Audio Files folder. Pro Tools natively supports audio files in either the WAV or AIFF format. However, for cross-compatibility purposes, WAV is the default file format for both Mac and Windows Pro Tools systems.

 Audio that you record in Pro Tools is saved only *in the Audio Files folder; it is not saved in the session file. When transferring sessions between systems, be sure to copy over the entire top-level session folder in order to include all associated audio files and other material needed for the session.*

Fade Files

The Fade Files folder contains separate fade file documents, which are created by Pro Tools whenever you apply volume fade-ins, fade-outs, and crossfades while editing a session (EDIT > FADES > CREATE). In the event that you move or copy a session and lose fade files, Pro Tools can re-create them automatically.

MIDI Files

MIDI data is normally stored within the Pro Tools session; as such, no MIDI files will exist outside the session document. However, MIDI files can be exported from Pro Tools using the Export > MIDI command. Exported MIDI files can be recognized by their *.mid* extensions.

Sibelius Files

If you work with scores inside Pro Tools (WINDOW > SCORE EDITOR), you can use either the Send to Sibelius command or the Export > Sibelius command to generate a score file that can be opened/edited with the full-featured Sibelius notation software. Exported Sibelius files can be recognized by their *.sib* extensions.

Region Groups

The Region Groups folder is the default directory that Pro Tools uses for any region groups you export from your Pro Tools session. If you do not export any region groups, this folder will remain empty and will be removed when you close the session; region groups used in your session are not stored in this folder unless they've been exported.

Rendered Files

Whenever you use rendered Elastic Audio processing, Pro Tools creates temporary files for the audio on the affected tracks. These temporary files are kept in an auto-created Rendered Files folder in the session folder. If you commit Rendered Elastic Audio processing to a track, a new file is written to disk in the Audio Files folder, and the temporary rendered file is deleted from the Rendered Files folder.

If you do not use Rendered Elastic Audio processing in your session, no Rendered Files folder will be created in the session folder.

Session File Backups

If you enable the AutoSave function in Pro Tools, the Session File Backups folder will be created automatically, and auto-saved session files will be stored in this location.

Video Files

The Video Files folder is used when you digitize a movie into Pro Tools using an Avid video peripheral, such as the Avid Mojo. When you import a movie that is already in digital form (such as a QuickTime or Avid video file) into Pro Tools, the session references that movie in its stored location and does not copy it into your current Pro Tools session folder.

 For maximum session portability, you might want to create a Video Files folder, if it does not already exist, and copy existing movies into it prior to importing them into your session.

Starting Pro Tools

Because Pro Tools systems are composed of both hardware and software, preparing your system for use might involve more than simply turning on your computer and launching the Pro Tools application. The larger the system, the more important it becomes to follow a specific startup sequence.

Powering Up Your Hardware

When starting your Pro Tools hardware, it's important to power up the system components in the proper order. Starting components out of sequence could cause a component to not be recognized, prevent the software from launching, or cause unexpected behavior.

The recommended sequence for starting a Pro Tools system is as follows:

1. Make sure all your equipment (including your computer) is off.
2. Turn on any external hard drives that use external power and wait about 10 seconds for them to spin up to speed.
3. Turn on any MIDI interfaces and MIDI devices (including any MIDI control surfaces) and synchronization peripherals.
4. Turn on your audio interface. Wait at least 15 seconds for the audio interface to initialize.
5. Start your computer.
6. Turn on your audio monitoring system, if applicable.

 Some audio interfaces, such as the Fast Track USB and the Pro Tools Mbox, get their power from the computer; these interfaces do not need to be powered up in advance.

 Additional steps will be required for Pro Tools\HD system startup. Consult the Getting Started guide that came with your system for details.

Using the PACE iLok System

Pro Tools 9 software is protected with an iLok key, as are many other Avid third-party software products and plug-ins. Using an iLok key for Pro Tools enables you to use a single key for all of your plug-ins and software options.

The iLok is a USB smart key that contains licenses for your protected software products. Pro Tools 9 is compatible with the original iLok key as well as the newer, second-generation iLok key. The original iLok design stored more than 100 separate licenses from multiple software vendors on a single key; the new design will store up to 500 separate licenses. The iLok enables you to carry your software licenses with you wherever you go in a portable, convenient, and hassle-free key. Details and tools for managing your iLok keys and licenses are available at www.ilok.com.

Because your Pro Tools software requires iLok authorization, you'll need to insert your iLok key into an available USB port on your computer before launching Pro Tools 9.

The PACE iLok key (original design, left; new design, right)

Launching Pro Tools

Pro Tools software can be launched by double-clicking on the application icon on the system's internal drive or by double-clicking on a shortcut to the application. In Windows systems, the application is typically installed under C:\Program Files\Digidesign\Pro Tools, and a shortcut is placed on the desktop. In the Mac OS, the application is typically placed under Applications\Digidesign\Pro Tools.

The Pro Tools application icon

 On Windows systems, Pro Tools may also be available from the Start menu at the lower-left corner of the display.

 Mac users might want to create a shortcut to the Pro Tools application on the Dock. To do so, simply drag the application icon onto the Dock.

When you launch Pro Tools, the application starts with no session open. From this point, you can change settings that affect the application's overall performance, depending on your needs. (Note that you might have to dismiss the Quick Start dialog box first; see the "Quick Start Dialog Box" section in Chapter 3.)

Optimizing Host-Based Pro Tools Performance

Pro Tools 9 systems take advantage of the computer's processing capacity (called *host-based processing*) to carry out operations such as recording, playback, mixing, and Real-Time AudioSuite (RTAS) plug-in processing (effects and virtual instruments). Pro Tools|HD systems use dedicated DSP hardware for most of their audio processing power; however, they can also use host-based processing capacity for RTAS plug-in processing.

While the default system settings are adequate for most processing tasks, Pro Tools lets you adjust the performance of a system by changing settings that affect its host-based processing capacity (the Hardware Buffer Size and the CPU Usage Limit).

Hardware Buffer Size

The Hardware Buffer Size (H/W Buffer Size) controls the size of the hardware cache used to handle host-based tasks, such as RTAS plug-in processing.

- Lower Hardware Buffer Size settings reduce monitoring latency and are useful when you are recording live input.
- Higher Hardware Buffer Size settings allow for more audio processing and effects and are useful when you are mixing and using more RTAS plug-ins.

 The H/W Buffer Size setting does not affect TDM processing, which is performed by dedicated DSP hardware on Pro Tools|HD systems.

CPU Usage Limit

The CPU Usage Limit controls the percentage of the computer's processing power allocated to Pro Tools host processing tasks.

- Lower CPU Usage Limit settings limit the effect of Pro Tools processing on other processing-intensive tasks, such as screen redraws, and are useful when you are experiencing slow system response or when you are running other applications at the same time as Pro Tools.
- Higher CPU Usage Limit settings allocate more processing power to Pro Tools and are useful for playing back large sessions or using more RTAS plug-ins.

Modifying Hardware Buffer Size and/or CPU Usage Limit Settings

Adjustments to the Hardware Buffer Size and CPU Usage Limit can be made in the Playback Engine dialog box, as follows:

1. Choose SETUP > PLAYBACK ENGINE.
2. From the H/W Buffer Size pop-up menu, select the audio buffer size in samples—lower the setting to reduce latency; raise it to increase processing power for plug-ins.
3. From the CPU Usage Limit pop-up menu, select the percentage of CPU processing to allocate to Pro Tools—lower the setting to increase system response; raise it to increase processing power for Pro Tools.
4. Click OK.

 Additional details on the Playback Engine dialog box are covered in the Pro Tools 110 course.

Pro Tools Playback Engine dialog box

The Pro Tools Software Interface

Before beginning to work on a session, you should have some basic familiarity with the Pro Tools software interface. The software interface is displayed once you create or open a session by choosing FILE > NEW SESSION, FILE > OPEN SESSION, or FILE > OPEN RECENT. Details on creating and opening sessions are provided in Chapter 3, "Creating Your First Session."

This section introduces you to the menu structure and main windows in Pro Tools 9.

The Menu Structure

Among the first things you see upon launching Pro Tools is the menu system across the top of the screen. Learning how the menus are organized will save you a lot of time when you are trying to find a specific Pro Tools function. Following is a brief description of each menu.

File Menu

File menu commands let you create and maintain Pro Tools sessions. The File menu includes options for opening, creating, and saving sessions; bouncing tracks; and importing and exporting session components.

Edit Menu

Edit menu commands allow you to edit and manipulate the current selection and to affect data in the Timeline. The Edit menu includes options for copying and pasting; duplicating, repeating, and shifting selections; trimming, separating, and healing regions; and performing similar operations.

View Menu

View menu commands control how Pro Tools windows, tracks, and track data are displayed. Some View menu commands toggle the display of various component parts of Pro Tools windows. Select the command to display a component or view feature; deselect the command to hide it.

 Though commonly confused, the View menu and the Window menu serve distinctly different functions. Commands in the View menu affect parts of a window or change how the elements within a window are displayed. By contrast, commands in the Window menu show or hide entire windows or arrange the windows on the screen.

Track Menu

Track menu commands let you set up and maintain tracks in a Pro Tools session. The Track menu includes track-based operations, such as options for creating, duplicating, grouping, deleting, and modifying tracks and track settings.

Region Menu

Region menu commands allow you to work with Pro Tools *regions*. Regions are essentially "pointers" to available audio or MIDI files or file segments. The Region menu includes options for arranging, grouping, looping, quantizing, warping, and otherwise modifying regions and region settings.

In Pro Tools HD (and Pro Tools with the Complete Production Toolkit 2), certain Region menu commands are also available for working with Video regions.

Event Menu

The Event menu contains commands for modifying the time and tempo settings of your Pro Tools session, for working with MIDI and audio events and operations, and for adjusting various properties of MIDI recordings.

AudioSuite Menu

The AudioSuite menu allows you to access all AudioSuite plug-ins currently installed in your system's Plug-Ins folder. AudioSuite plug-ins apply non-real-time, file-based processing to selections in Pro Tools. AudioSuite processing applies a plug-in effect permanently, replacing a selection with a new audio file.

Options Menu

The Options menu commands let you select several editing, recording, monitoring, playback, and display options. From this menu, you can enable loop recording, turn on pre- and post-roll, engage Dynamic Transport mode, set scrolling options, and make other similar choices.

 The Options menu displays independent functions that toggle on or off. Menu items with a check mark next to them are currently on, or enabled; items without a check mark are off, or disabled. Selecting an item toggles its state on/off.

Setup Menu

The Setup menu lets you configure various Pro Tools hardware and software parameters. It includes options for configuring your peripheral devices, such as audio interfaces; configuring host-based processing options; setting disk allocations; mapping I/O settings; configuring session and MIDI settings; configuring Click/Countoff behavior; and modifying your Pro Tools preferences.

 All items under the Setup menu display a dialog box when selected. The choices in the Setup menu allow you to configure functions or operations that involve multiple settings.

Window Menu

Window menu commands allow you to display various Pro Tools windows and palettes. The Window menu includes commands for toggling the Edit, Mix, and Transport windows; the Pro Tools Task Manager; the Workspace and Project browsers; and the Window Configurations, Automation, Memory Locations, Video, Color Palette, Undo History, and other displays.

Help Menu

The Help menu provides links to important Pro Tools documentation, including Keyboard Shortcuts, the Audio Plug-Ins Guide, the Pro Tools Menus Guide, and the Pro Tools Reference Guide.

Main Pro Tools Windows

Pro Tools software provides a host of windows and palettes you can use to perform a variety of tasks and functions. The three primary windows that you will need to be familiar with to begin working with Pro Tools are the Edit window, the Mix window, and the Transport window. Pro Tools also includes two additional types of main windows: the MIDI Editor window and the Score Editor window.

Edit Window

The Edit window provides a timeline display of audio, MIDI data, video, and mixer automation for recording, editing, and arranging tracks. It displays waveforms for the audio in your session and is the main window that you will use to work directly with audio, MIDI, and video files in Pro Tools. Each Audio and MIDI track displayed in the Edit window has controls for Record Enable, Solo, Mute, and Automation Mode.

— Toolbar

— Timeline Display

— Tracks Display

— Side columns

Pro Tools Edit window

Edit Tools

Pro Tools provides several Edit tools in the toolbar area at the top of the Edit window. The Edit tools are used to select, move, trim, and otherwise modify regions in Pro Tools. The functionality of each Edit tool is described in the "Edit Tool Functions" section later in this chapter.

Edit tool buttons

Edit Modes

Pro Tools provides selector buttons in the toolbar area at the top of the Edit window for activating each of its four Edit modes. The Edit modes (Shuffle, Spot, Slip, and Grid) affect the movement and placement of audio and MIDI regions (and individual MIDI notes). The Edit modes also affect how commands such as Copy and Paste function and how the various Edit tools (Trim, Selector, Grabber, and Pencil) work. The Edit modes are described in the "Edit Mode Features" section later in this chapter.

Edit mode buttons

Edit Window Side Columns

The Edit window includes columns on the left and right sides that provide additional view and display options for your session data. Along the left side of the Edit window is a vertical column that contains the Track List and Edit Group List. The Track List is at the top of the column and contains a pop-up menu used to display and sort tracks. Directly beneath the Track List is the Edit Group List, where the track grouping status is displayed. (Track grouping is covered in the Pro Tools 110 course.) Both lists in the left-side column contain display areas and pop-up menus for their respective functions.

Along the right side of the Edit window is a separate vertical column that contains the Region List. The Region List includes a pop-up menu and display area for the audio and MIDI files and file segments (regions) that are currently available in the session. On Pro Tools|HD systems and Pro Tools systems with Complete Production Toolkit 2, the Region List will also display Video files and regions.

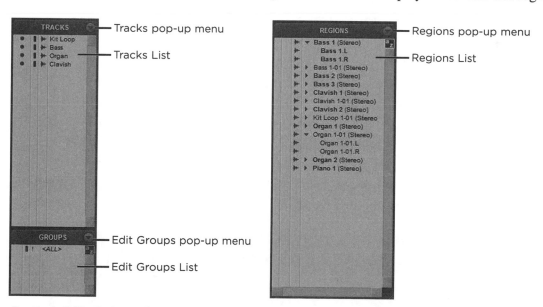

Pro Tools Edit window columns

Pro Tools lets you customize the display of Edit window side columns to accommodate your needs at any given point in your project. You can show and hide the left and right columns independently or adjust their display widths and heights as needed. By sizing or hiding these columns, you can control the amount of horizontal display area that is available for your track views in the Edit window, as well as simplify the Edit window view.

To show or hide either the left or right side column, do the following:

- Click the arrow icon located in the bottom corner corresponding to the column you want to show or hide. The arrow icon will reverse to point in the opposite direction, and the column will slide into or out of view.
- Click the corresponding arrow icon again to return to the previous view.
  Or
- Double-click with your pointer positioned over the column separator (where the cursor changes to a double-headed arrow). The column will slide into or out of view.

To adjust column width or height, follow these steps:

1. Position your pointer over the column separator where the cursor changes into a double-headed arrow.
2. Click and drag on the column separator to adjust its position as needed.

Ruler Views

Rulers are horizontal displays that appear in the Timeline display area of the Edit window, just above your tracks display. Pro Tools' Rulers provide measurement indicators in a variety of useful increments to help you identify specific locations in your session's Timeline. You can display or hide any combination of the following Rulers in the Edit window:

- **Bars:Beats.** This Ruler is useful for music editors, composers, and musicians.
- **Min:Sec.** This Ruler is useful for radio or those who need to measure in absolute time.
- **Samples.** This Ruler displays the system's smallest editing resolution.
- **Time Code and Time Code 2.** These Rulers are primarily used for video and film post-production and some professional music applications.
- **Feet+Frames.** This Ruler is also used for video and film post-production work.
- **Tempo.** This Ruler allows you to specify changes in tempo within the session.
- **Key Signature.** This Ruler allows you to specify key changes within the session.
- **Chord Symbols.** This Ruler allows you to add chord symbols to the session to indicate chord changes.
- **Meter.** This Ruler allows you to specify changes in meter within the session.
- **Markers.** This Ruler allows you to create markers to identify and recall important track locations and view settings within the session.

Pro Tools Ruler displays

Additional information on Rulers is provided in the "Time Scales and Rulers" section later in this chapter.

Customizing the Toolbar

Pro Tools allows users to customize the toolbar in the Edit window using the Edit Window Toolbar menu in the upper-right corner of the window. This menu lets you show or hide various controls and displays in the toolbar. You can also move toolbar controls and arrange them according to your preferences.

 You can show and hide control and display elements in the MIDI Editor and Score Editor windows using the same methods.

To show or hide a control or display, click on the EDIT WINDOW TOOLBAR menu icon (or right-click on the toolbar background) and select or deselect an item from the menu.

Using the Edit Window Toolbar menu to show or hide parts of the window

The display elements available under the Edit Window Toolbar menu include the following:

- **Zoom controls.** When selected, the Zoom controls are displayed in the Edit window toolbar.

Zoom controls in the Edit window

- **Transport.** When selected, the Transport controls are displayed in the Edit window toolbar.

Transport controls in the Edit window

- **MIDI controls.** When selected, the MIDI controls are displayed in the Edit window toolbar.

MIDI controls in the Edit window

To move a set of controls in the toolbar, CTRL-CLICK (Windows) or COMMAND-CLICK (Mac) on a non-active part of the toolbar near to the controls you wish to move and drag the set to a new area of the toolbar. For example, if you prefer the Zoom controls to be located the right of the Edit tools in the toolbar, simply Ctrl-click (Windows) or Command-click (Mac) and drag them to that location.

Moving controls in the Edit window toolbar

Mix Window

The Mix window provides a mixer-like environment for recording and mixing audio. In the Mix window, tracks appear as mixer strips (also called *channel strips*). Each track displayed in the Mix window has controls for inserts, sends, input and output assignments, Automation Mode selection, panning, and volume. The channel strips also provide buttons for enabling record, toggling solo and mute on and off, and selecting voice assignments and mix groups.

Pro Tools Mix window

Signal Routing Controls

The top portion of each channel strip in the Mix window provides controls for routing signals into and out of the track. These controls include Insert selectors, Send selectors, Input selectors, and Output selectors. Insert selectors can be used to add real-time effects processing to a track using one of your loaded plug-ins. Send selectors can be used to route a track's signal to an available bus path or output path. The Input and Output selectors are used to route input and output signals from your audio interface for recording or playback.

Insert selectors

Send selectors

Input selector

Output selector

Signal routing controls

Record and Playback Controls

Immediately beneath the signal routing controls in the Mix window is a series of controls that are used to set record and playback options. These controls include the Automation Mode selector; the Pan controls; the Track Record Enable, Solo, and Mute buttons; and the Volume Fader for each track. The Automation Mode selector can be used to enable various options for Pro Tools' automatable parameters. The Pan controls can be used to position the output of a track within a stereo field (or output pair). The buttons for Track Record Enable, Solo, and Mute can be used to activate and deactivate each of these functions for a track during record and playback operations. The Volume Fader can be used to adjust the playback/monitoring level of a track.

 The Volume Fader in the Mix window does not affect the input gain (record level) of a signal being recorded. The signal level must be set appropriately at the source or adjusted using a preamp or gain-equipped audio interface.

Automation Mode selector

Pan controls

Record Enable, Solo, and Mute buttons

Volume fader

Record and playback controls

Mix Window Side Column

The Mix window includes a single column located on the left side that provides additional view and display options for your session data. The Mix window side column contains the Track List and Mix Group List. The Track List is at the top of the column and is used to display and sort tracks. Directly beneath the Track List is the Mix Group List, where the track grouping status is displayed. (Track grouping is covered in the Pro Tools 110 course.) Both lists in the Mix window side column contain display areas and pop-up menus for their respective functions.

— Tracks pop-up menu

— Tracks List

— Mix Groups pop-up menu

— Mix Groups List

Pro Tools Mix window column

As with the Edit window side columns, Pro Tools lets you customize the display of the Mix window side column as needed. You can show and hide the side column, adjust the display width, and adjust the relative height of the lists in the same manner as the columns in the Edit window.

Transport Window

The Transport window provides buttons for various transport functions that operate similarly to the controls on a CD or DVD player. (These are the same Transport controls that can optionally be displayed in the Edit window toolbar.) The Transport window can also be set to display counters (Location Indicators) and MIDI controls. The Location Indicators in the Transport window mirror the Main and Sub Counters at the top of the Edit window in normal operation.

Transport controls   Counters   MIDI controls

— Transport window menu icon

The Transport window, showing Transport controls, counters, and MIDI controls in Expanded Transport display

Controls and display elements in the Transport window can be shown/hidden using options under the main View > Transport menu or the Transport window menu.

Counters

Enabling the counters in the Transport window will display the Location Indicators to the right of the Transport controls. The Location Indicators provide information for navigation and editing via a Main Location Indicator and a Sub Location Indicator. The Main and Sub Location Indicators can be set for different Time Scale formats (such as Samples, Bars|Beats, or Minutes:Seconds).

The Main Location Indicator in the Transport window provides a convenient way to navigate to a specific time location. To navigate with the Main Location Indicator, follow these steps:

1. Click in the MAIN LOCATION INDICATOR.
2. Type in a location.
3. Press ENTER (Windows) or RETURN (Mac). The Timeline insertion point will automatically move to the new location.

MIDI Controls

The Transport window includes a MIDI controls section, providing options for playing back your session and recording MIDI data. The MIDI controls let you set options for triggering MIDI recording, playing metronome clicks, overdubbing MIDI, using a tempo map, and setting the tempo and meter. The functions of the MIDI controls are described in more detail in the "MIDI Control Features" section later in this chapter.

Additional Editor Windows

Although the primary Edit window works well for general editing operations, Pro Tools provides two additional types of editor windows focused on specific editing and presentation tasks. These are the MIDI Editor window and the Score Editor window.

MIDI Editor Window

Pro Tools provides MIDI Editor windows for detailed MIDI composition and editing tasks. MIDI Editor windows can show MIDI data and automation data for Auxiliary Input, Instrument, and MIDI tracks. You can open several separate MIDI Editor windows simultaneously, each providing a different view of the MIDI data in your Pro Tools session. You can also display a "docked" MIDI Editor window (also known as the *MIDI Editor view*) at the bottom of the primary Edit window.

MIDI Editor windows display and let you edit MIDI data for one or more MIDI and Instrument tracks. When displaying multiple tracks, the MIDI Editor window superimposes the notes from each of the tracks in the MIDI Notes pane. The MIDI Editor window can also display automation and controller lanes for velocity stalks, volume automation playlists, and other continuous controller and automation data.

 Automation playlists are discussed in Chapter 9.

MIDI Notes
pane

Automation
and
Controller
lanes

MIDI Editor window

Score Editor Window

The Score Editor window lets you view, edit, arrange, and print MIDI data from your session as music notation. The Score Editor transcribes MIDI notes in real time and provides tools for navigating and editing in Notation view. It also provides Notation Display Track settings to specify how individual MIDI and Instrument tracks appear in the Score Editor. You can set the page layout and staff spacing and specify the title and composer for the score using the Score Setup window.

Score Editor window

Window Management

The Pro Tools Window menu provides commands to tile or cascade all open windows. These commands do not affect floating windows or the Transport window, but all other windows will rearrange automatically according to the selected command.

The Tile command arranges open windows in a tiled pattern on the screen, resizing each window as needed to fit. Two other commands, Tile Vertical and Tile Horizontal, resize windows uniformly, creating evenly distributed patterns. The Tile Vertical command arranges windows as narrow vertical strips, side by side; whereas the Tile Horizontal command arranges windows as long horizontal strips, stacked top to bottom. These two commands are not available when too many windows are open to display at once.

The Cascade command arranges open windows in a cascading pattern on the screen. The windows are overlaid on top of one another and resized to near full-screen. Only the top and left edges of underlying windows remain visible behind the foreground window.

Tool Tips and Additional Help

The Help menu provides links to the Pro Tools Help system, online resources, and various other reference files that are installed with Pro Tools.

In addition to the Help menu, the Pro Tools user interface provides Tool Tips in all main windows to help you solve any question that you may come across in Pro Tools. When you park the cursor for a few seconds over an abbreviated name (such as a track name or an output assignment) or over an unlabeled icon or tool, Pro Tools will display the full name of the item or its function.

Tool Tips are an optional display element controlled via the Tool Tips Display options in the Display Preferences pane (SETUP > PREFERENCES, DISPLAY tab). Tool Tips settings provide two options: *Function* shows the basic function of the item, and *Details* shows the complete name of an abbreviated name or item. Tool Tips can be set to display either or both of these options, or they can be turned off altogether.

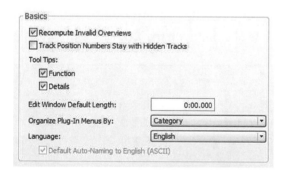

Basics section of the Display Preferences pane showing selected Tool Tips options

Edit Tool Functions

The Edit tools located in the toolbar area at the top of the Edit window provide access to Pro Tools' powerful audio and MIDI editing functions. The Edit tools include the Zoomer tool, the Trimmer tool, the Selector tool, the Grabber tool, the Scrubber tool, the Pencil tool, and the Smart Tool.

Zoomer Tool

Use the ZOOMER tool to zoom in and out on a particular area within a track. Zooming in is often helpful to examine a region or waveform closely.

Normal Zoom mode

The Zoomer tool offers two modes: Normal Zoom and Single Zoom mode.

- In Normal Zoom mode, the Zoomer tool remains selected after zooming.
- In Single Zoom mode, the previously selected tool is automatically reselected after zooming.

Single Zoom mode

To use the Zoomer tool, select it and click on the desired point within the track onto which you want to zoom in. Each click zooms all tracks in by one level, and the Edit window is centered on the zoom point.

To zoom in on a particular area in the Edit window, drag with the ZOOMER tool over the area you want to view. As you drag, a grey box will appear, indicating the range on which you will be zooming in. Release the mouse to fill the window with the selected portion of the waveform.

> *You can also use the ZOOMER tool for Marquee Zooming, allowing you to zoom in on a waveform both horizontally and vertically. To use Marquee Zooming, CTRL-DRAG (Windows) or COMMAND-DRAG (Mac) with the ZOOMER tool.*

To zoom out, hold ALT (Windows) or OPTION (Mac) while clicking with the ZOOMER tool.

REVERSE AN OPERATION WITH THE ALT/OPTION KEY

The Alt/Option modifier (Windows/Mac, respectively) provides several standard functions in Pro Tools. Among these is the Reverse Operation function. By adding the Alt/Option modifier to a keyboard or Edit tool action, you can cause Pro Tools to perform the reverse or opposite action. Try adding this key with the Trimmer tool to reverse the trim direction or with the Pencil tool when editing MIDI notes to use it as an eraser.

> *Double-click on the ZOOMER tool to get a full track view that fills the Edit window with the longest visible track in the session.*

Trimmer Tool

Use the TRIMMER tool to trim excess audio, MIDI, or video content from the beginning or end of a continuous section of program material, or *region*. The Trimmer tool modifies regions nondestructively, leaving the underlying source audio or video files unchanged. This tool allows you to quickly crop a region or to adjust the cropping on a region to re-expose material up to the entire length of the underlying source file. The first time you trim an uncropped region, Pro Tools automatically adds a new item to the Region List corresponding to the newly created subset region. The subset region is given a new name in order to differentiate it from the original.

Standard Trimmer tool

 The Trimmer tool button also provides access to the Time Compression/Expansion (TCE) Trimmer, the Loop Trimmer, and the Scrub Trimmer (Pro Tools HD only). These additional Trimmer tools are covered in detail in the 200-level Pro Tools courses.

Selector Tool

Use the SELECTOR tool to position the playback cursor or to select an area in a track for playback or editing. To position the playback cursor, click with the SELECTOR tool at the point where you want playback to begin. To select an area for playback or editing, drag with the SELECTOR tool across any area on one or more tracks. To add to or remove from an existing selection, hold the SHIFT key and click (or click and drag) to the left or right.

Selector tool

The Selector tool selects horizontally and vertically, allowing selections across multiple tracks in a single operation. Selected areas appear highlighted in the Edit window. In addition, the selection is indicated by a dark overlay in the Timeline area at the top of the window.

Selection across multiple tracks

You can use the Selector tool to quickly make a lengthy selection, as follows:

1. Click with the SELECTOR tool to position the playback cursor where you want the selection to start.
2. Scroll to the desired endpoint using the scroll bar at the bottom of the Edit window.
3. Shift-click at the desired endpoint to complete the selection.

Grabber Tool

Use the GRABBER tool to select an entire region with a single mouse click, to move regions along the Timeline within their current tracks, and to move regions between tracks.

Grabber tool button

To select a region, click anywhere on the region in the Edit window using the GRABBER tool. To move a region along the Timeline, click anywhere on the region and drag to the left or right with the GRABBER tool. Dragging a region vertically with the Grabber tool will move the region to another track in your session.

The Grabber tool can be used to position regions in a variety of ways, depending on the Edit mode that is currently selected. Regions can be moved freely along the Timeline in Slip mode or can be positioned numerically via a dialog box using Spot mode. Regions can also be made to snap to other regions or to Timeline increments using Shuffle or Grid mode, respectively. An overview of the Edit modes is provided in the "Edit Mode Features" section later in this chapter.

 The Grabber tool button also provides access to the Separation Grabber and Object Grabber tools. These additional Grabber tools are covered in the Pro Tools 201 course.

Scrubber Tool

Use the SCRUBBER tool to "scrub" slowly across Audio tracks in the Edit window to find a particular moment or audio event. Scrubbing originated in tape editing as a process of rocking the tape back and forth past the playhead to locate a precise position (usually for the sake of performing a splice). By scrubbing back and forth over an audio waveform in Pro Tools, you can listen closely and zero in on an exact edit point.

Scrubber tool

To scrub audio or MIDI in Pro Tools, click on a track in the Edit window with the SCRUBBER tool and drag left or right to begin playback at that point. Playback speed and direction vary with mouse movement. Scrubbing becomes smoother as you increase the magnification of the screen. For best results and more precise scrubbing, zoom in on the material you want to scrub.

 Dragging the Scrubber tool between two adjacent mono or stereo Audio tracks allows you to scrub the two tracks together.

Pencil Tool

You can use the PENCIL tool to destructively "redraw" waveform data. This feature is most commonly used to repair a pop or click in an audio file. A pop or click appears as a sudden sharp spike in a waveform. This tool becomes active only when the Edit window is zoomed in to the sample level.

Pencil tool

The Pencil tool is also useful for creating and editing MIDI data. The Pencil tool shapes (Freehand, Line, Triangle, Square, and Random) can be used to enter pitches with varying durations and velocities. (Note velocities are determined by the Pencil shape.) The various Pencil tool shapes can be particularly useful for drawing and editing different types of automation or MIDI control data—common examples include using Line for volume, Triangle for pan, Freehand for pitch bend, and Square or Random for velocity.

Smart Tool

Use the SMART TOOL to provide instant access to the Selector, Grabber, and Trimmer tools and to perform fades and crossfades. The position of the cursor in relation to a region or note or within an automation playlist determines how the Smart Tool functions.

Smart Tool in the Edit window

To use the SMART TOOL as a Selector, position the tool over the middle of an audio region, in the upper half. To use it as a Grabber, position it in the lower half. For the Trimmer tool, position the SMART TOOL near the region's start or end point.

The Smart Tool can also be used to create fade-ins, fade-outs, and crossfades.

 The functions of the Smart Tool are covered in detail in the Pro Tools 201 course.

Edit Mode Features

Pro Tools has four Edit modes: Shuffle, Spot, Slip, and Grid. The Edit mode is selected by clicking the corresponding mode button on the left side of the toolbar area in the Edit window. The Snap to Grid feature is a special Edit mode that lets you combine edit selections constrained by the Grid with any other Edit mode.

Edit mode buttons

 *You can also use function keys **F1** (Shuffle), **F2** (Slip), **F3** (Spot), and **F4** (Grid) to set the Edit mode.*

The Edit mode affects the movement and placement of audio regions, MIDI regions and notes, and video regions or clips. It also affects how commands such as Copy and Paste function, as well as how the various Edit tools work (Trimmer, Selector, Grabber, and Pencil).

Shuffle Mode

In Shuffle mode, region movement is constrained by other regions, and any changes you make affect the placement of subsequent regions on the track. When you move a region in Shuffle mode, it will snap to the previous or next region on the track. Additionally, when you perform an edit (trim, cut/delete, or paste material), all regions to the right will slide along the Timeline in train-car fashion to make space (when adding material) or to close a gap (when removing material).

Use Shuffle mode as a convenient way to make regions line up next to each other, without overlapping or leaving silence between them.

Slip Mode

In Slip mode, you can move, trim, cut, or paste regions freely within a track without affecting the placement of other regions on the track. In this mode, you can place a region anywhere on a track, leaving space between it and other regions, if desired. It is also possible to move a region so that it overlaps or completely covers another region.

Use Slip mode when you want the Trimmer, Selector, Grabber, and Pencil tools to work without restrictions to placement in time.

Spot Mode

In Spot mode, you can move or place regions at precise locations by specifying the destination location in a dialog box. As in Slip mode, edit operations do not affect the placement of other regions on the track.

When Spot mode is enabled, Pro Tools prompts you with a dialog box when working with regions, allowing you to specify the start, end, duration, or other relevant parameters. Use Spot mode when you want to control the placement or duration of a region using precise numerical values.

Grid Mode

In Grid mode, regions and MIDI notes that are moved, trimmed, or inserted will snap to the nearest time increment using the currently selected Time Scale and Grid size. Grid mode can be applied using either Absolute or Relative positioning options (see Chapter 8 for details).

Use Grid mode for making precise edits and aligning regions and selections using precise time intervals.

Snap to Grid

Snap to Grid is a special mode that allows you to make selections on the Grid while in Shuffle, Slip, or Spot mode. In any of these modes, when Snap to Grid is enabled, Edit selections and cursor placement are constrained by the Grid; however, region editing and placement are based on the active Edit mode.

For example, in Shuffle mode with Snap to Grid enabled, you can make a selection in a region based on the Grid. If you then cut the selection, any regions to the right of the edit would shuffle to the left, filling the resulting gap.

Shuffle mode with Snap to Grid enabled

Time Scales and Rulers

Every Pro Tools session uses a Main Time Scale and a Sub Time Scale. The Main Time Scale is the time format used for Transport functions; selection Start, End, and Length fields; and Grid and Nudge values. The Sub Time Scale provides additional timing reference and can be displayed along with the Main Time Scale in the Counters areas of the Edit window and the Transport window.

Pro Tools also provides various Rulers to help you navigate along the Timeline. Rulers can be displayed for a variety of time formats, including but not limited to the time formats used for the Main Time Scale and Sub Time Scale. Rulers appear in the Timeline display area at the top of the Edit window.

Main Time Scale

When the Main Time Scale in a Pro Tools session is set to Min:Sec, Timeline locations are represented in minutes and seconds relative to the start point of the session. When set to Bars|Beats, Timeline locations are represented in bars, beats, and ticks relative to the start point of the session (Bar 1, Beat 1).

The Main Time Scale determines the timebase units used for the following:

- The Main Counter in the Edit window
- The Main Location Indicator in the Transport window
- Selection Start, End, and Length values
- Pre- and Post-Roll amounts
- Initial Grid and Nudge values

The Main Time Scale can be set to Bars|Beats, Minutes:Seconds, Time Code, Feet+Frames, or Samples. To set the Main Time Scale, do one of the following:

- Select the desired timebase using the VIEW > MAIN COUNTER menu.

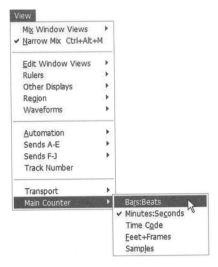

Main Counter menu

- Select the desired timebase from the MAIN TIME SCALE pop-up menu for the Main Counter at the top of the Edit window.

Main Time Scale pop-up menu

- If a Ruler is displayed for the desired timebase, click on its name so it becomes highlighted.

Switching the Main Time Scale using Rulers

Sub Time Scale

The Sub Time Scale in a Pro Tools session is set to Samples by default, meaning that Timeline locations are represented as sample-based values, relative to the start point of the session. The Sub Time Scale provides a convenient secondary timing reference.

Like the Main Time Scale, the Sub Time Scale can be set to Bars|Beats, Minutes:Seconds, Time Code, Feet+Frames, or Samples. To display the Sub Time Scale in the Edit menu, select SHOW SUB COUNTER from the Main Time Scale pop-up menu. To set the Sub Time Scale, select the desired timebase from the Sub Time Scale pop-up menu.

Sub Time Scale pop-up menu

Ruler Display Options

Pro Tools provides two types of Rulers that can be displayed in the Edit window: *Timebase Rulers* and *Conductor Rulers*.

The Pro Tools Timebase Rulers include the following:

- Bars|Beats
- Min:Sec
- Samples
- Time Code
- Time Code 2
- Feet+Frames

 Timebase Rulers are commonly referred to as Timelines *in the industry.*

The Pro Tools Conductor Rulers include the following:

- Markers
- Tempo
- Meter
- Key
- Chords

You can customize your sessions to display only the Timebase and Conductor Rulers you want to work with. To display a Ruler, do one of the following:

- Choose VIEW > RULERS and select the desired Ruler from the submenu.
- Click the RULER VIEW SELECTOR and select the desired Ruler from the pop-up menu.

Ruler View selector and pop-up menu

To remove a Ruler from the display, do one of the following:

- Choose VIEW > RULERS and click on a checked Ruler to deselect it.
- From the Ruler View selector pop-up menu, click on a checked item to deselect it.

Clicking on a Ruler to deselect it

- ALT-CLICK (Windows) or OPTION-CLICK (Mac) directly over the Ruler's nameplate in the Timeline display area.

Alt-clicking/Option-clicking on the Samples Ruler nameplate to hide the Ruler

HIDE VIEWS WITH THE ALT/OPTION KEY

A handy feature of the Alt/Option key (Windows/Mac, respectively) is the Hide Views function. By holding the Alt/Option key while clicking on the nameplate of a Ruler or Edit window column view, you can cause Pro Tools to instantly hide that Ruler or column view.

 The Ruler that corresponds to the session's Main Time Scale cannot be deselected/hidden. (The Main Time Scale Ruler is indicated by blue highlighting in the Ruler name.)

You also have the option to change the display order of the Rulers, arranging them as needed to best fit your work style. To change the display order for the Rulers, do the following:

- Click directly on the Ruler's nameplate and drag up or down to the desired location.

In the following example, the Min:Secs Ruler is moved below the Samples Ruler:

Rulers before and after moving the Min:Secs display

MIDI Control Features

The Edit and Transport windows provide access to various MIDI controls with options for playing back your session and recording MIDI data. The available MIDI controls include Wait for Note, Metronome, MIDI Merge, Tempo Ruler Enable, Countoff, Meter, and Tempo.

- Countoff controls
- Meter display
- Tempo field
- Tempo Ruler Enable (Conductor)

Wait for Note   Metronome   MIDI Merge

MIDI controls in the Transport window

Wait for Note

When Wait for Note is selected, recording does not begin until a MIDI event is received. This ensures that you begin recording when you're ready to play and that the first MIDI event is recorded precisely at the beginning of the record range.

 You can set a preference in the MIDI Preferences page (SETUP > PREFERENCES > MIDI) to use the F11 key for Wait for Note.

Metronome

When the Metronome button is selected, a metronome will sound during playback and recording, as specified by the settings in the Click/Countoff Options dialog box (SETUP > CLICK/COUNTOFF). The simplest way to enable metronome playback is to set up a click track for your session, as described in Chapter 4.

To modify the click settings, choose SETUP > CLICK/COUNTOFF or double-click the METRONOME button in the Edit or Transport window. Enter the desired settings in the Click area of the Click/Countoff Options dialog box.

Click/Countoff Options dialog box

With the Numeric Keypad mode set to Transport (default), you can press **[7]** *to enable the Click.*

 To set the mode for the numeric keypad, choose Setup > Preferences > Operation. *Select the desired mode under Numeric Keypad in the Transport section.*

Countoff Controls

When Count Off is selected (highlighted) in the MIDI controls section, Pro Tools counts off a specified number of bars (measures) before playback or recording begins. The number of bars used for Count Off is indicated in the Count Off field.

To change the Count Off settings, choose Setup > Click/Countoff or double-click the Count Off field in the Edit or Transport window. Enter the desired settings in the Countoff area of the Click/Countoff Options dialog box.

 With the Numeric Keypad mode set to Transport, you can press **[8]** *to enable the Countoff.*

MIDI Merge Mode

When MIDI Merge is selected (MIDI Merge mode), recorded MIDI data will be merged with existing track material, overdubbing the track. When deselected (Replace mode), recorded MIDI data will replace existing track material.

To engage MIDI Merge mode, click on the **MIDI Merge** button in the Edit or Transport window. Click a second time to return to Replace mode.

 With the Numeric Keypad mode set to Transport, you can press **[9]** *to enable MIDI Merge.*

Tempo Ruler Enable

When selected, Pro Tools uses the tempo map defined in the Tempo Ruler to control the tempo during playback and recording. When deselected, Pro Tools switches to Manual Tempo mode and ignores the tempo map.

In Manual Tempo mode, you can enter a BPM value in the Tempo field or tap in the tempo as follows:

1. Click the Tempo Ruler Enable button (a.k.a. the Conductor button) so it becomes unhighlighted.
2. Click in the Tempo field so it becomes highlighted.
3. Tap the **T** key on your computer keyboard repeatedly at the new tempo.

To compute the new tempo, Pro Tools averages the last eight (or fewer) taps to determine the correct tempo. The computed BPM value appears in the Tempo field.

The tempo can also be adjusted by typing a value directly into the Tempo field when you are in Manual Tempo mode.

Meter Display

The Meter display indicates the session's current meter based on the play location. Double-click the Meter display to open the Meter Change dialog box.

Tempo Field

The Tempo field displays the session's current tempo based on the play location. In Manual Tempo mode, you can enter a BPM value directly into this field. In addition, when the Tempo field is selected, you can tap in a tempo from a MIDI controller or from the computer keyboard using the **T** key.

Tempo Resolution Selector

The Tempo Resolution selector is located immediately to the left of the Tempo field and is used to set the note value that gets the beat. (The default value is a quarter note.) Changing this value will change the song playback tempo, in that the beat duration will change while BPM remains constant.

 ——— Tempo Resolution selector

Tempo Resolution selector in the MIDI Controls section (Edit window or Transport window)

To change the note value assigned to a beat, click on the TEMPO RESOLUTION selector and choose a new note value from the drop-down list.

PART II

Working with Sessions

Components

Overview

Part II provides information and instructions for working with Pro Tools sessions to accomplish common audio production tasks. In the early chapters, you will learn processes for creating and configuring sessions, creating audio and MIDI recordings, and keeping session files organized. As you progress through the chapters, you will learn how to import audio and movie files, how to set up virtual instrument plug-ins, how to use selection and navigation techniques to work with audio and MIDI recordings, and how to edit your work using Edit modes, edit commands, and moving and trimming operations. In the final chapters, you will learn about Pro Tools' mixing and automation functions, plug-in operations, and mixdown and bouncing operations, as well as suggestions for burning a completed mix on CD.

Chapter 3

Creating Your First Session

This chapter covers the basics of working with Pro Tools sessions. It introduces session configuration options, playback and navigation options, and session saving and opening operations.

Objectives

After you complete this chapter, you will be able to:

- Choose appropriate session parameters for a project
- Create and name tracks
- Recognize the difference between the playback cursor and the edit cursor
- Navigate your session for playback and editing
- Save, locate, and open sessions on available hard drives

Introduction

Before you can begin working with audio or MIDI in Pro Tools, you need to have a Pro Tools session open. This chapter covers the basics of creating a session, adding tracks to your session, navigating your session, and saving and reopening sessions.

Quick Start

When you first launch Pro Tools, the Quick Start dialog box is displayed, giving you quick access to options for creating or opening a session. The Quick Start dialog box lets you choose any of the following four actions:

- Create a new session from a template.
- Create a new blank session.
- Open any of the 10 most recent sessions.
- Open any other session on your system.

 Press **CTRL+UP** ARROW *or* **DOWN** ARROW *(Windows) or* **COMMAND+UP** ARROW *or* **DOWN** ARROW *(Mac) to select different session Quick Start options.*

Quick Start dialog box

Creating and Configuring a Pro Tools Session

From the Quick Start dialog box, you can begin a new recording project either by selecting **CREATE SESSION FROM TEMPLATE** and choosing a session template from the list or by selecting **CREATE BLANK SESSION**. As discussed in Chapter 2, creating a session sets up a standard hierarchy of folders for the session and its associated files. The characteristics of your recording will be determined by the session parameter settings. To specify these settings, click the **SESSION PARAMETERS** reveal button in the Quick Start dialog box. The dialog box will expand to display configurable audio and I/O parameters.

Session parameters in the Quick Start dialog box

PRO TOOLS SESSION TEMPLATES

The Pro Tools installer disc includes factory session templates that are pre-configured with common track and mixer setups. You can use these templates and/or create your own to avoid having to configure your studio setup from scratch every time you start a new session.

 To create a new session when the Quick Start dialog box is not being displayed, choose **FILE > NEW SESSION**. *The New Session dialog box will appear, allowing you to specify the session parameters.*

Choosing Session Parameter Settings

The session parameter settings include selections for audio file type, sample rate, I/O settings, and bit depth.

Audio File Type

Pro Tools stores audio as WAV or AIFF files. WAV is the default file type on all platforms. Use the default (WAV) format unless you intend to work primarily with imported files in another format.

Sample Rate

Pro Tools supports sample rates up to 192 kHz with a compatible audio interface. To optimize the file sizes in your session, choose the lowest sample rate that meets the needs of the project.

A sample rate of 44.1 kHz, the industry standard for audio CDs, is often adequate for home- and project-studio recordings. Higher sample rates can be chosen for demanding projects, to capture a greater frequency response from the source audio and to minimize sound degradation throughout the project lifecycle. However, with higher sample rates come greater disk space requirements for your session. (See Table 3.1 in the "Bit Depth" section of this chapter.)

For more details on sample rates, see the "How Sample Rate Affects Frequency Resolution" section in Chapter 1.

I/O Settings

Pro Tools provides preset input and output configurations for Stereo Mix or various surround sound options (Pro Tools HD and Pro Tools with the Complete Production Toolkit 2), such as 5.1 Mix I/O. You can also choose Last Used to load the settings from your last session. Use the settings that match the intended output of your final mix. For the Pro Tools 101 course, we will use the Stereo Mix setting only.

 Use the STEREO MIX setting whenever you are recording music or other audio intended for a general consumer market, such as music to be burned to audio CDs or to be posted as MP3 files.

Bit Depth

Pro Tools allows you to record in 16-bit or 24-bit audio resolution. The 16-bit option generates smaller files and is typically adequate for basic recordings destined for audio CDs. The 24-bit option provides a greater dynamic range in your recorded audio (see the "How Bit Depth Affects Amplitude Resolution" section in Chapter 1) and lowers the noise floor. This option should be used for high-end recordings that include very quiet passages (such as a classical orchestra piece), recordings that require intensive processing, and recordings intended for media that support higher resolution audio, such as DVD.

 For the highest quality audio, record at 24 bits and properly dither down, if needed, during the final mix. Dithering is covered in the Pro Tools 110 course.

Table 3.1 shows the relationship between sample rate, bit depth, and hard disk space consumption for the standard configurations supported in Pro Tools.

Table 3.1 Audio Recording Storage Requirements

Session Sample Rate	Session Bit Depth	Megabytes/Track Minute (Mono)	Megabytes/Track Minute (Stereo)
44.1 kHz	16-bit	5 MB	10 MB
44.1 kHz	24-bit	7.5 MB	15 MB
48 kHz	16-bit	5.5 MB	11 MB
48 kHz	24-bit	8.2 MB	16.4 MB
88.2 kHz	16-bit	10 MB	20 MB
88.2 kHz	24-bit	15 MB	30 MB
96 kHz	16-bit	11 MB	22 MB
96 kHz	24-bit	16.5 MB	33 MB
176.4 kHz	16-bit	20 MB	40 MB
176.4 kHz	24-bit	30 MB	60 MB
192 kHz	16-bit	22 MB	44 MB
192 kHz	24-bit	33 MB	66 MB

Creating the Session

After choosing your session parameters and clicking **OK** in the Quick Start dialog box (or the New Session dialog box), you will be prompted to choose a save location and a name for the new session.

Dialog box for naming and saving a session

Using the dialog box, navigate to a valid audio drive, enter a name, and click **SAVE** to save your session-related files to the selected location. The new Pro Tools session will open, with no tracks in the Edit and Mix windows.

 You can configure Pro Tools to automatically add a click track to new sessions. Choose **SETUP > PREFERENCES** *and select the* **MIDI** *tab. Enable the option for* **AUTOMATICALLY CREATE CLICK TRACK IN NEW SESSIONS**.

Adding Tracks

Once you've created a new session, you will need to create and name new tracks. In Pro Tools, tracks are where audio, MIDI, and automation data are recorded and edited. Audio and MIDI data can be edited into regions that are copied or repeated in different locations to create loops, to rearrange sections or entire songs, or to assemble material from multiple takes. You add tracks to a Pro Tools session using the New Tracks dialog box.

The New Tracks dialog box

To add tracks to your session, choose **TRACK > NEW** to open the New Tracks dialog box and then choose the number of tracks and the track format, type, and timebase using the dialog box controls.

Track Number

The New Tracks dialog box allows you to add multiple tracks to your session simultaneously. To add multiple tracks with the same format, type, and timebase, enter the number of tracks to add in the Track Total field. To add multiple tracks using different configurations, click on the **ADD ROW** button (plus sign).

You can simultaneously add as many tracks with as many different configurations as your session will allow.

 *Tracks will be added to your session in the order shown in the New Tracks dialog box. To rearrange the track order, click on the **MOVE ROW** control and drag the row to a new position.*

Arranging tracks using the Move Row control

Track Format

Within the New Tracks dialog box, you can choose a format for the track or tracks you are adding to your session. Available options include mono, stereo, or multi-channel formats, depending on the type of track you are adding and the type of system you are using. Stereo tracks provide the added benefit of automatically linking both channels for editing, mixing, and region renaming, although separate control over each individual channel of the stereo pair is not possible.

Track Type

Track types supported in Pro Tools include the following:

- Audio tracks
- MIDI tracks
- Instrument tracks

- Video tracks (Complete Production Toolkit 2 or Pro Tools HD required for multiple tracks)
- Auxiliary inputs
- VCA Masters (Complete Production Toolkit 2 or Pro Tools HD only)
- Master faders

Any combination of the supported track types can be added using the New Tracks dialog box.

 Standard Pro Tools software without Complete Production Toolkit 2 does not include Video tracks in the New Tracks dialog box, since only a single Video track is supported. A Video track will be created only if you import video into your session.

Audio Tracks

Audio tracks allow you to import/record and edit an audio signal as a waveform. Audio tracks can be mono, stereo, or any supported multi-channel format.

Host-based Pro Tools systems can create up to 128 voiceable tracks in a session (up to 96 active), while Pro Tools|HD systems can create up to 512 such tracks (up to 192 voiced); however, the session sample rate, the number of voices your hardware supports, and the continuity of your audio will determine how many tracks you can actually play back and record simultaneously.

 Pro Tools uses the host computer's CPU to mix and process Audio tracks. Computers with faster clock speeds yield higher track counts and more plug-in processing.

MIDI Tracks

MIDI tracks store MIDI note and controller data. Pro Tools includes an integrated MIDI sequencer that lets you import/record and edit MIDI data in much the same way that you perform these operations when working with audio files. MIDI data appears in tracks in the Pro Tools Edit window, referencing the same Timeline as Audio tracks.

Note that you do not specify a track format (mono or stereo) for MIDI tracks, since no audio passes through the track; MIDI tracks are data-only.

Instrument Tracks

Instrument tracks combine the functions of MIDI tracks and auxiliary inputs (see the upcoming "Auxiliary Inputs" section) into a single track type, making them ideal for composing with virtual instrument plug-ins, sound modules, and all your other MIDI devices.

Video Tracks

Video tracks let you add or import video to the Timeline. Pro Tools lets you add or import one Video track per session and use a single video clip on the track. Pro Tools systems with Complete Production Toolkit 2, and systems with Pro Tools|HD hardware or Pro Tools|HD Native hardware, let you add multiple Video tracks to the Timeline and use multiple video files and Video regions on each Video track. Only one Video track can be active, or *online*, at any time.

Auxiliary Inputs

An Aux Input track can be used as an effects return, a destination for a submix, an input to monitor or process live audio (such as the output of a synthesizer triggered from a MIDI source), or a control point for any other audio routing task. Auxiliary inputs can be mono, stereo, or any supported multi-channel format.

VCA Master Tracks

VCA Master tracks are available in Pro Tools HD software only, or in Pro Tools software with Complete Production Toolkit 2. These tracks emulate the operation of voltage-controlled amplifier channels on analog consoles. Traditional VCA channel faders are used to control, group, or offset the signal levels of other channels on the console. In similar fashion, a Pro Tools VCA Master track is associated with a Mix group, and the controls of the tracks in the Mix group can then be modified by the controls on the VCA Master.

   VCA Masters are covered in the Pro Tools 201 course.

Master Faders

A master fader is a single fader used to control hardware output levels and bus paths. Master Fader tracks control the overall level of the Audio tracks that are routed to the session's main output paths or busses. In Pro Tools, you can create a Master Fader track for mono, stereo, or any supported multi-channel format.

   Example: *Suppose you have 24 tracks in a session with Tracks 1 through 8 routed to Analog Output 1–2, Tracks 9 through 16 routed to Analog Output 3–4, and Tracks 17 through 24 routed to Analog Output 5–6. You might want to create three master faders, one to control each of the output pairs.*

Timebase

The Track *Timebase* refers to the type of Time Scale that material on the track is associated with. All track types can be set to either sample-based (for the Samples Time Scale) or tick-based (for the Bars|Beats Time Scale), with different tracks set to different timebases, as needed.

Audio tracks are sample-based by default, meaning that audio regions and events have absolute locations on the Timeline, correlated to specific sample locations. Material on sample-based tracks maintains a constant absolute position on the track, regardless of tempo or meter changes specified in the session.

By contrast, MIDI and Instrument tracks are tick-based by default, meaning that MIDI regions and events are fixed to bar and beat positions and move relative to the sample Timeline as meter and tempo changes occur.

Although Audio tracks are sample-based by default, Elastic Audio–enabled tracks can be switched to tick-based in order to automatically follow tempo changes in your session and conform to the session's tempo map.

You select whether a track is sample-based or tick-based when you create it; however, you can change timebases later as needed.

Sample-based editing and tick-based editing are covered in more detail in the Pro Tools 110 and 210M courses.

Naming Tracks

When you create tracks in Pro Tools, they are added to the session using generic names, such as Audio 1, Audio 2, MIDI 1, and so on. To change a track name to something more meaningful, double-click the track name within the Edit window or the Mix window. A dialog box will appear, allowing you to rename the track.

The Track Name dialog box

 You can also name a track by right-clicking on the track name and choosing RENAME *from the pop-up menu.*

Using the Track Name dialog box, you can also add comments to a track and cycle through the tracks in your session, renaming and adding comments to each, using the NEXT and PREVIOUS buttons. Comments you add will be displayed in the Comments area, if displayed, at the bottom of the channel strip (Mix window) or at the head of a track (Edit window).

 Press CTRL+LEFT/RIGHT ARROW *(Windows) or* COMMAND+LEFT/RIGHT ARROW *(Mac) in the Track Name dialog box to cycle through your tracks and rename each without leaving the keyboard.*

Deleting Tracks

When you delete tracks, your audio or MIDI region data will remain in the Region List, but your arrangement of the regions on the deleted track (the track's playlist) will be lost. This is also true of video regions in Pro Tools HD or Pro Tools with Complete Production Toolkit 2.

 The Track Delete command cannot be undone.

To delete a track, follow these steps:

1. Click the track nameplate to select the track; Shift-click or Ctrl-click (Windows)/Command-click (Mac) to select multiple tracks.
2. Choose TRACK > DELETE.

3. If all selected tracks are empty, they will be deleted immediately; if any tracks contain data, you will be prompted with a verification dialog box. Click DELETE to permanently remove the selected tracks from the session.

 You can also right-click on a track name and choose DELETE *from the pop-up menu to remove all selected tracks.*

Adding Audio to Your Session

Once you have created one or more Audio tracks in your session, you can begin adding audio, either by recording to your track(s) or by importing existing audio files. When you record audio or import audio from a hard drive (or other volume) into tracks in your session, Pro Tools also places the audio files in the Region List.

Audio recording is covered in Chapter 4, and audio importing is covered in Chapter 5.

The Playback Cursor and the Edit Cursor

The Edit window displays two different cursors: a *playback* cursor and an *edit* cursor. The two cursors are linked by default; however, you can unlink them to meet the needs of a particular situation. When unlinked, the different cursors allow you to play one area of your session while simultaneously editing an entirely different area. This can be useful when you are working with a film or video scene or when you are trying out edits within an area that you need to audition repeatedly.

Throughout this book, we will assume that the playback and edit cursors remain linked, unless otherwise noted.

 Workflows that involve unlinking the edit and playback cursors are included in the Pro Tools 210M and 310M courses.

To link or unlink the playback and edit cursors, choose OPTIONS > LINK TIMELINE AND EDIT SELECTION. The option should be checked (linked) for this course.

Playback Cursor

The playback cursor is a solid, non-blinking line that moves across the screen during playback and indicates where the current playback point is. The playback cursor's exact time location is displayed in the Main and Sub Counters in the Transport window (mirrored in Counters in the Edit window when LINK TIMELINE AND EDIT SELECTION is active).

Edit Cursor

The edit cursor is a flashing line that appears when you click the Selector tool in a track. The blinking edit cursor indicates the starting point for any editing tasks that you perform. By making a selection with the edit cursor, you define an area for Pro Tools to perform a desired editing task.

With the Timeline and Edit Selections linked and the Pro Tools Transport stopped, the playback cursor's location will always match the edit cursor's location.

Setting the Playback Point

With the Timeline and Edit Selections linked, you can set the playback point using the Selector tool by clicking directly on a track. To set the playback point on a track using the Selector tool, follow these steps:

1. In the Edit window, click the SELECTOR tool. The cursor will turn into an I-beam.
2. Click and release the mouse button at any point in an existing track.
3. Press the SPACE BAR to begin playback from this point.
4. To stop playback, press the SPACE BAR again.
5. To move to a different playback point in the track, click the SELECTOR at the new position and press the SPACE BAR again.

You can also set the playback point with any tool selected by clicking on any Ruler in the Timeline display area of the Edit window. This allows you to set the playback point without changing tools. Clicking on a Timebase Ruler provides a common way to set the playback point regardless of whether the Timeline and Edit Selections are linked.

Scrolling Options

Pro Tools offers several different display options that affect how the contents of the Edit window are displayed during playback and recording. The three options available on all Pro Tools systems are discussed in the following sections. Additional options that provide continuous scrolling are available on Pro Tools|HD systems and Pro Tools systems with Complete Production Toolkit 2.

No Scrolling

Scrolling can be turned off by choosing OPTIONS > SCROLLING > NO SCROLLING. This option prevents Pro Tools from scrolling the Edit window during playback and recording as the playback cursor moves off screen and does not reposition the window when playback or recording is stopped.

After Playback

To prevent scrolling during playback but have the Edit window reposition to the stop point during playback and recording, use the After Playback scrolling option. To select this option, choose OPTIONS > SCROLLING > AFTER PLAYBACK.

Page

To scroll the Edit window one screen (or "page") at a time as the playback cursor moves across the Timeline, enable the Page scrolling option. To select this option, choose OPTIONS > SCROLLING > PAGE.

When Page scrolling is enabled, the playback cursor moves across the Edit window until it reaches the right edge of the window. Each time the playback cursor reaches the right edge, the entire contents of the window are scrolled, one screen at a time, and the playback cursor continues from the left edge of the Edit window.

 When the zoom magnification of the Edit window is too high, Page scrolling may not function properly. If you experience problems, decrease the zoom magnification to enable Page scrolling.

Locating the Playback Cursor

At times, the playback cursor might be difficult to find in a session. For example, if the No Scrolling option is selected, the playback cursor will move off screen after it has played past the location currently visible in the Edit window.

To make navigation easier, Pro Tools provides a Playback Cursor Locator, which you can use to jump to the playback cursor when it is off screen.

If the playback cursor is not visible in the Edit window, the Playback Cursor Locator will appear in the Main Timebase Ruler, as follows:

- On the left if the playback cursor is located before the visible area
- On the right if the playback cursor is located after the visible area

Playback Cursor Locator

The Playback Cursor Locator is red when any track is record-enabled and blue when no tracks are record-enabled.

To locate the playback cursor when it is off screen, click the PLAYBACK CURSOR LOCATOR in the Main Timebase Ruler. The Edit window's waveform display will jump to the playback cursor's current onscreen location.

Saving, Locating, and Opening Existing Sessions

As with most software applications, Pro Tools provides commands for saving and opening your files under the File menu. The following sections describe the options for saving, locating, and opening your session files and other files related to your Pro Tools projects.

Saving a Session

While working in Pro Tools, it is important to save your work often. When you save a session using the two commands explained in the following sections, you are saving only the Pro Tools session file, not its associated files. (A session's audio and fade files are written directly to disk, so you don't have to save them independently.) Consequently, even very large sessions can be saved quickly.

Save Command

Saving can be done manually by choosing the Save command from the File menu. This saves the changes you have made since the last time you saved and writes the session in its current form over the old version. You cannot undo the Save command.

Save As Command

The Save As command is useful for saving a copy of the current session under a different name or in a different hard drive location. Because the Save As command closes the current session and lets you keep working on the renamed copy, it is particularly useful if you are experimenting and want to save successive stages of a session. This way, you can save each major step under a different name, such as Student Session-2, Student Session-2A, and so on. By working this way, you can always retrace your steps if you should want to go back to an earlier version.

To use the Save As feature, follow these steps:

1. Choose FILE > SAVE AS.
2. Type a new name for the session.
3. Click SAVE.

The renamed, newly saved session will then remain open for you to continue your work.

 A third Save command, Save Copy In, allows you to create a copy from your current session with different session parameters and place it, along with copies of all associated audio files, in a new location. The Save Copy In command is discussed in Chapter 10.

Locating and Opening a Session

Pro Tools provides specialized windows, called *DigiBase browsers*, that you can use to quickly locate, manage, and open Pro Tools sessions and related media files. DigiBase browsers provide more meaningful search, navigation, file information, and audition capabilities than standard operating system–level functions.

If you know the location of the session you want to open, you can do so directly from the File menu (choose FILE > OPEN SESSION). For recently used sessions, choose FILE > OPEN RECENT and select the session that you wish to open from the submenu. In other cases, you can use the DigiBase *Workspace* browser to help locate a session on your system.

Locating a Session

The DigiBase Workspace browser has a powerful search tool that lets you search for Pro Tools file types, such as session files, audio files, and video files.

To search for Pro Tools sessions in the DigiBase Workspace browser, follow these steps:

1. Choose WINDOW > WORKSPACE. The Workspace browser will open as the active window.
2. In the Workspace window, click the FIND button (magnifying glass) to show the search tools.

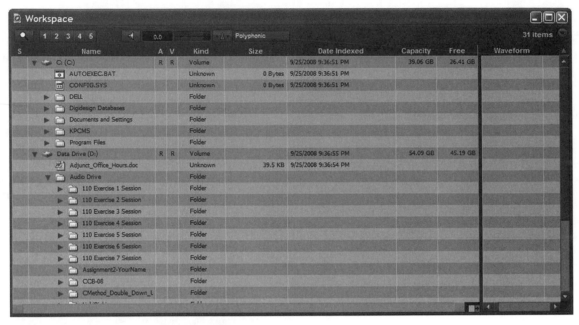

The DigiBase Workspace browser window

Clicking the Find button in the Workspace browser

3. Select the volumes or folders you want to search by selecting the appropriate check boxes in the Workspace window. Note that you can navigate through the file system by clicking the triangle icons to expand or collapse volumes and folders.

Selecting a folder to search

4. Click the drop-down button in the Kind column and select SESSION FILE.

5. Click the SEARCH button. The search results will be shown in the bottom half of the Workspace browser.

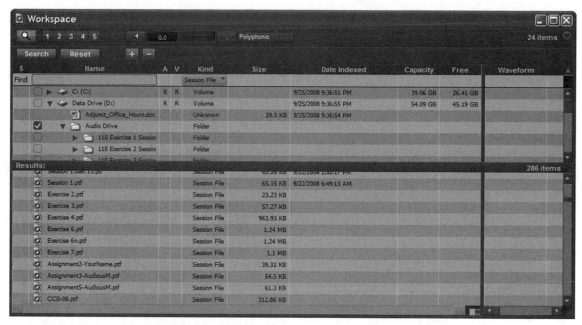

Search results shown in the Workspace browser

Opening a Session

Once you have located the session you are interested in, you can open the session directly from the DigiBase Workspace browser window. (You can also open Pro Tools sessions from the computer's hard drive by double-clicking on the session file in an Explorer or Finder window.)

 Pro Tools can have only one session open at a time. If you attempt to open a session while another session is open, Pro Tools will prompt you to save the current session and close it before opening the selected session.

To open a Pro Tools session using a DigiBase browser, follow these steps:

1. Locate the session file you want to open in the Workspace browser.
2. Double-click the session file.

The Pro Tools session will open with all windows and display options appearing exactly as saved. Any previously created tracks will appear in the Edit and Mix windows, and all audio and MIDI regions associated with the session will appear in the Region List at the right of the Edit window.

 If the Edit or Mix window is not displayed in a session you have opened, you can display it by choosing the corresponding command in the Window menu.

Chapter 4

Making Your First Audio Recording

This chapter covers the steps required to begin recording audio in your Pro Tools sessions. It also describes the types of audio regions your session will include and covers processes for keeping your regions and audio files organized.

Objectives

After you complete this chapter, you will be able to:

- Set up Pro Tools hardware and software for recording audio
- Create and configure a click track
- Record audio onto tracks in your session
- Recognize whole-file regions and subset regions
- Organize your regions and audio files after recording to minimize clutter and optimize your session

Introduction

Many Pro Tools projects require extensive audio recording. After all, multi-track recording is a cornerstone of what Pro Tools is all about. Whether your projects involve a simple setup in a home studio or an elaborate system in a professional environment, knowing how to get your audio onto tracks in Pro Tools is the first step to creating a successful recording.

Before Recording

Before you begin recording in a session, you should ensure that your system has enough storage space for the project. The amount of storage space consumed by audio regions in a project will vary, depending on the bit depth and sample rate of the session. (See the "Analog-to-Digital Conversion" section in Chapter 1 for a detailed discussion of bit depth and sample rate.)

Audio Storage Requirements

Pro Tools records all audio using sample rates ranging from 44.1 kHz to 192 kHz, with bit depths of 16-bit or 24-bit. At a sample rate of 44.1 kHz, each track consumes 5 megabytes (MB) of disk space per minute for 16-bit audio (mono) and 7.5 MB per minute for 24-bit audio (mono). With increasing bit depth and sample rates, hard disk space consumption increases correspondingly; recording at a sample rate of 88.2 kHz, therefore, consumes twice as much space as recording at 44.1 kHz. Similarly, recording in stereo consumes twice the space of recording in mono.

 Table 3.1 in Chapter 3 shows storage consumption at the different data rates supported by Pro Tools.

CALCULATING FILE SIZES

The sample rate and bit depth of the audio you record are directly related to the size of the resulting files. In fact, you can calculate file sizes in mathematical terms using these two parameters:

Sample Rate × Bit Depth = Bits per Second

Or, stated another way:

Sample Rate × Bit Depth × 60 = Bits per Minute

In the binary world of computers, 8 bits make a byte, 1024 bytes make a kilobyte (KB), and 1024 KB make a megabyte (MB). Therefore, this equation can be restated as follows:

(Sample Rate × Bit Depth × 60) √ (8 bits per byte × 1024 bytes per kilobyte × 1024 kilobytes per megabyte) = Megabytes (MB) per Minute

Reducing terms gives us the following:

Sample Rate × Bit Depth √ 139,810 = MB per Minute

So by way of example, recording audio at a sample rate of 44,100 samples per second with a bit depth of 24 bits per sample would generate files that consume space at the following rate:

44,100 × 24 √ 139,810 = 7.57 MB per Minute

Disk Space Window

With a session running, you can monitor storage space and estimate the amount of available record time remaining for your project using the Disk Space window.

To access the disk space window, choose WINDOW > DISK SPACE.

Disk Space window

The Disk Space window shows the number of continuous track minutes available on each mounted hard drive, using the current session's sample rate and bit depth.

Preparing to Record

Once you have created a session, added an Audio track (or tracks) to record onto, and verified that you have adequate disk space available for your project, you will need to prepare your hardware and software for recording. If your session does not already include a click track, you might want to add one to use as a tempo reference while recording. Whether or not you use a click track, the general processes you will use to prepare for recording audio are as follows:

1. Check the hardware connections.
2. Record-enable the Audio track(s).
3. Set the track input path, level, and pan.

Creating a Click Track (Optional)

When you're working with a song or other composition that is bar- and beat-based, you might want to record tracks while listening to a MIDI-generated metronome click in Pro Tools. This ensures that recorded material, both MIDI and audio, will align with your session's bar and beat boundaries.

Aligning track material with beats allows you to take advantage of many useful MIDI editing functions in Pro Tools. It also enables you to arrange your song in sections by copying and pasting measures in Grid mode.

To set up a click track, use the TRACK > CREATE CLICK TRACK command. This command inserts the Click plug-in on a new Auxiliary Input track. The Click plug-in is a mono plug-in that creates an audio metronome click during session playback. You can use this audio click as a tempo reference when performing and recording. The Click plug-in receives its tempo and meter data from the Pro Tools application, enabling it to follow any changes in tempo and meter that have been set in a session. Several click sound presets are included for you to choose from.

To create a click track, do the following:

• Choose TRACK > CREATE CLICK TRACK. A new click track will be created in your session.

To configure the Click plug-in, do the following:

1. Choose **OPTIONS > CLICK** to enable the Click option, if not already active (or enable the Metronome button in the Transport window).

2. From the Insert panel for the click track (Mix or Edit window), click on the **CLICK** insert nameplate. The Click plug-in window will open.

The Click plug-in window

 Details on inserts and plug-ins are presented in Chapter 9.

3. Click on the drop-down labeled **<FACTORY DEFAULT>** to select a click sound preset, and set other options as desired.

   • **Accented.** Control the output level for the accented beat (Beat 1 of each bar) of the audio click.

   • **Unaccented Beats.** Control the output level for the unaccented beats of the audio click.

4. Click the **CLOSE** icon in the upper-right corner (Windows) or upper-left corner (Mac) to exit the Click plug-in window.

5. Choose **SETUP > CLICK/COUNTOFF** to open the Click/Countoff Options dialog box; set the Click and Countoff options as desired.

Click/Countoff Options dialog box

 The Note, Velocity, Duration, and Output options in this dialog box are used with MIDI instrument–based clicks and do not affect the Click plug-in.

When you begin playback, a click is generated according to the tempo and meter of the current session and the settings in the Click/Countoff Options dialog box.

Checking Hardware Connections

Recording audio involves connecting an instrument, microphone, or other sound source to your Pro Tools system. Most audio interfaces have inputs designated for different sound sources and input types. Before starting to record, you should verify that your sound source is connected to the appropriate inputs of the audio interface and that the signal is being passed through correctly. For basic recording, it is simplest to use the lowest available inputs on your audio interface that match your needs (for example, Input 1 for a mono source or Inputs 1 and 2 for a stereo pair).

If necessary, check the configuration of your audio interface and/or the Hardware Setup of your system to ensure correct routing of inputs or to change existing settings. Depending on your audio interface, you can use physical controls or switches, the controls in the Hardware Setup dialog box, or a separate control panel to define which physical inputs and outputs on your audio interface are routed to available inputs and outputs in Pro Tools.

 Example: Suppose you are using an Mbox with a guitar and bass connected to the front-panel instrument inputs and microphones connected to the rear-panel XLR/TRS inputs. Using the source selector switches on the front panel, you can choose which source (front or rear) is routed to each Pro Tools input.

Record-Enabling Tracks

To set up a Pro Tools Audio track for recording, click the track's RECORD ENABLE button in either the Edit window or the Mix window. The button will flash red when the track is record-enabled.

When a track has been record-enabled, the Track Fader turns red, indicating that it is now functioning as a record monitor level control.

 To record-enable multiple Audio tracks, click the RECORD ENABLE buttons on additional tracks. To record-enable all tracks of a particular type in the session, Alt-click (Windows) or Option-click (Mac OS) on any track's RECORD ENABLE button.

Record Enable buttons: Mix window and Edit window

Setting Input Path, Level, and Pan

With your sound source connected to the inputs of your Pro Tools interface, you are now ready to set Pro Tools to receive a signal from your source and to pass the signal through the system for recording and monitoring purposes.

Input Path

Each Audio track has an *Audio Input Path selector*, which allows you to route a signal from an input on your interface to the track for recording. To set the incoming signal, do the following:

1. Locate the channel strip for the track you will record to in the Mix window.
2. Verify that the input displayed on the Input Path selector matches the input that your sound source is plugged into on your audio interface.

The Input Path selector in the Mix window

3. If necessary, click the INPUT PATH SELECTOR to make changes, selecting the correct input path from the pop-up menu. (Note: Stereo tracks will have a pair of inputs routed to the track.)

Input Path selector pop-up menu

 Example: *Suppose you are recording a vocalist and acoustic guitar accompaniment onto Tracks 1 and 2 of your session, with the vocalist's mic plugged into Input 1 of your Mbox and the guitar mic plugged into Input 2. In the Pro Tools Mix window, you should have the Input Path selector for your first track set to* **A 1 (MONO)** *(to receive signal from Input 1) and the Input Path selector for your second track set to* **A 2 (MONO)** *(to receive signal from Input 2).*

Input Level

As a general rule, input levels should be adjusted to obtain a strong, clean signal without clipping. Unlike when recording to tape, however, you do not need to record at the highest possible level in Pro Tools. Recording too hot can leave little room for subsequent gain-based processing (such as EQ) and can lead to digital clipping, which is always detrimental to audio quality. For best results, aim for an average peak input level around –6 dB, keeping the track meter in the yellow range. To do this, adjust the level of your analog source while monitoring the indicator lights on your onscreen track meter.

Adjusting the input level will typically require you to change the source volume, adjust the microphone placement, or modify the incoming signal strength using a mixer or pre-amplifier, because record levels cannot be adjusted within Pro Tools. Note that although a track's Volume Fader can be used to increase or decrease playback levels, the Volume Fader *does not* affect record levels.

Many Pro Tools, M-Audio, and third-party I/O devices provide pre-amplifier gains for their inputs. For all other I/O devices, record levels are set entirely from the source or pre-I/O signal processing.

In the case of direct digital recording, which involves a one-to-one transfer, the source levels are copied directly to Pro Tools, typically with no level adjustment possible. (Some digital playback devices support digital output gain adjustment, allowing levels to be modified at the source.)

Pan Position

To set the pan position of the incoming signal (the placement of the signal in the stereo field), change the position of the Pan knob(s) for the track in the Mix window. The pan is initially set to >0<, signifying the center of the stereo field. Pan settings range from <100 (hard left) to 100> (hard right). Setting the pan affects the stereo placement of a signal for monitoring and playback purposes only; it has no effect on how the audio files are actually recorded.

Recording and Managing Audio

With your sound source routed to one or more tracks and the desired tracks record-enabled, you are ready to begin recording audio. Pro Tools offers a variety of recording modes that can be used in different audio recording situations. We will use the default mode (Nondestructive Record) for all work done in this course.

 Other record modes are covered in the Pro Tools 110, 201, and 210M/210P courses.

To begin recording audio, do the following:

1. Display the Transport window, if it is not already showing (**WINDOW > TRANSPORT**).
2. To display or hide the expanded view, click the **EXPANDED VIEW** toggle button in the upper-right corner (Windows) or upper-left corner (Mac) of the Transport window, or click the **TRANSPORT WINDOW** menu icon and select **EXPANDED TRANSPORT**.
3. Verify that one or more tracks have been record-enabled. (See the "Record-Enabling Tracks" section earlier in this chapter.)

4. Click the RECORD button in the Transport window to enter Record Ready mode. The button will turn red and begin to flash.

Record button
(active)

The Transport window in Record Ready mode

5. When you're ready, click PLAY in the Transport window to begin recording (or press the SPACE BAR).

 You can also press CTRL+SPACE BAR *(Windows),* COMMAND+SPACE BAR *(Mac), or* F12 *to start recording immediately without first entering Record Ready mode.*

6. When you have finished your record take, click the STOP button in the Transport window (or press the SPACE BAR).

Organizing after Recording

You should complete several housekeeping steps immediately after making a successful audio recording to stay organized and to prevent accidents while editing.

Return to Playback Mode

Returning record-enabled tracks to Playback mode will prevent unintended recording onto those tracks during subsequent operations in your session. To return a track to Playback mode and adjust the playback settings, do the following:

1. Click the RECORD ENABLE button on the Audio track to take it out of Record Ready mode. The track's Volume Fader will now function as a playback level control rather than as an input-monitoring level control.

2. Click PLAY in the Transport window.

3. Adjust the playback level and panning as necessary.

 If you have overloaded your audio inputs during recording and caused clipping, the topmost indicator on the level meter will stay lit. Click the indicator light to clear it.

Organize Audio Files and Regions

Each time you record audio into Pro Tools, you create a single audio file that appears in both the Region List and the Track Playlist. An *audio file* is an entire unedited, continuous audio recording. Audio files—or *whole-file regions*, as they are known in Pro Tools—are written and stored externally from your session file. Organizing audio files involves maintaining information both within the Pro Tools session and within the external files.

When you record audio into Pro Tools, the audio files are stored in your session's Audio Files folder by default.

As you begin to edit, you also create smaller, more manageable pieces of the original sound file, called *subset regions*, or simply *regions*. An audio subset region is an electronic pointer, normally stored within the session document, that references some portion of an audio file. Regions can range in length from one sample up to a maximum of two hours. Subset regions do not store audio information directly, but instead store information used to display, edit, and play back audio information contained in the whole-file region. Organizing audio subset regions is generally internal to Pro Tools only.

Recognizing Audio Files and Regions

The Region List in the Edit window shows all whole-file regions and subset regions that have been used in your session.

Pro Tools lists all whole-file regions in boldface type and all subset regions in normal type. When sound files are recorded onto stereo Audio tracks, in addition to appearing in boldface type, the word *stereo* is shown in parentheses at the end of the file name. Examples of these file and region types are shown in the following figure.

Audio files and regions in the Region List

Note that regions on stereo Audio tracks also allow you to view both left and right channels of the region separately by clicking the disclosure triangle.

Audio regions represent pieces of audio data that can be moved or edited within Pro Tools. They are created during normal editing, either by the user or automatically by Pro Tools, and can refer to any type of audio, such as music, dialogue, sound effects, Foley, or automated dialogue replacement (ADR).

Whole-file regions and subset regions can also appear in the Track Playlist. As shown in the following figure, each audio region on a track is displayed using a solid rectangle to clearly delineate the region boundaries.

Audio regions as displayed in a Track Playlist

Naming Audio Files and Regions

During recording and editing, Pro Tools gives your audio files and regions default file names. At times, you might want to change the names of the files and/or regions in your session to make them easier to recognize and more meaningful for your purposes.

Default Naming Conventions

When you record audio on a track, Pro Tools names the resulting file (a whole-file region) using the name of the Audio track followed by an underscore and the take number for that track (a sequential number based on the number of times you've recorded on that track). Following are examples of the file names Pro Tools automatically creates after recording for the first time on a mono track and on a stereo track:

      Audio 1_01   Where *Audio 1* is the mono track name and *01* is the take number

      Music 1_01 (Stereo)   Where *Music 1* is the stereo track name and *01* is the take number

When you edit a whole-file region on a track, Pro Tools retains the original file and creates a new, edited region, appending a hyphen followed by the edit number (a sequential number based on the number of edits you have created from that whole-file region) onto the end of the region name. Following are examples of the region names Pro Tools automatically creates for the first edit to whole-file regions on a mono track and on a stereo track:

      Audio 1_02-01   Where *Audio 1_02* is a whole-file region on a mono track and *01* is the edit number for that region

      Music 1_02-01 (Stereo) Where *Music 1_02* is a whole-file region on a stereo track and *01* is the edit number for that region

Changing File and Region Names

You can change the default name that Pro Tools assigns to a whole-file region or a subset region at any time. To rename a region, do one of the following:

- Double-click the file or region in the Edit window (with the **Grabber** tool) or in the Region List.

 *Double-clicking on a MIDI region opens the MIDI Editor window by default. This behavior can be changed using the associated Preferences setting (**Setup** > **Preferences** > **MIDI** tab).*

- Right-click on the file or region in the Edit window or Region List and select **Rename** from the pop-up menu.

The Name dialog box will open.

The Name dialog box

When renaming a whole-file region, you can select from the following options in the Name dialog box:

- **Name Region Only.** Renames the file region in Pro Tools but leaves the original file name on the hard drive unchanged.
- **Name Region and Disk File.** Renames the region in Pro Tools and renames the file on the hard drive as well.

Note that when you rename a stereo file or region, both corresponding left and right channels are renamed accordingly.

Removing Audio Regions and Deleting Audio Files

Pro Tools makes an important distinction between removing regions from a session and deleting files from a hard drive:

- When you remove a region from a session, the parent audio file remains on the hard drive and can be used in other regions elsewhere in the session or in other sessions.
- When you delete an audio file from the hard drive, all regions referring to that file are removed from the session, and the file is permanently deleted.

Removing Audio Regions

As your Region List grows in your session, you might want to periodically remove the audio regions you no longer need, in order to reduce clutter. However, because removing audio regions does not delete the audio files, it will have no effect on hard drive usage of the session.

To remove unwanted audio regions from the Region List, do the following:

1. Select the regions in the Region List that you want to clear. To select multiple regions, **CTRL-CLICK** (Windows) or **COMMAND-CLICK** (Mac) on regions individually; to select a continuous range, **SHIFT-CLICK** on the top and bottom of the range.
2. Choose **CLEAR** from the Regions pop-up menu.

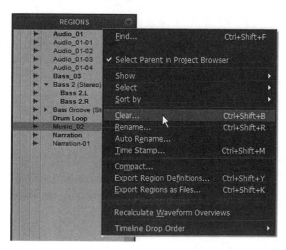

Regions pop-up menu

3. In the resulting Clear Regions dialog box, click REMOVE to remove the regions from the session, while leaving the audio files of any whole-file regions that are cleared on the hard drive.

The Clear Regions dialog box

Pro Tools requires that all regions used on any Track Playlist, in the Undo queue, or on the Clipboard remain in the Region List. If you attempt to remove a region that has been placed on a track, on the Clipboard, or in the Undo queue, the following warning appears:

Clear warning dialog box

Choose one of the following:

- **Yes.** This option clears the region from the Region List and the corresponding track, Undo queue, or Clipboard.
- **No.** This option cancels the Clear command.

Deleting Audio Files

As you work on your session, you will probably accumulate unwanted whole-file regions from test recordings or unusable takes. As you reduce clutter in your Region List, you might want to delete these unneeded audio files from your hard drive.

By removing audio files from the hard drive, you can free up additional drive space and reduce the overall storage requirements of your session. In addition to utilizing hard drive space more effectively, this will also help reduce the file backup time of your sessions.

To remove regions from the Region List and delete any associated audio files from the hard drive permanently, do the following:

1. Complete Steps 1 and 2 in the "Removing Audio Regions" section earlier in this chapter.
2. In the Clear Regions dialog box, click DELETE to remove the selected regions from the Region List *and* permanently delete the files for any selected whole-file regions from your hard drive.

 The Delete option permanently and irreversibly deletes audio files from your hard drive for the current session and all other sessions that reference the audio file. It cannot be undone. Use this command with caution.

Just like when you are removing audio regions, if you attempt to delete a file that has been placed on a track, on the Clipboard, or in the Undo queue, you will receive a warning message.

- Click **YES** to permanently remove the file from the session and from the hard drive.
- Click **NO** to leave the file untouched in the session and on the hard drive.

Pro Tools will prevent you from permanently deleting an audio file that is referenced by subset regions within the same session. If you attempt to delete an audio file that is referenced by other regions in the session, the following dialog box will appear:

Dialog box displayed when unable to delete

- Click **YES** to remove the whole-file region from the Region List, while leaving the audio file on the hard drive.
- Click **NO** to leave the whole-file region untouched in the Region List and on the hard drive.

If no other confirmation dialog box appears first, Pro Tools will prompt you with the following warning before completing the Delete command:

Delete warning dialog box

- Click **YES** to permanently remove the file from the session and from the hard drive.
- Click **NO** to leave the file untouched in the session and on the hard drive.

 *To bypass repeated warnings when you are clearing or deleting multiple files or regions, **ALT-CLICK** (Windows) or **OPTION-CLICK** (Mac) on the **YES** or **NO** button. This will prevent multiple warnings from appearing.*

Chapter 5

Importing Media into Your Session

This chapter introduces various processes for importing audio and video files into a Pro Tools session. It describes file formats and types that can be imported, explains the functions of the Import Audio dialog box and other methods of importing audio, and discusses importing video files.

Objectives

After you complete this chapter, you will be able to:

- Determine whether the bit depth, sample rate, and format of an audio file are compatible with your session
- Understand how Pro Tools treats stereo files
- Understand the functions of each part of the Import Audio dialog box
- Import audio files to the Region List or to Audio tracks in the Edit window
- Import video files to a Video track in the Edit window

Introduction

Many music and post-production projects require you to work with media files that have been created outside of your current session. Whether you need to import music loops, add tracks recorded by others, copy audio sound effects files from a CD, or place a video clip in your session, you will need to know how to use the import options provided in Pro Tools.

Considerations Prior to Import

Pro Tools allows you to import audio and video files that already reside on a hard drive (or other volume) into your session. You can import media using one of several techniques, depending upon the type of media you are importing. Pro Tools can read some file formats directly and can convert many other audio formats on import. Prior to importing a file, you should understand whether the file can be read by your session and how the file will change if it needs to be converted.

Bit Depth, Sample Rate, and File Format

The types of media files that you can successfully import into a Pro Tools session will depend in part on how your session was originally configured. Some important considerations for audio files include the bit depth, sample rate, and native file format of your session and of the files you plan to import. Important considerations for video files include the frame rate, sample rate, and file format.

Audio Bit Depth and Sample Rate

The bit depth (or bit resolution) of a Pro Tools session will be either 16-bit or 24-bit, and the sample rate may be any of the following: 44.1 kHz, 48 kHz, 88.2 kHz, 96 kHz, 176.4 kHz, or 192 kHz. These settings are specified when a session is created. (See the "Choosing Session Parameter Settings" section in Chapter 3.) The bit depth and sample rate of an imported file must match those of the current session in order to play back correctly.

Audio File Formats

The native audio file formats used in a Pro Tools session include Audio Interchange File Format (AIFF) and Waveform Audio File Format (WAV). You specify the audio file format when the session is created. (See the "Choosing Session Parameter Settings" section in Chapter 3.)

 To determine the bit depth, sample rate, and file format of an open session, choose SETUP > SESSION.

Pro Tools recognizes compatible file formats that match the sample rate and bit depth of your session, allowing you to add them to the Region List without requiring any file translation. All WAV and AIFF files can coexist in a session without requiring conversion. However, any files in another format as well as any files that have a different bit depth or sample rate from the session, regardless of format, must be converted.

Pro Tools will convert files on import, if necessary. Pro Tools can import many common audio file formats, including the following:

- **Sound Designer II (SD II).** SD II is a monophonic or stereo interleaved file format supported on Macintosh systems only. This format supports only 44.1- and 48-kHz sample rates and can be imported into sessions on either platform with conversion.

- **Audio Interchange File Format (AIFF).** This file format is used primarily on Macintosh systems, although the Windows versions of Pro Tools also support this file format. AIFF files can be recorded directly or imported without requiring conversion. The AIFF file format is commonly used with multimedia software programs for Macintosh, such as Final Cut, and is the standard audio file format used by Apple's QuickTime software.

- **Audio Interchange File Compressed (AIFC).** An updated variant of the original AIFF audio file standard for the Macintosh, AIFC allows users to apply audio compression standards to AIFF files. In Avid systems, AIFC file compression is usually turned off; as such, there is essentially no difference between the Avid AIFC format and the standard AIFF file format.

- **Waveform Audio File Format (WAV/WAVE).** Pro Tools reads and plays back any standard WAV (WAVE) format files. However, it records and exports WAV files exclusively in the Broadcast WAV or BWF format. (Like other WAV files, BWF files are denoted by the *.wav* extension.) BWF files store timestamps in a way that makes them ideal for file interchange operations. BWF is the default file format for both Mac and Windows-based Pro Tools systems. BWF/WAV files can be recorded directly and imported (without conversion) on either platform, allowing seamless audio file exchange between Mac and Windows.

- **MP3 (MPEG-1 Layer-3).** This file format remains popular for Internet audio. MP3 files are supported on all common computer platforms and employ file compression of 10:1, while still maintaining reasonable audio quality. Because of their small size and cross-platform support, they are well suited for use in email messages, web publishing, bulk file transfer, and storage. MP3 files must be converted for import to a Pro Tools session.

- **Windows Media Audio (WMA).** The WMA Standard format is becoming increasingly widespread and is second only to MP3 in popularity for compressed audio. The newer WMA Professional format offers higher quality and scales well at smaller file sizes; this format also supports multi-channel surround-sound files, sample rates up to 96 kHz, and 24-bit resolution. Pro Tools converts WMA files on import.

Video File Formats

Pro Tools can import video files in the QuickTime format. Pro Tools HD and Pro Tools with Complete Production Toolkit 2 can also import Avid video files. Windows systems also have the ability to import Windows Media (VC-1 AP) files.

Before you import a video file, you should verify the correct frame rate and sample rate, when applicable.

 QuickTime software is required for working with QuickTime files in Pro Tools. If you do not have the software installed on your system, you can obtain a free download from the Apple website (www.apple.com).

Configuration of Stereo Files

No universal stereo file configuration standard exists for software programs on Mac and Windows systems. However, two main stereo file configuration formats are common on both platforms: split stereo and interleaved stereo.

These two stereo file formats have no audible difference between them. The difference is primarily in how the audio is stored in the files. Either format can be imported into Pro Tools, although Pro Tools treats the two formats differently.

- **Split stereo.** In split stereo files, the stereo information is split between two separate mono files for the left and right channels. The split stereo file format is supported on Pro Tools systems (and Avid picture-editing systems); files in this format can be imported directly into a session. The split stereo file format is primarily used for Sound Designer II, AIFF/AIFC, and WAV/BWF files.
- **Interleaved stereo.** In an interleaved stereo file, the stereo information is combined (interleaved) into one single file that contains both left and right channel information. The stereo interleaved file format is not directly compatible with Pro Tools. When interleaved stereo files are imported into a session, Pro Tools rewrites (or translates) the file into corresponding split stereo files. Stereo interleaved files are primarily used for MP3 files and by software programs such as Adaptec/Roxio Toast, Apple Final Cut Pro, and QuickTime.

Importing interleaved stereo sound files is a non-destructive process, meaning it will not destroy or overwrite the original file. Instead, Pro Tools copies the left and right channel information from the original interleaved file into separate split stereo mono file pairs. These files are then placed in the Region List as stereo file pairs, with a corresponding notation of .L and .R appended to each file name.

Importing Audio

When you import audio from a hard drive (or other volume) into your session, Pro Tools places the audio files in the Region List. Pro Tools provides several options for importing audio into a session.

Import Audio Dialog Box

Audio files and regions can be imported directly to the Region List or imported to new tracks using the Import Audio dialog box. This dialog box can be used to add, copy, and/or convert audio files for use in your session.

The Import Audio dialog box includes seven main areas.

- **File navigation.** A standard navigation bar at the top of the dialog box combined with the navigation display window on the left side allows you to locate and select audio files within an available hard drive or other volume.
- **File properties.** The area below the navigation window lists the file type, length, size, bit depth, sample rate, and number of channels (1=mono, 2=stereo interleaved) for the file selected in the navigation window.

— Navigation bar

— Navigation display window

— File regions window

— Region import window

— Region select buttons

— Audition controls

— File properties

— Comments

Import Audio dialog box (Windows)

- **Comments.** The area along the bottom of the dialog box describes how the selected file can be imported into the session and provides other information about the file's use in the session.

- **File regions.** The file regions window in the middle of the dialog box shows the currently selected file and lists the whole-file region (parent soundfile) and the internal subset regions (pointers to portions of the parent soundfile) that have been created from the original source file. Two types of icons can appear in the window, indicating whether the item is an audio file or an audio region.

  - **Audio file.** An icon that looks like a document with the upper-left corner turned down and dual audio waveforms is used to identify an audio file.

  - **Audio region.** An icon that looks like reverse highlighted dual-audio waveforms is used to identify an audio region.

—— Audio File icon

—— Audio Region icon

File and region icons in the Import Audio dialog box

- **Region select buttons.** The Add Region and Convert Region/Copy Region buttons below the file regions window are used to select audio to add, copy, or convert for use in your session. Clicking one of these buttons adds the selected audio file or region to the region import window on the right side of the dialog box.
- **Audition controls.** The controls beneath the region select buttons allow you to start, stop, rewind, and fast-forward playback of the currently selected file or region.
- **Region import.** The area on the right side of the dialog box displays the audio files and regions that you have selected to import to the Region List of your current session and the import method that will be used. You can remove regions from this list using the buttons beneath the display window.

Importing Audio with the Import Command

Audio files can be imported to tracks or directly to the Region List, making the files available to be placed into tracks later.

To import audio, follow these steps:

1. Choose FILE > IMPORT > AUDIO. The Import Audio dialog box will appear.
2. Select an audio file in the navigation window to display its properties and any subset regions it contains.
3. Place a file or region in the region import window by clicking any of the following buttons:
   - **Add/Add All.** Use these buttons to add files or regions that match the format, bit depth, and sample rate of your session to the Region List. Regions that do not match the sample rate of the current session can also be added using these buttons, but they will not play back at the correct speed and pitch.

 The Add and Add All buttons reference the original audio file(s) and do not copy them into your session's Audio Files folder. If the original files are moved or become unavailable, or if the session is transferred to a different system, the session may no longer be able to play the referenced files.

   - **Copy/Copy All.** Use these buttons to copy and add files or regions that match the format, bit depth, and sample rate of your session to the Region List. The Copy/Copy All buttons change to Convert/Convert All buttons when the selected audio region does not match the sample rate or bit depth of the current session.
   - **Convert/Convert All.** Use these buttons to copy and convert files or regions that do not match the format, bit depth, or sample rate of your session. All converted files will automatically be copied into new files that match the file format, bit depth, and sample rate of your session, with the correct speed, length, and pitch.
4. Click DONE to begin importing the audio to your session.
5. If any audio files or regions are being copied or converted, a dialog box will appear, prompting you to select a target destination for the newly created files. In the CHOOSE A DESTINATION FOLDER dialog box, the Audio Files folder for the current session will be selected by default; you can choose an alternate folder or directory location, if desired. Navigate to the desired folder location and choose USE CURRENT FOLDER.

6. When the AUDIO IMPORT OPTIONS dialog box appears, do one of the following:

- Select NEW TRACK and choose a start location from the drop-down list. New Audio tracks will be created for each separate region you import, and each region will be placed at the specified location on its track. The imported audio will also appear in the Region List.

- Select REGION LIST to import the audio to the Region List for later use. The imported audio will appear in the Region List in the session but will not be added to any tracks during import.

The Audio Import Options dialog box

Importing Audio with DigiBase Browsers

As discussed in Chapter 3, Pro Tools provides specialized DigiBase browsers that you can use to quickly locate, manage, and open Pro Tools sessions and compatible files. DigiBase browsers provide powerful search, navigation, file information, and audition capabilities for Pro Tools.

You can import audio into Pro Tools by dragging files into a session from a DigiBase browser window. All files imported in this manner are automatically converted to match the file format, bit depth, and sample rate of the session, if needed. If no conversion is necessary, the original files will be referenced and not copied.

Like the Import Audio dialog box, the DigiBase Workspace browser can be used to import audio directly into the Region List or to import audio into new tracks in a session.

Importing to the Region List

To import audio directly into the Region List using the DigiBase Workspace browser, follow these steps:

1. Choose WINDOW > WORKSPACE.

2. To refine file choices so you can pick from only audio files in specific locations, follow these steps:

   a. In the Workspace window, click the FIND button (magnifying glass) on the left side of the toolbar. When the button is activated, the toolbar will expand to display the Search tools, and the browser window will divide into two panes.

Clicking the Find button in the Workspace browser

b. Select the volumes and/or folders you want to search by selecting/deselecting the check boxes in the top pane. Note that you can drill down through the file system by clicking the arrow icons to expand volumes and folders.

Selecting a search location

c. Click the drop-down button in the KIND column and select AUDIO FILE.

d. Click the SEARCH button. The search results will be shown in the bottom half of the Workspace browser.

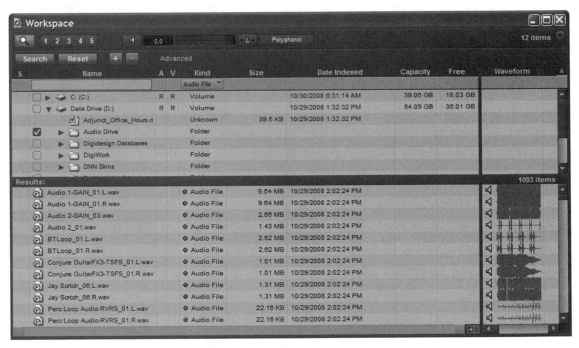

Search results displayed in the Workspace browser

3. Drag the audio files you want to import from the Workspace browser onto the Region List.

The files are automatically converted to the file format, bit depth, and sample rate of the session, if necessary, and will appear in the Region List.

 Imported audio that matches the session sample rate and bit depth will be referenced in its original location and not copied into the current session's Audio Files folder. To force-copy a file, hold ALT *(Windows) or* OPTION *(Mac) while dragging the file to the Region List.*

Importing to Tracks

To import audio to tracks using the DigiBase Workspace browser, follow these steps:

1. Choose WINDOW > WORKSPACE and use the Workspace browser to locate the audio files you want to import. (See Step 2 in the preceding "Importing to the Region List" section.)
2. Drag the audio files from the browser onto an existing track or tracks in the Pro Tools Edit window.

The files will be automatically converted to the file format, bit depth, and sample rate of the session, if necessary, and will appear on the selected track or tracks.

 To create new tracks for audio when importing from the Workspace browser, Shift-drag the audio files from the Workspace browser to the Edit window or drag the files to the Track List. Each of the imported audio files will appear on a new track.

Batch Importing Audio

With a Pro Tools session open, you can quickly import multiple audio files directly into the session. Files that have a different bit depth or sample rate from the session will automatically be converted on import, as will any files with a non-native file format.

To batch import files, follow these steps:

1. With a Pro Tools session open, browse the files on available volumes using your operating system's Explorer or Finder window.
2. Locate the audio files you want to import and drag them onto the Pro Tools application icon or its alias/shortcut.

Each of the files will appear in the Region List in the session.

Importing Audio from an Audio CD

Pro Tools lets you import tracks from an audio CD using the DigiBase drag-and-drop feature. Since the transfer is made in the digital domain, there is no signal loss. The sample rate for audio CDs is 44.1 kHz. Therefore, if your session's sample rate is set to 48 kHz or higher, Pro Tools will convert the sample rate for the imported audio. Before importing CD audio, set the Sample Rate Conversion Quality Preference accordingly (choose SETUP > PREFERENCES and select the PROCESSING tab).

To transfer audio from an audio CD using a DigiBase browser, follow these steps:

1. Insert the audio CD into your CD-ROM drive.
2. From within your Pro Tools session, choose WINDOW > WORKSPACE.

3. Browse to the CD and select the audio track(s) you want to import.

4. Drag the file(s) onto the Region List, Track List, or Tracks Display area in the Edit window of the current session.

Importing Video

To import a video file into Pro Tools, follow these steps:

1. Check the time code settings of the session to make sure they match those of the movie you want to import and then save the session.

2. Choose FILE > IMPORT > VIDEO. A dialog box will open, allowing you to select the video file to import.

3. Navigate to and select the desired QuickTime movie or other video file that is compatible with your system.

4. Click OPEN. The Video Import Options dialog box will appear.

The Video Import Options dialog box

5. Select the desired import options as follows:

   • Select a start location from the LOCATION drop-down list.

   • If you wish to import audio embedded in a QuickTime movie, select IMPORT AUDIO FROM FILE.

6. Click OK.

Pro Tools will import the movie and display it in its own Video track in the Edit window as well as in a floating Video window. The first frame of the movie will be automatically placed at the selected start time in your session, unless otherwise specified during import. If you chose to import audio, you will be prompted to choose a destination folder for the audio file. After you've selected the desired folder, the audio will appear in a new Audio track in the session.

Depending on the setting of your Video track view, the movie will display in the Edit window as blocks or as a picture-icon (picon) "thumbnail" overview of the frames of the movie it represents. The Video track will show greater or lesser detail depending on your current zoom level in the Edit window—the closer in you zoom, the greater the number of individual frames that are displayed in the Video track; the farther out you zoom, the fewer the number of individual frames that are visible.

The Video track behaves much like a Pro Tools audio or MIDI track in that you can move the Video region with the Grabber or other editing tools. This allows you to offset the movie to any start point.

Only one video file can be associated with a standard Pro Tools session at a time. If you want to import a different movie into a session, repeat the preceding steps. The new movie will replace the original in the session.

Pro Tools HD and Pro Tools with Complete Production Toolkit 2 let you use multiple Video tracks in your session and add multiple video files and Video regions to each Video track. However, only one Video track can be *active* at any time.

The Video track will take its name from the imported video file. Video tracks can subsequently be renamed, in the same manner as other tracks in your session. (See the "Naming Tracks" section in Chapter 3 for details.) However, if you later import a new video file, the track will be renamed to match the imported file.

 Using Frames view to view movie content in the Video track may cause your computer to exhibit reduced or sluggish performance. If this happens, switch the Video track to Blocks view. You can also hide the Video track to further optimize performance, if necessary.

Chapter 6

Making Your First MIDI Recording

This chapter covers the basics of recording and working with MIDI data in Pro Tools. It describes how to set up and record onto MIDI-compatible tracks, how to use virtual instrument plug-ins, and how to select different views for the MIDI data on your tracks.

Objectives

After you complete this chapter, you will be able to:

- Understand the basics of the MIDI protocol
- Identify the two types of MIDI-compatible tracks that Pro Tools provides
- Recognize the difference between sample-based operation and tick-based operation
- Set the Main Time Scale to Bars|Beats
- Prepare a system to record MIDI data
- Set up a virtual instrument to play MIDI data recorded on an Instrument track

Introduction

Recording and editing MIDI data is similar to working with audio; many of the tools, modes, and menu functions work in a similar fashion. However, MIDI data is fundamentally different from audio; therefore, some of the processes and operations you use to work with this data will be different. This chapter introduces Pro Tools features that will allow you to record and edit MIDI data in ways that are specific to this protocol.

MIDI Basics

MIDI, or *Musical Instrument Digital Interface*, is a protocol for connecting electronic instruments, performance controllers, and computers so they can communicate with one another. MIDI data is different from data stored in an audio file in that MIDI data does not represent sound waves; instead, it represents information about a performance, such as the pitch, duration, volume, and order of notes to be played.

MIDI devices transmit performance data via MIDI messages, which are composed of 8-bit numbers (or *bytes*) and include information such as *note* or *pitch number* (indicating an individual note in a scale) and *velocity* (typically affecting an individual note's volume). Up to 16 separate channels of MIDI information can be sent over a single MIDI cable, allowing a single cable path to control multiple MIDI devices or to control a single device that is capable of multi-channel (also known as *multi-timbral*) operation.

THE FORMAT OF A MIDI MESSAGE

The most significant bit of a MIDI message byte is reserved to distinguish between status bytes and data bytes. The remaining seven bits represent the unique data of the message byte, encompassing a range of values from 0 to 127. The maximum length for a standard MIDI message is three bytes, consisting of one status byte and one or more data bytes.

Status Byte	Data Byte 1	Data Byte 2
1tttnnnn	0xxxxxxx	0xxxxxxx

Where:

  t is used to specify the type of status message being sent

  n is used to specify the associated MIDI Channel Number

  x is used to specify the associated data value, such as a note number (pitch) or velocity value

---

Many other kinds of information can be conveyed via MIDI messages, such as pan and general MIDI volume information for instruments that support these, as well as program change events, or commands that tell MIDI instruments which of their available sounds, or *patches*, to use.

A *MIDI sequencer* allows you to store, edit, and play back MIDI information that can be used to control MIDI-compatible devices, such as synthesizers, sound modules, and drum machines. These devices don't have to be external hardware devices—a growing number of software synthesis and sampling packages are available, enabling you to add internal devices to your host computer.

MIDI in Pro Tools

Pro Tools includes an integrated MIDI sequencer that lets you import, record, and edit MIDI in much the same way that you work with audio. MIDI data appears in tracks in the Pro Tools Edit window, referencing the same Timeline as your Audio tracks. Corresponding channel strips appear in the Pro Tools Mix window and include familiar mixer-style controls that affect MIDI data in the track. MIDI Editor windows are also available in Pro Tools for detailed MIDI composition and editing tasks.

As you learned in Chapter 3, Pro Tools provides two types of tracks for working with MIDI data: MIDI tracks and Instrument tracks.

- A *MIDI track* stores MIDI note, instrument, and controller data only; no audio can pass through a MIDI track. MIDI tracks are often used in conjunction with Auxiliary Input tracks for monitoring and playback of a synthesizer or virtual instrument associated with MIDI data.

- An *Instrument track* provides MIDI and audio capability in a single channel strip. Like MIDI tracks, Instrument tracks store note, instrument, and controller data. Instrument tracks can also route audio signals for monitoring and playback of an instrument associated with the MIDI data on the track. This capability simplifies the process of recording, editing, and monitoring MIDI data.

Creating MIDI-Compatible Tracks

If your session does not already contain them, you will have to create one or more MIDI-compatible tracks for your MIDI recording. The type of track you use (MIDI track or Instrument track) will depend on how you prefer to work with your MIDI devices. Some considerations include whether you will be using a virtual instrument with the track (see the "Using Virtual Instruments" section later in this chapter) and the complexity of your setup. For basic MIDI recording or working with virtual instruments, you will probably find Instrument tracks to be easier to use, due to the simplified manner in which they allow you to route audio from your MIDI devices through your session.

To add MIDI-compatible tracks, do the following:

1. Chose TRACK > NEW to open the New Tracks dialog box.
2. Input the number of desired tracks in the TRACK TOTAL field.
3. Select either MIDI TRACK or INSTRUMENT TRACK in the Track Type drop-down list. The Track Time Base drop-down will default to Ticks.
4. For Instrument tracks, choose between MONO and STEREO in the Track Format drop-down list. (Additional multi-channel formats are available with Pro Tools HD software and Pro Tools with Complete Production Toolkit 2.)
5. Click CREATE.

Creating stereo Instrument tracks in the New Tracks dialog box

When you create a track for working with MIDI data, the track timebase defaults to Ticks, indicating that the track uses tick-based timing (also known as *bar-and-beat-based timing*). MIDI operations are typically bar-and-beat-based, whereas audio operations are typically sample-based.

Sample-Based Operation versus Tick-Based Operation

The differences between sample-based operation and tick-based operation are essentially the differences between how audio data is stored and how MIDI data is stored.

Sample-Based Operation

In sample-based operation, recorded information is tied to fixed points in time relative to the beginning of the session. In Chapter 4, you learned how to record audio in Pro Tools. Recorded audio data is stored in audio files as individual audio samples. In Pro Tools, the corresponding audio regions are represented on sample-based tracks by default. Audio material that resides on sample-based tracks is located at particular sample locations on the Timeline. You can think of these sample-based locations as *absolute locations* in time, measured by the number of samples that have elapsed since the beginning of the session. The audio material will not move from its absolute locations in time if the session tempo is later modified—though the audio regions' *relative* bar and beat locations in the session will change.

Audio tracks can also be set to tick-based operation to perform specialized functions, such as tempo matching for REX-like region groups or Elastic Audio. For the purposes of this course, whenever we discuss recording and editing audio, we will assume sample-based operation unless otherwise stated.

Tick-Based Operation

In tick-based operation, recorded information is tied to specific Bar|Beat locations in an arrangement. When you record MIDI data, Pro Tools uses tick-based timing to determine the locations of your MIDI events. MIDI events are recorded relative to particular bar and beat locations within the composition (such as bar 16, beat 1), and their absolute locations adjust based on the session tempo—if the tempo increases, the MIDI data will play back faster, and individual events will occur earlier in time; if the tempo decreases, the MIDI data will play back slower, and the same events will occur later in time. The Elastic Audio capabilities in Pro Tools provide the same functionality for audio on tick-based tracks, enabling audio regions to automatically compress or expand to conform to the session tempo.

Pro Tools subdivides the bars and beats in your session into ticks, with 960 ticks comprising a quarter note. Timing can thus be specified with a precision (or resolution) of up to 1/960th of a quarter note when using tick-based operation. You can think of the tick-based locations as *relative locations* in time, measured by the number of bars, beats, and ticks that have elapsed since the beginning of the session. A tick-based event maintains its rhythmic location relative to other tick-based events in the song if the session tempo is later modified—but a tempo change will cause the event to occur earlier or later in *absolute* time, thereby changing its location relative to any sample-based audio in the session.

Tick-based tracks and data coexist with sample-based tracks and data within the same Pro Tools session.

 Pro Tools displays relationships between audio and MIDI accurately in the Edit window at all zoom levels, with MIDI event durations drawn proportionally to the Timeline, according to tempo.

Though MIDI tracks are typically tick-based, they can also be set to sample-based to perform specialized functions. For the purposes of this course, whenever we discuss MIDI recording and editing, we will assume tick-based operation unless otherwise stated.

 Sample-based MIDI operations are discussed in the Pro Tools 110 and 310M courses.

Time Scale and Rulers for Working with MIDI

When you are working with MIDI data in a session, you will frequently reference the Bars|Beats Time Scale. This Time Scale can be displayed in the Location Indicators at the top of the Edit window and is represented on the Bars|Beats Ruler. You will also commonly work with tempo, meter, and key signature settings, which are displayed in the Tempo, Meter, and Key Signature Rulers, respectively.

Setting the Timebase Ruler and Main Time Scale

For MIDI recording and editing, you will find it helpful to display the Bars|Beats Timebase Ruler and to set the Main Time Scale to Bars|Beats. This will let you reference any recorded material, track selections, and edits to the bar numbers and beats of the project.

To set the Timebase Ruler and Main Time Scale, do the following:

1. Display the Bars|Beats Ruler by choosing VIEW > RULERS > BARS:BEATS.
2. Set the Main Time Scale to Bars|Beats by doing one of the following:
   - Click on BARS|BEATS in the Ruler View area of the Edit window.
   - Select VIEW > MAIN COUNTER > BARS:BEATS.
   - Click on the MAIN COUNTER SELECTOR in either the Edit window or the Transport window and select BARS|BEATS from the pop-up menu.

Main Counter selector in the Edit window

Selecting Bars|Beats from the Main Counter pop-up menu

 Refer to Chapter 2 for more information on the Main Time Scale.

The Bars|Beats Time Scale displays information in the following format:

1|1|000 (Bar Number|Beat Number|Tick Number)

The first number in this format represents the bar number with respect to the zero point on the session Timeline. The second number represents the beat number within the current bar. The final number represents the tick number within the current beat, based on the division of 960 ticks per quarter note.

Tempo, Meter, and Key Signature Rulers

The Tempo, Meter, and Key Signature Rulers allow you to specify the default tempo, meter, and key signature for your session and to set tempo, meter, and key changes at any point along the session Timeline. To display the Tempo, Meter, and Key Signature Rulers, choose VIEW > RULERS > TEMPO, VIEW > RULERS > METER, and VIEW > RULERS > KEY SIGNATURE, respectively.

Preparing to Record MIDI

Once you have added MIDI-compatible tracks to your session, you will need to prepare your MIDI device and software for recording. The general processes you will use to prepare for recording MIDI are as follows:

1. Connect a MIDI device.
2. Enable input from the MIDI device.
3. Check the track inputs/outputs.
4. Record-enable the track(s).
5. Set record options.

Connecting a MIDI Device

Recording MIDI data typically involves connecting a keyboard, a drum machine, or another MIDI device as an input to your Pro Tools system. Before starting to record, you should verify that the MIDI device you will use for input (also called a *MIDI controller*) is connected to your system through an input on your MIDI interface or a USB port on your computer, if applicable. You might also need to connect a MIDI output from your interface as a return to this device or as an input to a separate MIDI device, such as a synthesizer, for monitoring and playback purposes.

 Example: For basic recording in a home or project studio, you can connect a MIDI cable from the MIDI Out port on the back of a keyboard to the MIDI In port on an Mbox or similar interface. For monitoring and playback purposes, you can also connect the MIDI Out port of the Mbox to the MIDI In port on the keyboard (assuming onboard sound capabilities) or to a separate synthesizer unit.

 Connecting a MIDI device to Pro Tools with a USB cable provides both MIDI input and MIDI output for the device.

Enabling Input from the MIDI Device

To record from a MIDI controller in Pro Tools, the controller (input device) or MIDI interface must be enabled in the MIDI Input Enable dialog box.

To verify that the input device or MIDI interface is enabled, do the following:

1. Choose SETUP > MIDI > INPUT DEVICES. The MIDI Input Enable dialog box will open.

MIDI Input Enable dialog box

2. In the MIDI Input Enable dialog box, verify that the MIDI device or MIDI interface you will record from is selected.

3. When you are finished, click OK.

 Devices do not need to be selected to receive MIDI data being output from Pro Tools. For example, a device used exclusively as a sound module does not need to be selected in the MIDI Input Enable dialog box.

Checking MIDI Inputs/Outputs

Next you will need to configure the inputs and outputs of your MIDI-compatible track(s) with the appropriate settings to route the MIDI signals into and out of the tracks.

MIDI Input

The MIDI Input selector in the Edit or Mix window for a MIDI-compatible track is the functional equivalent to the Audio Input Path selector for an Audio track. This selector determines which incoming MIDI data gets recorded onto the track in Pro Tools.

On MIDI tracks, the MIDI Input selector is located in the track display (Edit window) or channel strip (Mix window), where the Audio Input Path selector would be on an Audio track. On Instrument tracks, however, the MIDI Input selector appears in the Instrument MIDI controls section. This section of the track display or channel strip is used only for Instrument tracks and needs to be displayed separately.

MIDI Input selector (Instrument track)

MIDI Input selector (MIDI track)

The MIDI Input selector as it appears in a MIDI track and an Instrument track

To display the Instrument MIDI controls, do one of the following:

- Choose VIEW > MIX WINDOW > INSTRUMENTS. The Instrument MIDI controls will appear at the top of the channel strip.
- Choose VIEW > EDIT WINDOW > INSTRUMENTS. The Instrument MIDI controls will appear at the head of the track display.

The MIDI Input selectors for MIDI-compatible tracks are set to All by default, such that the MIDI signals from all connected and enabled input devices are received in the track. If you prefer, you can set the MIDI Input to a specific device (port) and channel to more tightly control the routing of MIDI data.

To limit the MIDI input on a track to a specific device, do the following:

1. Click on the **MIDI INPUT SELECTOR** in the Edit or Mix window.
2. Select the MIDI device or interface and port that you want to route to the track.
3. Do one of the following:
   - Select ALL CHANNELS to route all channels from the selected device to the track.
   - Select a specific channel to route only the data being transmitted on that channel to the track.

MIDI Output

The MIDI Output selector for a MIDI-compatible track determines which device or port is used for monitoring and playing back MIDI data. Live MIDI signals can be routed to an audio sound source for monitoring purposes when MIDI Thru is enabled. (See the "MIDI Thru" section later in this chapter.) Similarly, recorded MIDI signals can be routed to an audio sound source for playback purposes. You use the MIDI Output selector to configure the device or port and the MIDI channel that the signal is routed to for both of these purposes. On MIDI tracks, the MIDI Output selector is located where the Audio Output Path selector would be on an Audio track; on Instrument tracks, it is located in the Instrument MIDI controls section of the channel strip (Mix window) or track display (Edit window).

To set the MIDI Output, do the following:

1. Click on the **MIDI OUTPUT SELECTOR** in the Edit or Mix window.
2. Select the instrument or port and channel you wish to route the output to for MIDI playback.

Record-Enabling MIDI-Compatible Tracks

The process you use to enable recording on a Pro Tools MIDI track or Instrument track is the same as you use for an Audio track: Simply click the track's **RECORD ENABLE** button in either the Edit window or the Mix window. As with an Audio track, the Record Enable button flashes red when a MIDI-compatible track is record-ready.

Setting Record Options

Pro Tools provides various record options that are specific to working with MIDI data. You will need to set the MIDI Controls, quantizing, and MIDI Thru options as desired prior to beginning to record onto your MIDI tracks.

MIDI Controls

As discussed in Chapter 2, the Pro Tools Transport window or Edit window can be set to show MIDI Controls that you can use when recording MIDI data.

To display MIDI Controls in the Pro Tools Transport window, do the following:

1. Select **WINDOW > TRANSPORT** to display the Transport window, if it is not currently showing.
2. Select **VIEW > TRANSPORT > MIDI CONTROLS** to display the MIDI Controls, if they are not currently showing.

 *The MIDI Controls can also be displayed in the Edit window. Choose **MIDI CONTROLS** from the Edit Window Toolbar menu in the upper-right corner of the window.*

Before you begin recording MIDI data, you can take any of the following optional steps to set the MIDI Controls:

1. Enable **WAIT FOR NOTE** and/or **COUNT OFF** in the Transport window or Edit window, if desired. Use Wait for Note to begin recording automatically when you begin playing; use Count Off to count off a specified number of measures before recording begins.
2. Enable the **METRONOME**, if desired, and specify the settings in the Click/Countoff Options dialog box (**SETUP > CLICK/COUNTOFF**).

 The simplest way to enable playback of the metronome click is to set up a click track. See the "Creating a Click Track" section in Chapter 4 for details.

3. Disable **MIDI MERGE** for initial recording. Once you have recorded a MIDI pass that you want to keep, you can enable this control to layer additional MIDI data on top of the existing recording.

4. Set the tempo for recording by doing one of the following:

    *   Engage the **TEMPO RULER ENABLE** button (Conductor Track) to follow the tempo map defined in the Tempo Ruler. See the "Setting the Default Tempo" section later in this chapter for more information.

    *   Disengage the **TEMPO RULER ENABLE** button (Conductor Track) to set the tempo using the Tempo field in the Transport window or Edit window.

5. Set the meter as needed by double-clicking the **CURRENT METER** display. See the "Setting the Default Meter" section later in this chapter for more information.

The functions of each of the MIDI Controls are described in detail in the "MIDI Controls" section in Chapter 2.

Input Quantize

The Input Quantize feature enables you to automatically align, or *quantize*, all recorded MIDI notes to a specified timing grid. This creates a style of recording similar to working with a hardware sequencer or drum machine. Do not use this feature if you want to preserve the original "feel" of the performance.

To enable Input Quantize, do the following:

1. Choose **EVENT > EVENT OPERATIONS > INPUT QUANTIZE.** The Event Operations window will open with Input Quantize selected in the Operation drop-down list.

The Event Operations window

2. Select the ENABLE INPUT QUANTIZE option.

3. In the WHAT TO QUANTIZE section of the window, choose the MIDI note attributes to quantize:

   • **Attacks.** Aligns note start points to the nearest grid value (commonly used).

   • **Releases.** Aligns note end points to the nearest grid value (used only for specific situations).

   • **Preserve Note Duration.** Preserves the note durations of the performance by moving end points in concert with start points. If this option is not selected, note start and end points can be moved independently, changing the duration of the note.

4. Set the quantize grid to the smallest note value that will be played. All notes in the performance will be aligned to the nearest value on this grid.

5. In the OPTIONS section of the Input Quantize window, select any other desired options.

MIDI Thru

To monitor MIDI-compatible tracks while recording, you need to enable MIDI Thru. When it is enabled, Pro Tools routes the MIDI signals it receives from your controllers out to the devices and channels assigned by the MIDI Output selectors for your MIDI-compatible tracks.

To enable MIDI Thru, select OPTIONS > MIDI THRU.

 When using MIDI Thru, you might need to disable Local Control on your MIDI keyboard controller. Otherwise, your keyboard could receive double MIDI notes, which can lead to stuck notes.

 You must enable MIDI Thru when using an Instrument track to record MIDI data; if MIDI Thru is not enabled, the track will not receive a MIDI signal.

Using Virtual Instruments

Virtual instruments are the software equivalents of outboard synthesizers or sound modules. Many virtual instruments are available for Pro Tools in the form of real-time plug-ins. The Xpand!², Boom, and Structure Free plug-ins are examples of virtual instruments installed as standard components of Pro Tools.

Virtual instrument plug-ins can be added to Auxiliary Input tracks or Instrument tracks and triggered by MIDI events routed through the respective tracks.

For basic recording with a virtual instrument, you will want to create an Instrument track and connect a MIDI controller as described earlier in this chapter.

Placing a Virtual Instrument on an Instrument Track

A virtual instrument plug-in can be placed directly on an Instrument track, allowing the instrument to be triggered by the MIDI data on the track during playback or by MIDI data passing through the track for live input monitoring.

To add a virtual instrument such as Xpand!², Boom, or Structure Free to an Instrument track in Pro Tools, do the following:

1. Display the track inserts, if not already displayed, by choosing VIEW > MIX WINDOW or VIEW > EDIT WINDOW and selecting INSERTS.

2. Click an insert on the Instrument track, choose PLUG-IN > INSTRUMENT, and select the virtual instrument to use on the track. The track's MIDI Output will automatically be assigned to the virtual instrument plug-in, and the instrument's user interface will open.

Selecting the Xpand!² virtual instrument plug-in

 Stereo Instrument tracks provide two options for plug-ins: multi-channel plug-ins and multi-mono plug-ins. Choose multi-channel plug-ins for stereo virtual instruments; choose multi-mono plug-ins for mono virtual instruments.

3. Assign the appropriate hardware outputs, if not already selected, using the AUDIO OUTPUT PATH selector (for monitoring and playback purposes).

4. Set the track's VOLUME FADER to the desired output level.

5. Play notes on your MIDI controller. The meters on the Instrument track will register the instrument's audio output.

 The MIDI signal received on an Instrument track is displayed by the MIDI meter in the Instrument MIDI Controls section of the channel strip or track display. If the MIDI meter on an Instrument track does not register a signal, verify that the MIDI output has been assigned with the MIDI Output selector.

Using Xpand!²

Xpand!² is an A.I.R. virtual instrument designed to provide fast access to high-quality sounds directly from within Pro Tools. Xpand!² comes equipped with more than 2,300 *Patches* (plug-in settings) and more than 1,200 combinable *Parts* (sound presets). The Xpand!² sound library includes synth pads, leads, acoustic and electric pianos, organs, strings, vocals, brass and woodwinds, mallet percussion, ethnic instruments, loops, and more.

Xpand!² provides four synthesizer slots (A, B, C, and D), each with individual MIDI channel, Mix, Arpeggiator, Modulation, and Effects settings. Each slot can hold one of the included preset Parts. Each Xpand!² Patch is composed of a blend of the individual Parts in slots A through D, which can be layered together to produce a rich, dynamic texture.

To use the Xpand!² plug-in, add the plug-in to an Instrument track as described in the "Placing a Virtual Instrument on an Instrument Track" section earlier in this chapter. The Xpand!² user interface will open, displaying selectors for each of the four parts.

The Xpand!² virtual instrument plug-in user interface

The plug-in initially opens to the <factory default> setting with a Part assigned for slot A only. Xpand!² includes numerous additional Patches to choose from, organized into folders by type.

To select a different Patch setting, click either the LIBRARIAN MENU or the PLUG-IN SETTINGS SELECT button in the plug-in window and navigate to the desired folder and Patch. Each Patch calls up a preset Xpand!² configuration.

Librarian Menu

Plug-in Settings select button

Plug-in controls for selecting a different Xpand!² patch

Each of the Xpand!² sound Parts can be turned on or off at any time by clicking on the On/Off power indicator above the Part letter. (When toggled off, the power indicator turns a dimmed gray color.) Slot assignments can also be changed individually by clicking on the sound selector in the Xpand!² user interface.

Clicking on the power indicator to turn off sound Part B

Clicking on the sound selector to change the Part assigned to slot A

Using Boom

Boom is a virtual drum machine featuring a broad range of percussion sounds. The Boom user interface
provides a simple, drum-machine-style pattern sequencer. Boom comes with 10 drum kits inspired by
classic electronic drum machines.

To use the Boom plug-in, add the plug-in to an Instrument track as described in the "Placing a Virtual
Instrument on an Instrument Track" section earlier in this chapter. The Boom user interface will open,
displaying the pattern for the <factory default> preset.

The Boom virtual instrument plug-in user interface

The Matrix Display on the left side of the plug-in window presents a visual overview of the current
pattern in Boom's sequencer. The Matrix provides a way to work with patterns and to keep track of
the step that Boom is playing at any given time. Each lit LED in the sequencer corresponds to an

instrument that is sequenced to play at that step. The brighter the LED, the higher the velocity of the instrument trigger. You can click each LED directly to add a note on that step. Successive clicks toggle through velocity levels or toggle the note on/off.

The Boom Matrix Display

The Kit Selector menu at the bottom of the plug-in window provides access to the 10 preset drum kits in Boom: Urban 1, Urban 2, Dance 1, Dance 2, Electro, Eight-O, Nine-O, Fat 8, Fat 9, and Retro.

The Boom Kit Selector menu

You can use MIDI data on your Instrument track to control Boom playback. Boom responds to two main ranges of MIDI notes:

- From C1–D#2, Boom plays each of the instruments in the current drum kit. This allows you to use Pro Tools' MIDI sequencer to create drum tracks, rather than using Boom's built-in pattern sequencer.
- From C3–D#4, each note triggers one of the 16 patterns in the current preset, switching between them on the fly.

Using Structure Free

Structure Free is a sample playback plug-in that brings various sample libraries to Pro Tools. Structure Free comes with 60 preset patches and a 64-voice multi-timbral sound engine. The Structure Free sample library includes drum kits, drum loops, bass and guitar patches, leads, electric pianos, organs, pads, and more.

Structure Free loads a variety of sample libraries, including native Structure, SampleCell, SampleCell II, Kontakt, Kontakt 2, and EXS 24. The plug-in supports all common bit depths, sample rates, and surround formats.

To use Structure Free, add the plug-in to a stereo Instrument track as described in the "Placing a Virtual Instrument on an Instrument Track" section earlier in this chapter. The Structure Free user interface will open with the Sine Wave Patch loaded.

Patch menu
Quick Browse menu
MIDI Channel selector

Patch List

Smart Knobs

The Structure Free sample player user interface

To select a different Patch preset, click the QUICK BROWSE menu and navigate to the desired folder and Patch. Each Patch calls up a preset Structure Free configuration.

Selecting a Patch from the Quick Browse menu

Additional Patches can be added to the preset using the Patch menu at the top of the Patch List. To add a Patch, select PATCH > ADD PATCH and navigate to the desired folder and Patch. To configure a new Patch to play back concurrent with existing patches, set its MIDI channel correspondingly (to MIDI Channel A1, for example).

Adding a Patch from the Patch menu

Selecting a MIDI channel from the MIDI Channel selector

Many of the Structure Free patches include *Key Switches*, special MIDI notes or keys that are assigned to change control values rather than trigger notes. Key Switches can toggle between different settings or mute parts within a Patch. For example, a Key Switch can be assigned to Smart Knobs that control effect settings, allowing you to mix in effects by pressing the corresponding key on your MIDI controller.

All available Key Switches appear blue on the screen keyboard. The currently activated Key Switch appears green.

Setting the Default Meter, Tempo, and Key Signature

Before you begin recording MIDI data, you will need to verify the meter and tempo settings for your session and make any necessary changes. You may also want to set the key signature for your session. The following sections describe how to set the meter, tempo, and key signature for your composition.

Setting the Default Meter

When you open a new session in Pro Tools, the meter defaults to 4/4. If you intend to record with the click and you are working with a different meter, make sure to set the default meter accordingly. Meter events, which can occur anywhere within a Pro Tools session, are registered and displayed using the Meter Ruler.

To set the default meter for a session, do the following:

1. With the Meter Ruler displayed in the Edit window, click on the **ADD METER CHANGE** button (or double-click on the **CURRENT METER** display in the Transport window). The Meter Change dialog box will open.

The Add Meter Change button on the Meter Ruler

The Meter Change dialog box

2. Enter the meter you will use for the session and enter 1|1|000 in the **LOCATION** field.
3. Choose a note value that corresponds to the desired click timing.
4. Click **OK** to insert the new meter event at the beginning of the session, replacing the default meter.

Setting the Default Tempo

When you open a new session in Pro Tools, the tempo defaults to 120 beats per minute (BPM). If you intend to record with the click, and you are working with a different tempo, make sure to set the default tempo accordingly. If you know the tempo you will use for the session, you can insert a tempo event at the beginning of the session.

Tempo events, which can occur anywhere within a Pro Tools session, are registered and displayed using the Tempo Ruler.

To set the default tempo, do the following:

1. With the Tempo Ruler displayed and the Tempo Ruler Enable option selected (see the "Tempo Map Mode" section later in this chapter), click on the ADD TEMPO CHANGE button.

The Add Tempo Change button on the Tempo Ruler

2. Enter the BPM value you will use for the session and enter 1|1|000 in the LOCATION field.

The Tempo Change dialog box

3. To base the beat on something other than the default quarter note, select the desired note value.

4. Click **OK** to insert the new tempo event at the beginning of the session, replacing the default tempo.

Tempo Map Mode

When you create a new Pro Tools session, the session is configured by default to follow the tempo map defined in the Tempo Ruler. The tempo map can be toggled on and off as needed. To use the tempo map, ensure that the TEMPO RULER ENABLE (Conductor Track) button is activated in the Transport or Edit window.

Enabling the Tempo Ruler in the Transport window

Manual Tempo Mode

In Manual Tempo mode, Pro Tools will ignore the tempo events in the Tempo Ruler. In this mode, the tempo can be adjusted by typing a value directly into the Current Tempo field in the Transport window. The tempo can also be tapped in using the T key on your computer. Manually adjusting the tempo during playback will momentarily interrupt playback.

To put Pro Tools into Manual Tempo mode, click to deselect the TEMPO RULER ENABLE button in the Transport window.

Setting the Default Key Signature

When you open a new session in Pro Tools, the key signature defaults to C major. If you intend to use the key signature functionality in Pro Tools, make sure to set the key signature for your session correctly. If you know the key you will use for the session, you can insert a Key Change event at the beginning of the session to change the default key of the session.

Key Change events, which can occur anywhere within a Pro Tools session, are registered and displayed using the Key Signature Ruler.

To set the default key signature, do the following:

1. With the Key Signature Ruler displayed, click on the ADD KEY SIGNATURE button.

The Add Key Signature button on the Key Signature Ruler

2. Select the mode (major or minor) and key signature you will use for the session and enter 1|1|000 in the FROM field.

The Key Change dialog box

3. Click **OK** to insert the Key Change event at the beginning of the session.

Recording MIDI

With a MIDI controller connected to your Pro Tools system, the MIDI signal routed to a MIDI-compatible track, and the track record-enabled, you are ready to begin recording.

To record to a MIDI-compatible track, do the following:

1. Display the Transport window, if it is not already showing (**WINDOW > TRANSPORT**).
2. In the Transport window, click the **RETURN TO ZERO** button so the start and end times are cleared. This ensures that you'll start recording from the beginning of the track.
3. Verify that one or more tracks have been record-enabled. (See the "Record-Enabling MIDI-Compatible Tracks" section earlier in this chapter.)
4. Click the **RECORD** button in the Transport window to enter Record Ready mode. The button will turn red and begin to flash. If you are using Wait for Note, the Play button will also flash green.

The Transport window in Record Ready mode

5. When you're ready, click PLAY in the Transport window, or if you're using Wait for Note, simply begin playing. Recording will begin.

 If you are using countoff, the Record and Play buttons will flash during the countoff, after which recording will begin.

6. When you have finished recording, click STOP.

To play back the track through a connected virtual instrument or outboard device, do the following:

1. Click the RECORD ENABLE button on the Instrument track to disable recording.
2. In the Transport window, click the RETURN TO ZERO button.
3. Click PLAY in the Transport window to begin playback.

Viewing MIDI Data on MIDI-Compatible Tracks

After you've completed a recording, your MIDI data will appear in the Edit window, arranged in a Track Playlist, against the same Timeline as audio. Your MIDI information can be viewed in a variety of ways in Pro Tools, allowing you to perform editing tasks that affect different attributes of the data. The Edit window allows you to select from several view formats, including *Notes* view, *Regions* view, and *Velocity* view. Alternatively, you can view and work with your MIDI data in a MIDI Editor window, giving you access to multiple types of data at once.

 You can quickly toggle between Notes and Regions views in the Edit window by pressing START+– (Windows) or CONTROL+– (Mac) whenever your insertion point is located in a MIDI-compatible track.

MIDI-compatible tracks and Audio tracks in the Edit window

MIDI Regions View

MIDI data is initially displayed in Regions view by default. MIDI Regions view shows MIDI notes grouped together into regions, similar to regions on Audio tracks. MIDI regions act as containers for the MIDI data that falls within the region boundaries. While notes are visible in Regions view, they cannot be individually edited in this view.

An Instrument track in Regions view

MIDI regions can be selected, copied, cut, and trimmed in the same way as audio regions, allowing you to quickly arrange song phrases or sections.

To switch to Regions view, do one of the following:

- Click anywhere in the track with the **SELECTOR** tool and press **START+-** (Windows) or **CONTROL+-** (Mac) to toggle to Regions view. Depending on the currently selected view, you might have to toggle twice.
- Click on the **TRACK VIEW SELECTOR** for the track and choose **REGIONS** from the pop-up list.

Selecting Regions view from the Track View selector pop-up menu

 *When Zoom Toggle is active, pressing **START+-** (Windows) or **CONTROL+-** (Mac) will toggle between Notes view and Velocity view.*

MIDI Notes View

MIDI Notes view shows individual MIDI notes in a piano-roll format, with pitch shown on the vertical axis and durations shown on the horizontal axis. The pitch range displayed in a track depends on the track height and the current zoom value. A mini-keyboard on the left side of the track allows you to scroll up or down to see all pitches in the track.

Mini keyboard with scroll arrows

When a track's notes do not fit within the track's current height, notes above or below the viewed area are shown as single-pixel lines at the very top and bottom of the track display.

 You can audition pitches on the mini-keyboard by clicking on any key in Notes view. The selected note is played through your connected virtual instrument or outboard device.

If a MIDI-compatible track has been set to a different view, you can easily change back to Notes view using the key command or the Track View selector.

To switch to Notes view, do one of the following:

- Click anywhere in the track with the SELECTOR tool and press START+- (Windows) or CONTROL+- (Mac) to toggle to Notes view.
- Click on the TRACK VIEW SELECTOR for the track and choose NOTES from the pop-up list.

Velocity View

The MIDI Velocity view shows the attack velocity of each note in the MIDI track with a vertical indicator called a *velocity stalk*. Velocity stalks can be dragged up or down, individually or in groups, to change the velocities of their associated notes.

MIDI track in Velocity view

MIDI Editor Window Views

MIDI data on your tracks can also be viewed using a MIDI Editor window. MIDI Editor windows can show MIDI data and automation data simultaneously for all of your Auxiliary Input, Instrument, and MIDI tracks. When displaying multiple tracks, the MIDI Editor window superimposes the MIDI notes from each of the tracks in the MIDI Notes pane. The MIDI Editor window can also display automation and controller lanes at the bottom of the window for velocity stalks, volume automation playlists, and other continuous controller and automation data.

MIDI notes, velocity stalks, and volume automation displayed in a MIDI Editor window

To display MIDI data in a MIDI Editor window, do one of the following:

- Double-click on a MIDI region in the Edit window (Regions view) with the Grabber tool.
- Select WINDOW > MIDI EDITOR or press START+= (Windows) or CONTROL+= (Mac).

MIDI Editor windows allow you to toggle between Notes view and Notation view for the displayed MIDI and Instrument tracks. To toggle the view, click on the NOTATION DISPLAY ENABLE button on the left side of the MIDI Editor window toolbar.

Toggling to Notation view in the MIDI Editor window

Chapter 7

Selecting and Navigating

This chapter covers various selection and navigation techniques that are available in Pro Tools. It includes descriptions of how to use Timeline and Edit selections, how to modify your session view (including setting track sizes and zoom displays), and how to use memory markers for quickly navigating to preset locations and views in your session.

Objectives

After you complete this chapter, you will be able to:

- Navigate a session with the Universe view
- Recognize the difference between a Timeline selection and an Edit selection
- Mark and adjust selection in and out points
- Use the Tab key to navigate a Track Playlist
- Adjust the session view for different needs
- Add, delete, and work with marker memory locations

Introduction

Understanding selection and navigation techniques can dramatically improve your efficiency in working with Pro Tools. Whether you need to audition material you have just added to your session or you need to edit a transition between regions, being able to quickly find and select the right material is of key importance. The sections in this chapter introduce you to various processes that you can use to streamline your work in all phases of your project.

Using the Universe View

Pro Tools provides a Universe view that can be displayed at the top of the Edit window. The Universe view displays an overview of your entire session, providing a miniature representation of all video, audio, and MIDI material on your displayed tracks.

Material residing on each track is represented by a single horizontal line in the Universe view that is the same color as the regions on the track. Since Aux Inputs, VCA tracks (Pro Tools HD only), and Master Faders do not contain any audio, they are represented as blank areas in the Universe view.

To toggle the display of the Universe view, do the following:

- Choose VIEW > OTHER DISPLAYS > UNIVERSE.

Universe view

Universe view in the Edit window

Resizing the Universe

You can resize the height of the Universe view to fit the total number of tracks in the session or to show more of the Edit window.

To resize the height of the Universe view, do the following:

1. Click the area between the bottom of the Universe view and the top of the Timebase Rulers. The cursor will change to a double-headed arrow, indicating that you can resize the Universe view area.
2. Drag up or down to change the height of the Universe view.

If you resize the Universe view to less than its minimum size, the view will toggle off. This provides another method of hiding the view. When you toggle the view on again, it will restore to its previous height.

The Current View Indicator

The area of the session that is currently displayed in the Edit window is represented by a white rectangular frame in the Universe view.

If you change the display in the Edit window—by zooming, scrolling, hiding or showing tracks, or changing track heights—the framed area in the Universe view will relocate and resize accordingly. During playback, if the Edit window is set to scroll, the framed area in the Universe view will also scroll.

Current view indicator frame

Framed area in the Universe view

Moving and Scrolling from the Universe View

By clicking in the Universe view, you can scroll the material displayed in the Edit window horizontally, vertically, or both. This provides a simple method of navigating within your session and controlling which sections of your tracks are visible in the Edit window.

To navigate the session using the Universe view, do the following:

1. If the Universe view is not currently displayed, choose VIEW > OTHER DISPLAYS > UNIVERSE.
2. Do one of the following:
   - Click anywhere in the Universe view to move the framed area. The Edit window will update accordingly, jumping to the framed location.
   - Click and drag on the framed area. The Edit window will scroll in real time to match your movements in the Universe view.

Types of Selection

Once you've navigated to the area where you would like to work, you will often need to make a specific selection. Pro Tools provides two types of selections: *Timeline selections* and *Edit selections*. Timeline selections can be made from any Timebase Ruler and are used to set a playback or record range. Edit selections can be made in any track or in multiple tracks and are used to set an edit range.

Timeline Selections

At any time while working in your Pro Tools session, you can create a Timeline selection. Timeline selections are frequently made by dragging with the Selector tool and can also be created or adjusted using the Timeline Selection fields in the Transport window or the Timeline Selection Markers in the Main Timebase Ruler.

 With Link Timeline and Edit Selection enabled, a Timeline selection is also made whenever you select audio or MIDI data on a track. See the "Edit Selections" section later in this chapter.

Selecting with the Timebase Rulers

To make a Timeline selection with the Rulers, do the following:

1. With any tool selected, move your pointer over a TIMEBASE RULER in the Edit window. The SELECTOR tool will become active.

2. Click and drag with the SELECTOR tool in any Timebase Ruler to select the desired area of the Timeline.

Making a Timeline selection with the Selector tool

The Timeline selection is indicated in the Main Timebase Ruler by blue Timeline Selection Markers (red if a track is record-enabled). The start, end, and length values for the Timeline selection are also displayed in the Timeline Selection fields in the Transport window.

Timeline selection as indicated in the Timebase Rulers and the Transport window

Selecting with the Timeline Selection Fields (Transport Window)

You can use the Timeline Selection fields in the Transport window to create a new selection or to adjust a selection numerically from the keyboard.

To create a new selection using the Timeline Selection fields:

1. Click on the first field in the **START** Location Indicator to activate it. The selected field will become highlighted.

Field selected in the Transport window

2. Enter the desired value or use the **UP** or **DOWN** arrow keys on the keyboard to increment or decrement the value one unit at a time.

3. Click on each successive field to select it (or use the **LEFT** and **RIGHT** arrow keys on the keyboard to cycle through the fields).

4. Enter the desired value in each field or select a value using the **UP** or **DOWN** arrow keys.

5. Press **RETURN** or **ENTER** to confirm your entry and move the insertion point to the specified location.

6. Do one of the following to complete the selection:

   - Repeat this process, using the **END** fields to specify the end point for the Timeline selection. The Length indicator fields will update accordingly.

   - Repeat this process, using the **LENGTH** fields to specify the duration of the Timeline selection. The End indicator fields will update accordingly.

 When you type a value in a Timeline Selection field or an Edit Selection field, Pro Tools will zero out all fields to the right of the changed field. To change a value without affecting the other fields (to move to a different bar but retain the beat and tick number, for example), select the value and press the UP or DOWN arrow key as needed.

 The plus (+) and minus (–) keys provide a calculator-like function, allowing you to add or subtract a number to offset the current field. To add to or subtract from a field, press PLUS or MINUS in any field, followed by the desired offset. Press RETURN or ENTER to calculate the new value or press ESCAPE to cancel.

Selecting with the Timeline Selection Markers

You can also use the Timeline Selection Markers on the Main Timebase Ruler to create a new selection or to adjust an existing selection. To set the Timeline selection by dragging the Timeline Selection Markers, do the following:

1. With any tool selected, move your pointer over a **TIMELINE SELECTION MARKER** in the Main Timebase Ruler. The Time Grabber tool will become active.

2. Drag the **TIMELINE SELECTION END MARKER** (up arrow) to set the end point.

3. Drag the TIMELINE SELECTION START MARKER (down arrow) to set the start point.

Dragging a Timeline Selection Marker

Edit Selections

When you are working with audio or MIDI data in your Pro Tools session, you can create an Edit selection to work with a portion of the material on a track. Edit selections are frequently made using the Grabber tool or the Selector tool. Edit selections can also be created or adjusted using the Edit Selection fields in the Edit window.

 With Link Timeline and Edit Selection enabled, an Edit selection is also made whenever you select an area on a Timebase Ruler. See the "Timeline Selections" section earlier in this chapter.

Selecting with the Grabber Tool

The Grabber tool includes three modes: the Time Grabber, the Separation Grabber, and the Object Grabber. Throughout this chapter, the discussion of the Grabber tool refers to the Time Grabber unless otherwise specified.

 Alternate tools, including the Separation Grabber and the Object Grabber, are discussed in the Pro Tools 201 course.

You can use the Grabber tool to make an Edit selection on any region that exists on a Track Playlist. To select a region with the Grabber tool, click once on the region you want to select. The selected region will be highlighted. To select multiple regions, click on the first of the regions you want to select and then Shift-click on the last region. Both regions will be selected, along with all regions in between them.

Selected regions can be moved, copied, cut, or deleted (cleared) from the track.

 When MIDI and Instrument tracks are set to Notes view, the Grabber tool selects individual MIDI notes or note ranges. To select MIDI regions, first set the track to Regions view (see the "MIDI Regions View" section in Chapter 6) and then click on a region to select it.

Selecting with the Selector Tool

Using the Selector tool, you can select any portion of audio or MIDI data on your tracks for editing. To make an Edit selection with the Selector tool, do one of the following:

- Click and drag across the area on the track that you want to select.
- Click once to define a starting point for the selection and then Shift-click to define an ending point for the selection.

The selected area becomes highlighted, and the selection can be moved, copied, cut, or deleted (cleared) from the track.

 Double-clicking with the Selector tool will select an entire region; triple-clicking will select the entire Track Playlist.

Selecting with the Edit Selection Fields (Edit Window)

You can use the Edit Selection fields in the Edit window to create a new selection or to adjust a selection numerically from the keyboard.

Edit Selection Fields

The Edit Selection fields in the Edit window

To create a new selection using the Edit Selection fields:

1. Click on the first field in the **START** Location Indicator to activate it. The selected field will be highlighted.

2. Enter the desired value or use the **UP** or **DOWN** arrow keys on the keyboard to increment or decrement the value one unit at a time.

3. Click on each successive field to select it (or use the **LEFT** and **RIGHT** arrow keys on the keyboard to cycle through the fields).

4. Enter the desired value in each field or select a value using the **UP** or **DOWN** arrow keys.

5. Press **RETURN** or **ENTER** to confirm your entry and move the insertion point to the location you have specified.

 Use the slash key (/) to rotate between the Start, End, and Length boxes in the Edit Selection fields. This shortcut also works for the Timeline Selection fields (Transport window).

6. Do one of the following:
   • Repeat this process, using the **END** fields to specify the end point for the Edit selection. The Length indicator fields will update accordingly.
   • Repeat this process, using the **LENGTH** fields to specify the duration of the Edit selection. The End indicator fields will update accordingly.

Working with Selections

Pro Tools provides various ways of making selections and adjusting the selection boundaries. The following sections describe some common selection techniques.

Creating Separate Timeline Selections and Edit Selections

The default setting in Pro Tools links Timeline selections and Edit selections together. This means that whenever you select an area on the Timeline, you simultaneously select the same area in each of your Track Playlists. Conversely, whenever you select a region or area in any Track Playlist, you simultaneously select the same area in the Timeline. This is often the easiest way to work because it allows you to easily play back areas as you adjust your selection and to easily re-record selected areas on a track.

However, in advanced workflows, you might encounter situations in which you want to unlink the Timeline selection from the Edit selection. You can link and unlink the Timeline selection and Edit selection using the Link Timeline and Edit Selection toggle button in the Edit window. This button is blue when the Timeline and Edit selections are linked.

Using the toggle button to link the Timeline and Edit selections

For the purposes of this book, we assume that selections are made with the Timeline and Edit selections linked. Workflows that require unlinking the Timeline and Edit selections are introduced in later courses.

Making Selections on Multiple Tracks

Edit selections can be extended across multiple tracks in several different ways. The method you use will depend on the needs of the situation.

Selecting Material on Adjacent Tracks

When you create a selection with the Selector tool, you can drag vertically to select the same area across several adjacent tracks.

Making a selection across multiple tracks using the Selector tool

Selecting Material on Nonadjacent Tracks

After creating a selection on one or more tracks, you can add the selection to an additional track by Shift-clicking on the Track Playlist with the Selector tool. This technique allows you to make selections on *nonadjacent* tracks.

Making a selection across nonadjacent tracks using Shift-click on a Track Playlist

Selecting Material on Selected Tracks

The Link Track and Edit Selection setting in Pro Tools provides an option for sharing Edit selections among tracks by selecting or deselecting the desired tracks. This option allows you to copy a selection to additional tracks, remove a selection from individual tracks, and move a selection among tracks by selecting or deselecting tracks as needed.

Enabling Link Track and Edit Selection

In normal operation, selecting a track in Pro Tools brings that track into focus for certain track-level operations, such as grouping, hiding, duplicating, making active/inactive, deleting, and so forth. To select a track, you simply click on the track nameplate in the Edit or Mix window. The track nameplate becomes highlighted to indicate that the track is selected.

Selecting a track in the Edit window by clicking the nameplate

By enabling the Link Track and Edit Selection setting (OPTIONS > LINK TRACK AND EDIT SELECTION), tracks that receive an Edit selection become selected automatically. Conversely, tracks that are selected after an Edit selection is made inherit the Edit selection.

The Edit selection can be linked or unlinked from selected tracks using the Link Track and Edit Selection toggle button in the Edit window. This button turns blue when the track selection and Edit selection are linked.

Using the toggle button to link the Edit selection to selected tracks

Using Link Track and Edit Selection to Modify Playlist Selections

To copy an Edit selection (or playlist selection) to additional tracks with Link Track and Edit Selection enabled, do one of the following:

- To select a range of adjacent tracks, Shift-click on the nameplate of the last track in the range. All tracks in the range will be selected and will inherit the Edit selection.
- To select nonadjacent tracks, Ctrl-click (Windows) or Command-click (Mac) on the nameplates of the desired tracks. Each clicked tracked will be selected and will inherit the Edit selection.

To remove an Edit selection from a track while retaining it on others, Ctrl-click (Windows) or Command-click (Mac) on the nameplate of the unwanted track to deselect it. The Edit selection will be removed from that track.

To move a selection to a different track, click on the nameplate of the desired destination track to select it. The Edit selection will be removed from the previously selected track(s) and placed on the newly selected track.

Marking Selection In and Out Points during Playback

Another useful selection technique involves using the arrow keys to select a range of material on the fly during real-time playback. This technique can be a great timesaver, as you can make selections while auditioning your session, such as when playing back a record take. To make a selection during real-time playback, do the following:

1. Using the SELECTOR tool, place the cursor near the desired starting point of the track on which you want to make a selection.
2. Begin playback of the track.
3. Press the DOWN arrow key on the keyboard at the point where you want your selection to start. The cursor will mark your starting point on the screen for you during playback.
4. Press the UP arrow key to end your selection. The selected area will be highlighted.
5. Stop playback.

Pressing an arrow key a second time during playback will update the starting/ending point and cancel the previously selected point.

If you press the UP arrow key to mark the selection end point without having pressed the DOWN arrow key, the starting playback point will be used as the start of the selection.

Using the Tab Key

When working in a track, you can use the Tab key to move the cursor to region boundaries on the Track Playlist. To advance the cursor to the next adjacent region boundary to the right, press the **TAB** key. To withdraw the cursor to the previous region boundary to the left, press **CTRL+TAB** (Windows) or **OPTION+TAB** (Mac). With each press of the Tab key, the cursor will move to the next successive region boundary.

Using the Tab key to make selections can be quite useful when you want your selection to start or end exactly on a region boundary, because it allows you to precisely locate the cursor to any region start or end point.

- To select from the current cursor position or extend a selection to the next region boundary to the right, press **SHIFT+TAB**.

- To select from the current cursor position or extend a selection to the previous region boundary to the left, press **CTRL+SHIFT+TAB** (Windows) or **OPTION+SHIFT+TAB** (Mac).

Cursor position

Starting cursor position

Result of pressing Shift+Tab (left) or Ctrl/Option+Shift+Tab (right)

 The Tab key is a repeater key; do not hold it down. Doing so will cause your selection to tab rapidly to successive region boundaries.

Tabbing to Transient Points

A variation on the standard Tab key behavior is provided by the Tab to Transients function. This function is extremely useful for finding the initial peak or modulation in an audio waveform, saving you time and trouble when locating the exact starting point of a sound or louder transition.

To use the Tab to Transients function, do the following:

1. Click on the **TAB TO TRANSIENTS** toggle button in the Edit window toolbar so that it becomes highlighted in blue.

Enabling the Tab to Transients function

2. Press the **TAB** key to move the cursor forward to the next transient to the right. Press **CTRL+TAB** (Windows) or **OPTION+TAB** (Mac) to move the cursor backward to the previous transient to the left.

Cursor advanced to the start of a kick drum hit using Tab to Transients

 The Tab to Transients threshold is set by Pro Tools and is not user-adjustable.

Using the Tab to Transients function is an easy way to make selections that start or end on a sound, because it allows you to locate the cursor immediately before an audio peak.

- To select from the current cursor position or extend a selection to the next transient to the right, press **SHIFT+TAB**.
- To select from the current cursor position or extend a selection to the previous transient to the left, press **CTRL+SHIFT+TAB** (Windows) or **OPTION+SHIFT+TAB** (Mac).

To disable the Tab to Transients function (so that the Tab key again moves to region boundaries), click the **TAB TO TRANSIENTS** toggle button so that it is no longer lit blue.

 *Press **CTRL+ALT+TAB** (Windows) or **COMMAND+OPTION+TAB** (Mac) to toggle the Tab to Transients function on and off.*

Adjusting the Session View

Pro Tools enables you to customize many aspects of your session display. You can change the display size of individual tracks, change the order in which tracks are displayed, change the Zoom settings for the current view, and create Zoom presets to store and recall commonly used magnification settings.

Adjusting Track Size

Pro Tools allows you to change the size of the track display in the Edit window by adjusting the track height. Track height can be adjusted on a track-by-track basis, allowing each track to be displayed at any of the following sizes:

- Micro
- Mini
- Small
- Medium
- Large
- Jumbo
- Extreme
- Fit to Window

Larger track heights are particularly useful for precision editing because they show more detail. Smaller track heights are useful for conserving screen space in large sessions.

Bass track at different heights (mini, medium, and large track sizes shown)

 Due to their small size, tracks using the micro or mini display options do not show Voice or Automation Mode selectors in the Edit window. These options remain available in the Mix window.

You can select a track height at any time by clicking on the Track Height selector or the amplitude scale area of the track, or you can adjust the height incrementally by dragging the lower boundary of the track.

To select a track height from a pop-up menu:

1. Click the mouse button anywhere within the amplitude scale area immediately to the right of the track meter or click directly on the TRACK HEIGHT SELECTOR button to the left of the track name.

Track Height   Amplitude
selector   scale area

The Track Height selector button and amplitude scale area

2. Choose the desired height from the pop-up menu.

The Track Height pop-up menu

To incrementally resize the track height using the lower boundary of the track:

1. Position your pointer over the lower boundary at the head of any track; the cursor will change into a double-headed arrow.

2. Click on the track boundary and drag up or down. The track height will change in continuous increments.

Press and hold **CTRL** *(Windows) or* **COMMAND** *(Mac) while adjusting track height for continuous, non-incremental adjustment.*

To set all tracks in the session to the same height, press the **ALT** *key (Windows) or* **OPTION** *key (Mac) while selecting the desired height on any track.*

Changing the Track Order

Pro Tools allows you to change the order of tracks in your session at any time to customize the onscreen layout. Changing the track order affects both the Mix and Edit windows, as well as the track layout on any connected control surface.

Arranging tracks in a logical order can simplify your navigation. This can be true even in relatively small sessions. Consider arranging the tracks in your session such that related tracks are displayed together, instruments are displayed in a logical order, or commonly used tracks are presented at the top. The order can be rearranged as needed as you work your way through the editing process.

To change the session's track order, do any of the following:

• In the Edit window, click on the track nameplate and drag the track above or below other tracks in the session.

• In the Mix window, click on the track nameplate and drag the track to the left or right of other tracks in the session.

• In the Track List, click on the track name and drag it to a higher or lower position in the list.

Clicking on a track nameplate and dragging the track to a new position (Mix window)

Track order after repositioning the track

Zoomer Tool

As discussed in Chapter 2, the Zoomer tool includes two modes: Normal Zoom and Single Zoom. Throughout this chapter, the discussion of the Zoomer tool refers to Normal Zoom mode, unless otherwise specified.

The Zoomer tool can be used to examine a waveform up close for precision editing.

The Zoomer tool in Normal Zoom mode

Zooming In and Out

To zoom in, centering on a certain point in a track, do the following:

1. If it is not already selected, click the ZOOMER tool. The pointer will display a magnifying glass with a plus sign when positioned over a track.

2. Click once at the desired point within the track. The waveform will enlarge within the track display, with the zoom point centered horizontally in the Edit window.

3. To zoom in further, click multiple times. Each successive click zooms all tracks in by one additional level.

To zoom back out, ALT-CLICK (Windows) or OPTION-CLICK (Mac) with the ZOOMER tool. While you are pressing the ALT or OPTION key, the cursor will display a magnifying glass with a minus sign when positioned over a track. Each successive click zooms out by one additional level, with the zoom point centered horizontally in the Edit window.

Zooming In on a Range

The Zoomer tool can also be used to zoom in on a particular range, enlarging the range to fill the visible area of the track. To zoom into a range, do the following:

1. If it is not already selected, click the ZOOMER tool to select it.

2. Click and drag with the magnifying glass over the horizontal portion of a track that you want to view up close. (To zoom horizontally and vertically, CTRL-drag [Windows] or COMMAND-drag [Mac]). As you drag, a dashed box will appear, indicating the range that you will be zooming in on.

3. Release the mouse. The display will fill the screen with the portion of the waveform you selected, zooming in horizontally to the same level on all tracks simultaneously.

> 🔅 *Double-click on the ZOOMER tool to get a full track view that fills the screen with the longest displayed track in the session.*

Zoom Toggle Button

The Zoom Toggle button is located immediately beneath the Zoomer tool in the toolbar area. Use the ZOOM TOGGLE button to toggle the view between the current zoom state and a preset/defined zoom state.

Zoom Toggle button

When Zoom Toggle is enabled, the Edit window displays the stored zoom state, as specified in the Zoom Toggle preferences. When Zoom Toggle is disabled, the Edit window reverts to the pre–Zoom Toggle view.

Zoom Toggle behavior varies, based on the Zoom Toggle settings selected in the Editing Preferences page (SETUP > PREFERENCES).

Horizontal and Vertical Zoom Buttons

The Edit window includes Zoom buttons in the toolbar area that allow you to adjust the track waveform or MIDI view without using the Zoomer tool. These buttons adjust the display zoom levels, keeping the insertion cursor or selection start point centered as it changes. Like the Zoomer tool, the Zoom buttons change only the display of the data and do not affect playback.

—Zoom buttons

The Zoom buttons in the Edit window toolbar

From left to right, the Zoom buttons are as follows:

- **Horizontal Zoom Out button.** This button changes the time display of all tracks in the session by shrinking the track Timeline, audio waveform views, and MIDI displays to show more time on screen, with less detail. This adjustment is useful for obtaining a "big-picture" view of your Track Playlists.

- **Audio Zoom In and Out button.** This button changes the waveform amplitude display of all Audio tracks in the session by enlarging or shrinking the track waveform views vertically, making the waveforms appear taller or shorter. Zooming in is useful to distinguish low-amplitude audio waveforms; zooming out is useful to distinguish high-amplitude audio waveforms.

- **MIDI Zoom In and Out button.** This button changes the display of MIDI data on all MIDI-compatible tracks in the session by modifying the note range shown in the track (represented by the track's mini-keyboard). Zooming in shows a narrower range of notes, with each note appearing fatter; zooming out shows a broader range of notes, with each note appearing thinner.

 The MIDI Zoom buttons do not affect tracks in Regions view.

- **Horizontal Zoom In button.** This button changes the time display of all tracks in the session by enlarging the track Timeline, audio waveform views, and MIDI displays to show less time across the screen, with greater detail. This adjustment is useful for distinguishing precise edit points and magnifying the Edit window display to a very high resolution.

 Click and drag on any one of the ZOOM buttons for continuous zooming.

 ALT-CLICK (Windows) or OPTION-CLICK (Mac) on any one of the ZOOM buttons to return to the previous zoom magnification.

Zoom Presets

Directly beneath the Zoom buttons are five buttons numbered 1 through 5. These are the Zoom Preset buttons, which are used to store and recall commonly used zoom magnifications. Each Zoom Preset can be updated to store a zoom setting of your choice. Custom presets are saved with your session.

— Zoom presets

Zoom Preset buttons 1 through 5

To store a zoom setting as a Zoom Preset, do the following:

1. Using either the **Zoom** buttons or the **Zoomer** tool, set the screen to the desired zoom display.
2. While pressing the **Ctrl** key (Windows) or the **Command** key (Mac), click one of the five **Zoom Preset** buttons, or click and hold a button and select **Save Zoom Preset** from the pop-up menu.

To recall a Zoom Preset, click your mouse directly on the preset number you want to recall. The zoom setting will be instantly recalled.

 You can also recall Zoom Presets 1 through 5 by pressing the Start key (Windows) or the Control key (Mac) followed by a numeral key (1 through 5) on your computer's alpha keyboard.

Adding Markers to Your Session

Markers can be used to bookmark locations in your session for quick recall. The following sections describe how to add and delete markers, how to use the Memory Locations window and other techniques to recall marker locations, and how to create selections using marker locations.

About Memory Locations

Pro Tools provides up to 999 memory locations, which can be used to store and recall a variety of commonly used display and edit settings. Like Zoom Presets, memory locations can store horizontal and vertical screen magnification settings. However, memory locations can also do much more.

Memory locations come in two main varieties: markers and selections. Markers are used to store locations on the Timeline (playback locations), while selections are used to store Edit selections (edit locations). In this chapter, we will work only with markers.

In addition to storing a Timeline selection, a marker can store a variety of additional information, such as the current zoom setting, track height settings, track show/hide status, and more. Timeline locations and other settings stored with a marker memory location are reestablished when the memory location is later recalled.

Creating a Marker

Markers can be added to a session at any time. Often you will be able to set markers at specified points when playback is stopped. Other times, you might find it useful to add markers on the fly during playback or recording.

Adding Markers at Specified Points

To create a marker at a specified point, do the following:

1. If it is not already displayed, choose VIEW > RULERS > MARKERS to display the Marker Ruler.

2. Place the cursor or make a selection at the desired location in the track.

3. Click the ADD MARKER/MEMORY LOCATION button (plus sign) at the head of the Marker Ruler. The New Memory Location dialog box will appear.

Adding a new marker using the Marker Ruler

4. Give the marker a descriptive name. You can also change the marker number, if desired.

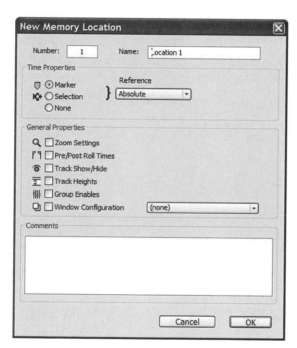

The New Memory Location dialog box

5. In the TIME PROPERTIES section of the dialog box, select MARKER.

6. In the REFERENCE pop-up menu, choose one of the following two options:

   • **Absolute.** This option sets the marker at a sample-based location on the Timeline. The marker will remain at a fixed location in time, regardless of session meter or tempo changes.

   • **Bar|Beat.** This option sets the marker at a tick-based location on the Timeline. The marker will maintain its relative position with respect to the bars and beats in the session, adjusting its absolute location with session meter or tempo changes.

7. (Optional) Under GENERAL PROPERTIES, select any options you wish to associate with the marker. For basic marking, the optional selections can all remain unchecked.

8. Click OK. A small yellow marker symbol corresponding to the memory location will appear in the Marker Ruler at the selected location.

Absolute marker symbol on the Marker Ruler

Adding Markers during Playback and Recording

Memory locations can be added during real-time playback and recording in much the same way as when playback is stopped. When added this way, the marker stores the cursor position at the time that the operation is initiated.

To create a marker during playback (or recording), do the following:

1. If it is not already displayed, choose VIEW > RULERS > MARKERS to display the Marker Ruler.

2. Start playback (or record) from the desired starting position.

3. Click the ADD MARKER/MEMORY LOCATION button (plus sign) at the head of the Marker Ruler. The New Memory Location dialog box will appear.

4. Select the desired options (see steps 4 through 7 in the previous section) and click OK.

 You can also add markers on the fly by pressing Enter on the numeric keypad during playback or recording.

The Memory Locations Window

The Memory Locations window can be used to view all markers and other memory locations that you have stored. To access the Memory Locations window, choose WINDOW > MEMORY LOCATIONS. The Memory Locations window will open.

The Memory Locations window

Recalling a Marker Location

To recall a marker location, do one of the following:

- In the MEMORY LOCATIONS window, click the entry for the desired marker location.
- On the numeric keypad, type a period, followed by the marker location number (1 through 999), and another period.
- Click the corresponding marker symbol in the MARKER RULER.

The marker location will be instantly recalled, and the playback cursor will be positioned at this spot.

Automatically Naming Marker Locations

To save time, you can have Pro Tools automatically name the marker locations you store during playback (and recording) so that you are not prompted with the Memory Locations dialog box each time you initiate a marker. With this feature enabled, Pro Tools gives a default name to all markers based on their number.

To enable auto-naming of marker locations during playback, do the following:

1. Display the Memory Locations window as described above (WINDOW > MEMORY LOCATIONS).
2. Open the Memory Locations menu by clicking on the menu button in the upper-right corner of the window.

The Memory Locations menu button

3. Select AUTO-NAME MEMORY LOCATION from the Memory Locations pop-up menu.

Selecting the auto-name option

To disable the Auto-Name Memory Location option, deselect AUTO-NAME MEMORY LOCATION from the Memory Locations menu.

 Markers can be edited and renamed at any time by double-clicking on the corresponding marker symbols in the Marker Ruler or in the Memory Locations window.

Deleting Marker Locations

To delete a single marker that you no longer need, do the following:

1. Display the Memory Locations window (WINDOW > MEMORY LOCATIONS).
2. Click on the entry that you want to delete.
3. Click on the MEMORY LOCATIONS menu button and choose CLEAR "MARKER NAME" from the pop-up menu. The selected marker will be deleted.

Removing the Bridge marker

 ALT-CLICK *(Windows) or* OPTION-CLICK *(Mac) on any entry in the Memory Locations window (or in the Marker Ruler) to instantly delete it.*

To delete multiple adjacent markers, select the markers by highlighting them on the Marker Ruler and press DELETE. Note that selections on the Marker Ruler must be made independently from Timeline or Edit selections.

A selection on the Marker Ruler

To delete all markers (and any other memory locations in the session), do the following:

1. Display the Memory Locations window (**WINDOW > MEMORY LOCATIONS**).
2. Click on the **MEMORY LOCATIONS** menu button and choose **DELETE ALL** from the pop-up menu. All memory locations will be cleared.

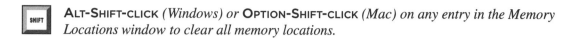 **ALT-SHIFT-CLICK** *(Windows) or* **OPTION-SHIFT-CLICK** *(Mac) on any entry in the Memory Locations window to clear all memory locations.*

Creating a Selection Using Markers

You can easily select between two previously created markers. This can be handy for quickly selecting song sections that you have marked, such as a verse, chorus, bridge, or guitar solo, for example.

To make a selection between two marker locations, do the following:

1. Click the first marker to recall the stored location.
2. Press the **SHIFT** key and click the second marker. The area between the two markers will become selected.

Chapter 8

Basic Editing Techniques

This chapter covers the basics of editing audio and MIDI data in Pro Tools. It provides details on playback options, Edit modes, edit commands, and moving and trimming operations. It also introduces techniques for creating fades and for undoing edit actions.

Objectives

After you complete this chapter, you will be able to:

- Set options for scrolling and looping during playback
- Understand the Pro Tools Edit modes
- Recognize the difference between Absolute Grid mode and Relative Grid mode
- Configure Grid and Nudge values
- Use standard editing commands to modify your playlists
- Understand the effects of Edit modes on moving and trimming operations
- Create fade-in, fade-out, and crossfade effects on your tracks

Introduction

Any time you add audio or MIDI data to the tracks in your session, you are likely to need to do some editing. Whether you need to adjust timing, smooth out a transition, or improve a performance, editing techniques will play a big part in transforming a session from a basic recording to a polished final product. The processes described in the following sections will help you make that transformation, enabling your recordings and compositions to sound their best.

Selecting Playback Options

To simplify your navigation and workflow, Pro Tools provides various playback options to choose from while working on your sessions. Two common options you will likely want to adjust from time to time include the scrolling options and the Loop Playback option.

Scrolling

As discussed in Chapter 3, Pro Tools 9 offers three scrolling options that determine how the contents of the Edit window are displayed during playback and recording. Use the setting that matches your needs for a particular task:

- **No Scrolling.** This option prevents the screen from following the position of the playback cursor. Use this option to keep the display located on an area that you are editing while playing back an area that starts or ends offscreen.
- **After Playback.** This option scrolls the screen to the point where playback ends, centering the end point on the screen. Use this option to locate an area that needs editing by auditioning your tracks. By stopping playback when you hear something amiss, your screen will automatically be scrolled to the area needing attention.
- **Page Scrolling.** This option scrolls the screen one page at a time during playback. Use this option to view the contents of your tracks as they are played back.

Additional details on scrolling options are provided in Chapter 3.

Loop Playback

During editing, you will often want to listen to a selection repeatedly. Loop Playback allows you to repeat your selection continuously, looping from the end of the selection back to the start without interruption. This allows you to easily review the continuity of an edit or transition point.

To use Loop Playback, do the following:

1. Select the desired audio or MIDI data.
2. Choose OPTIONS > LOOP PLAYBACK. The Playback button in the Edit window and Transport window will change to show a loop arrow.
3. Click PLAY or press the SPACE BAR to start continuous looped playback.

Transport window in Loop Playback

You can adjust the start and end points of the loop during playback by modifying your selection, as discussed in Chapter 7. By dragging the corresponding start/end markers in the Timeline Rulers, for example, you can resize your loop on either side. The loop will immediately play back from the start of the selection after you make an adjustment.

Area selected for Loop Playback

 Loop Playback requires a selection at least 0.5 seconds in length.

Using the Edit Modes

As you learned in Chapter 2, Pro Tools provides four Edit modes: Shuffle, Spot, Slip, and Grid. The Edit modes affect the movement and placement of audio and MIDI regions, the results of commands such as Copy and Paste, and the functions of the Edit tools. You will find each Edit mode useful for different purposes while editing your sessions.

- **Shuffle.** This mode allows you to shuffle the order of regions without adding space between them or having them overlap. Use Shuffle mode to rearrange adjacent parts in your session.

- **Slip.** This mode allows you to place a region anywhere on a track without affecting the placement of other regions, leaving space between regions or overlapping regions as desired. Use Slip mode to move or arrange the parts of your session freely.

- **Spot.** This mode allows you to specify exact locations using numerical values when moving, placing, or trimming regions. Use Spot mode to move the parts of your session to specific known destinations.

- **Grid.** This mode allows you to snap regions and MIDI notes to the nearest time increment on a grid, based on the currently selected Time Scale. Use Grid mode to fine-tune timing by aligning parts using defined timing intervals.

Pro Tools provides a combo-mode feature called Snap to Grid. This feature allows you to make selections based on the Grid while editing in Shuffle, Slip, or Spot mode.

You can activate the desired Edit mode at any time by clicking on the corresponding mode button in the toolbar area of the Edit window. To activate Snap to Grid, Shift-click on the Grid mode button when in any other mode.

The Edit mode buttons (Slip mode selected)

Shuffle, Slip, and Spot modes have only one option each and do not require any additional configuration before you use them. Grid mode provides two options to choose from, Absolute Grid and Relative Grid. The functions of both options are affected by the Grid configuration.

Shuffle Mode

In Shuffle mode, when you move or place regions on a track, their placement is constrained by other regions, and any edits you make to a region will affect the placement of subsequent regions on the track. Regions being moved or placed will automatically snap to the end of the preceding region, causing the two regions to butt up against each other. If a region is inserted between two existing regions, all subsequent regions on the track will move to the right to make space for the inserted region. Conversely, if a region is removed from between two existing regions, the subsequent regions on the track will move to the left to fill the void.

You can "shuffle" the order of regions in this mode, but you cannot separate them from each other, or add space between regions, and you cannot make them overlap as in Slip mode. However, any space between existing regions is maintained when the regions move as a result of insertions, deletions, or edits made earlier in the track.

When using the Trim tool in Shuffle mode, changing a region's start or end point will automatically move the subsequent regions by the amount added to or trimmed from the edited region.

 The placement and insertion of individual MIDI notes is not affected by Shuffle mode.

To activate Shuffle mode, click on the SHUFFLE button in the Edit window or press function key **F1**.

Slip Mode

In Slip mode, when you move, trim, cut, or paste regions, their placement is unconstrained by other regions on the track. Editing a region has no effect on subsequent regions, unless the edit causes regions to overlap, in which case the underlying region is trimmed out to accommodate the added material.

To activate Slip mode, click on the SLIP button in the Edit window or press function key **F2**.

Spot Mode

In Spot mode, you can move or place regions within a track at precise locations by specifying the desired destination numerically. As in Slip mode, edit operations do not affect the placement of other regions on the track.

Spot mode allows you to specify a destination based on any time format. You can also use Spot mode to capture an incoming time code address or to spot a region using its time stamps as reference points. This can be particularly useful when you are performing post-production tasks involving SMPTE frame locations.

When Spot mode is enabled, Pro Tools prompts you with a dialog box whenever a region is dragged from the Region List or a DigiBase browser or whenever you click on a region with the Grabber or Trimmer tool. When placing or moving a region, you specify a destination location for the region's start, sync point, or end by entering a value in the Start, Sync Point, or End field in the dialog box, respectively. When trimming a region, you specify the start or end points for the trim using the Start or End fields in the dialog box, respectively.

To activate Spot mode, click on the SPOT button in the Edit window or press function key **F3**.

Grid Mode

In Grid mode, you can make edits based on the timing interval defined by the Grid. (See the following "Configuring the Grid" section.) Selections and insertion points snap to Grid intervals, affecting cut, copy, and paste operations. Move and trim operations either align to the Grid or move in Grid increments relative to their origination point, depending on the option selected (Absolute or Relative).

- In Absolute Grid mode, moving any region snaps the region start to the Grid; trimming a region snaps the trimmed edge to the Grid. If a region's start point falls between Grid lines, moving the region will snap its start time to the nearest Grid line; trimming it will align the trimmed edge to the nearest Grid line. This mode is commonly used to ensure that regions start or end cleanly on the beat or on a subdivision of the beat.

- In Relative Grid mode, regions are moved and trimmed by Grid units. If a region's start point falls between Grid lines, the region will move in Grid increments, preserving its offset from the Grid. Likewise, the Trim tool will trim in Grid increments, preserving the starting point or ending point offset. This mode is commonly used to move regions by bars or beats while maintaining any offset relative to the beat.

To activate Grid mode using the last-used option, click the GRID button in the Edit window or press function key **F4**. To change the Grid mode from the last-used option, click and hold the GRID button and select the desired option from the pop-up selector, or press **F4** a second time to toggle the mode.

 You can temporarily suspend Grid mode and switch to Slip mode by holding down the CTRL key (Windows) or COMMAND key (Mac).

Snap To Grid

The Pro Tools Snap To Grid feature lets you make grid-based selections while working in Shuffle, Slip, or Spot mode. With Snap To Grid enabled, placing the Edit cursor and making Edit selections is constrained by the Grid, but any region editing you perform is based on the other selected Edit mode.

For example, in Shuffle mode with Snap To Grid enabled, any selections you make on audio regions will snap to Grid boundaries; however, if you cut a selection of audio, any regions to the right of the edit will shuffle to the left as normal in Shuffle mode.

To enable Snap To Grid, do the following:

1. Activate the Edit mode you wish to work in (Shuffle, Slip, or Spot).
2. Shift-click on the GRID mode button or press SHIFT+F4.

Snap To Grid in Shuffle mode

 Press **F1+F4** *to enable Snap To Grid and Shuffle mode, press* **F2+F4** *to enable Snap To Grid and Slip mode, and press* **F3+F4** *to enable Snap To Grid and Spot mode.*

Configuring the Grid

Pro Tools allows you to set a timing Grid, based on an interval of your choosing, to help maintain the timing of regions, notes, events, and selections as you edit your session. The Grid settings affect edit operations in Grid mode. (See the preceding "Grid Mode" section.) The Grid can also be used for display only, allowing it to serve as a visual reference without affecting edit operations.

Grid boundaries can be based on frames, bar and beat values, minutes or seconds, or a specified number of samples.

To configure the Grid, do the following:

1. Click the GRID VALUE pop-up selector in the toolbar area of the Edit window.

Grid Value pop-up selector

2. From the Grid Value pop-up menu, choose an appropriate TIME SCALE or choose REGIONS/MARKERS, which causes regions and selections to snap to existing region boundaries and memory location markers whenever they are in close proximity. The menu will close after you make a selection.

Selecting a Time Scale for the Grid

3. Click the GRID VALUE pop-up selector again to choose a corresponding Grid size; the options available will vary depending on the Time Scale selected in Step 2.

Grid-size options for each Time Scale

 The FOLLOW MAIN TIME SCALE option at the bottom of the Grid Value pop-up menu causes the grid to change automatically whenever the Main Time Scale is changed, using the Grid size last set for each Time Scale.

To maintain the Grid in a Time Scale that is different from your Main Time Scale, deselect this option.

Once you have set the Grid to an appropriate Time Scale and size, you have the option of displaying the Grid lines in the Edit window to serve as a visual reference. To display or hide Grid lines, click at the head of the currently selected main Timebase Ruler or click on the Grid indicator in the toolbar. The Grid lines will toggle on or off, and the Grid indicator will light green or become unlit to indicate that Grid lines are on or off, respectively.

Click the current Timebase Ruler or Grid indicator to toggle the Grid-line display

Editing Regions

Pro Tools offers a variety of standard editing commands, such as Copy and Paste, as well as several application-specific commands, such as Capture Region, Separate Region, and Heal Separation, that affect regions.

As discussed in Chapter 4, Pro Tools uses two types of regions: whole-file regions and subset regions. The editing techniques described in this section apply to both types of regions, unless otherwise specified.

Standard Editing Commands

Like most commercial applications, Pro Tools offers standard Cut, Copy, Paste, and Clear (delete) commands. The Pro Tools Duplicate and Repeat commands also offer standard functionality similar to that found in other media applications. Pro Tools performs each of these editing functions nondestructively, meaning that the operations won't alter your original audio files.

Each of these commands can be performed on a single track or on multiple tracks simultaneously, depending on the selection or the Clipboard contents. Edits can apply to the following material:

- Part of a region or parts of multiple regions (selected with the Selector tool)
- A whole region or multiple whole regions (selected with the Grabber tool)

Selections made for Cut, Copy, and Clear commands can cross multiple region boundaries, can include entire regions or partial regions, and can even include silence, if desired.

The effects of Paste, Duplicate, and Repeat operations vary depending on the Edit mode being used:

- In Shuffle mode, all audio or MIDI data that falls after the inserted selection will be moved later in the track(s) by the length of the insertion.
- In Slip mode, all audio and MIDI data remains in place, so inserted material replaces any existing material for the length of the insertion.

When you use any of the editing commands on audio selections within a region or regions, Pro Tools creates byproduct regions and automatically adds them to the Region List.

The Cut Command

Using the Cut command, you can cut a selected range, region, or series of regions from its current position and place the audio or MIDI data on the Clipboard to be pasted elsewhere.

To cut a selection and place the material on the Clipboard, do the following:

1. Make a selection of any length on a single track or multiple tracks.
2. Choose EDIT > CUT, or press CTRL+X (Windows) or COMMAND+X (Mac). The selected audio and/or MIDI data will be removed from the original location and copied to the Clipboard.

 When you cut or clear a selection in Shuffle mode, all audio to the right will slide over by the amount of time removed so that no gap remains.

The Copy Command

The Copy command is much like the Cut command, but instead of removing the selected range, it leaves the original and places a copy of it on the Clipboard so that you can paste it elsewhere.

To copy a selection, do the following:

1. Make a selection of any length on a single track or multiple tracks.
2. Choose EDIT > COPY, or press CTRL+C (Windows) or COMMAND+C (Mac). The selected audio and/or MIDI data will be copied to the Clipboard.

 When you place a selection on the computer's Clipboard using a Cut or Copy command, you replace any material previously stored on the Clipboard.

The Paste Command

Using the Paste command, you can insert the contents of the Clipboard into a location that you have chosen with the Selector. You can paste data only after something has been cut or copied to the Clipboard.

To use the Paste command, do the following:

1. Select the desired paste destination using one of the following methods:
   - Place the cursor (insertion point) on the desired destination track or tracks at the location where you want the start of the paste to occur.
   - Make a selection of any length on the desired destination track or tracks, with the beginning of the selection at the location where you want the start of the paste to occur.

 To paste on multiple tracks, you must make an insertion point or selection on each of the desired destination tracks.

2. Choose EDIT > PASTE, or press CTRL+V (Windows) or COMMAND+V (Mac). The material on the Clipboard will be pasted in, beginning at the selected start point.

 If the Clipboard contains material from multiple tracks, the data will be pasted in starting with the topmost track, and the selected destination tracks will be filled from top to bottom.

 To paste data immediately after a region, use the TAB key (with the Tab to Transient function turned off) to place the cursor exactly at the region's end.

The Clear Command

The Clear command allows you to remove any selected regions or any selected range of audio or MIDI data without placing the deleted audio on the Clipboard.

To clear a selection, do the following:

1. Make a selection of any length on a single track or multiple tracks.
2. Choose EDIT > CLEAR, or press CTRL+B (Windows) or COMMAND+B (Mac). This command has the same result as using the Delete key on the keyboard.

The Duplicate Command

The Duplicate command copies a selection within a single region, a selection that crosses multiple region boundaries (including space), a whole-file region, multiple regions, or any combination of these and places the selected audio or MIDI data immediately after the end of the selection. This command provides a handy way of quickly repeating a selection to extend a sound or create a simple looping effect—it is faster and more convenient than copying and pasting data to achieve the same result.

 For advanced looping effects, use the region looping features in Pro Tools.

 Region looping is covered in the Pro Tools 110 course.

To duplicate audio or MIDI data, do the following:

1. Make a selection of any length and content on one or more tracks.
2. (Optional) Play the selection using Loop Playback to ensure that it plays smoothly in succession, without glitches. If the selection plays smoothly when it loops, you can duplicate it without creating an audible edit point.
3. Adjust the selection as needed to create a smooth loop transition. You might want to zoom in to position the start and end of the selection on a zero crossing (a point of no amplitude in a waveform).
4. After you are satisfied with the selection, choose EDIT > DUPLICATE or press CTRL+D (Windows) or COMMAND+D (Mac). The selection will be duplicated and pasted at the end of the selected area or region.

The Repeat Command

The Repeat command is similar to Duplicate, but it allows you to specify the number of times the selected material will be duplicated.

To repeat a selection of audio or MIDI data multiple times, do the following:

1. Make a selection of any length and content on one or more tracks.
2. Choose EDIT > REPEAT or press ALT+R (Windows) or OPTION+R (Mac). The Repeat dialog box will open.

Repeat dialog box

3. Enter the desired number of repeat iterations and click **OK**. The selected material will be duplicated in succession immediately following the selection's end point, as specified in the Repeat dialog box.

Pro Tools–Specific Editing Commands

Pro Tools includes a number of editing commands that are specifically geared toward working with audio and MIDI regions. The following sections introduce commands for defining audio selections as regions, separating into two or more subset regions, and restoring regions that have been separated.

The Capture Region Command

The Capture Region command defines a selection as a new, independent region and adds it to the Region List without creating a separation in the source location. You can then reuse the captured region by dragging it from the Region List onto any Track Playlist. Selections to be captured as an independent region must be totally contained within a single source region. You cannot capture a selection that crosses one or more region boundaries.

To create a new region using the Capture Region command, do the following:

1. Make a selection of any length within an existing whole-file region or subset region.

2. Choose REGION > CAPTURE or press CTRL+R (Windows) or COMMAND+R (Mac). The Name dialog box will open.

The Name dialog box

3. Enter a name for the new region and click OK. The new region will appear in the Region List on the right side of the Edit window.

 You can rename a region at any time by double-clicking on the region name in the Region List or by double-clicking on the region in a Track Playlist using the Grabber tool.

The Separate Region Command

Separating a region is the process of breaking a region in two or separating a section of an original region into a new region.

You can separate a region for one of several purposes:

- To split a region into two separate regions at the insertion point. Use this process to split the source region into two new regions in the track, adding both to the Region List.

- To separate a selection from a parent region or from the material on either side of the selection. Use this process to separate a selection from its source region(s), creating new regions in the track and adding them to the Region List.

- To create multiple new regions from a selection, dividing the selection at Grid intervals or at transients. Use this process to automatically create regions based on a defined timing interval or based on audio events on the track.

Separating a region at the insertion point (before and after)

Separating a selection as a new region (before and after)

Separating a selection into new regions at Grid intervals (before and after)

When you separate regions, you create *byproduct* regions from the material remaining on either side of the selection. These new byproduct regions appear on the track and in the Region List with new edit numbers appended to the ends of their names.

To separate a region, do the following:

1. Make a selection of any length within a region or across multiple regions, or place the cursor (insertion point) at the location where you want a split to occur.

2. Do one of the following:

   • To create a separation at the insertion point or selection boundaries, choose **EDIT > SEPARATE REGION > AT SELECTION** or press **CTRL+E** (Windows) or **COMMAND+E** (Mac).

   • To create separations at each Grid boundary or transient, choose **EDIT > SEPARATE REGION > ON GRID** or **EDIT > SEPARATE REGION > AT TRANSIENTS**, respectively. The Pre-Separate Amount dialog box will open.

The Pre-Separate Amount dialog box

3. Enter the pre-separate amount in the dialog box, if needed, and click **OK**. This specifies the amount of pad time Pro Tools will include in the new regions before each Grid boundary or transient point.

Pro Tools creates new regions based on the selection start and end points. If the On Grid or At Transients option is chosen, Pro Tools will create additional regions within the selection at each Grid line or transient point. Pro Tools automatically names all resulting new regions by appending the next available edit number to the end of the original region name.

 To have Pro Tools display the Name dialog box for new regions created from a continuous selection, deselect the AUTO-NAME SEPARATED REGIONS *option in the Editing tab of the Pro Tools Preferences.*

The Heal Separation Command

If you've separated a region and you later decide to undo the separation, you can repair the separations and restore the original unedited material using the Heal Separation command. The Heal Separation command gives you a way to repair separated regions, provided that the regions are contiguous and their relative start and end points haven't changed since the separation.

To heal a separation between two or more contiguous regions, do the following:

1. Create a selection across the separation points of the regions to repair.

Selecting across separation points

2. Choose EDIT > HEAL SEPARATION or press CTRL+H (Windows) or COMMAND+H (Mac).

Selection after separations are healed

Moving and Trimming Regions

The following sections describe techniques for moving and trimming regions and discuss the effects of the Edit modes on these operations. The Nudge function is also introduced, along with the process for setting the Nudge value.

Using the Grabber Tool

The Grabber tool can be used to drag a region from the Region List or from an existing location on a Track Playlist. You can drag a region to a different location within the same track or to a different track.

The Grabber tool selected in the Edit toolbar

Moving Regions in Slip Mode

In Slip mode, you can move regions freely within a track or onto other tracks using the Grabber tool. You can place regions so that they overlap or so that there is space between the regions on a track. When you play back the track, there will be silence in any open areas. Table 8.1 shows the results of moving regions in Slip mode.

Table 8.1 Rules for Moving Regions in Slip Mode

Slip Mode Action	Result
When regions partially overlap	The audio on top trims the audio underneath.
When a smaller region is completely covered by a larger region	The smaller region is cleared from the track with no warning, although this action can be undone.
When a smaller region is placed inside a larger one	The smaller region will trim out the audio it covers, so that when it is dragged away, a hole (delete) results. The hole can be repaired using the Heal Separation command.

To move a region in Slip mode, do the following:

1. Select the GRABBER tool. The cursor will change into a hand.
2. Click on the region and drag it to the desired destination. An outline of the region will appear as you position it.
3. Release the mouse to position the region.

 As you drag regions, the Start, End, and Length Selection indicator boxes dynamically update to show you the result of the movement.

Moving Regions in Grid Mode

When using the Grabber tool in Grid mode, moving and dragging regions is constrained by the current Grid Value pop-up menu setting.

To move a region in Grid mode, do the following:

1. Verify that the Grid Time Scale and size have been set as desired. (See the "Configuring the Grid" section earlier in this chapter.)
2. Select the GRABBER tool. The cursor will change into a hand.
3. Click and drag the region to the desired destination. An outline of the region will appear on the track, snapping to each successive Grid line as you position the region.
4. Release the mouse to position the region.

Moving Regions in Shuffle Mode

In Shuffle mode, you can move regions within a track or onto another track, but their movement is constrained by other regions. When moved, regions automatically snap to each other like magnets. You can shuffle their order, but you cannot leave space between regions or overlap them.

To move a region in Shuffle mode, do the following:

1. Select the GRABBER tool. The cursor will change into a hand.
2. Drag a region to the desired destination. The insertion point will snap between the start and end points of existing regions on the track as you position the region.
3. Release the mouse to position the start of the region at the insertion point. Adjacent regions reposition themselves as needed to accommodate the region and to close up the space left at its point of origin.

Moving Regions in Spot Mode

Spotting is the process of placing regions at predetermined time locations within your tracks based on exact Time Scale units, such as Min:Secs, Bars|Beats, or SMPTE time code.

To move and place a region in Spot mode, do the following:

1. Select the GRABBER tool. The cursor will change into a hand.
2. Click on the desired region or drag a region from the Region List. The Spot Dialog box will appear.

The Spot Dialog box

3. Choose the desired TIME SCALE from the Time Scale pop-up menu. (The menu selection defaults to the Main Time Scale of the session.)
4. Enter the new location in either the START or END field and click OK. (Other options for this dialog box are covered in later courses.) The region's start or end point will align to the specified location.

Using the Trim Functions

Regions can be trimmed using either the Trim tool or the Trim command. The Trim functions allow you to shorten or lengthen regions as desired by trimming their heads or tails.

The Trim Tool

The Trim tool can be used to dynamically adjust the length of a region. By trimming the head or tail of a region, you can eliminate unwanted audio that precedes or follows any audio that you want to retain.

The Trim tool selected in the Edit toolbar

To trim a region, do the following:

1. If needed, use the ZOOMER tool to zoom in on the area you want to trim.
2. Click the TRIM tool (standard).
3. Move the cursor over the audio region you want to trim. The cursor will change to a left trim shape or a right trim shape on either side of the region's midpoint.

Left Trim (from start)	Right Trim (from end)

Trim tool, as displayed on either side of the region midpoint

4. Click the cursor on the left side to trim the region head or on the right side to trim the region tail; drag toward the center to shorten the region or away from the center to extend the region. As you drag, the region outline will preview the trim effect.
5. Release the mouse button to accept the trim. The region will update to display the new length.

 To reverse the direction of the Trim tool so that you can trim in either direction without having to trim past the midpoint, press ALT (Windows) or OPTION (Mac) before trimming a region.

Trimming with the Edit Modes

The function of the Trim tool is affected by the currently selected Edit mode. Slip, Shuffle, Spot, and Grid modes all affect trimming differently.

- **Trimming with Shuffle mode.** In Shuffle mode, trimming the head or tail of a region will cause all regions after the trim to move earlier or later, respectively, by the amount of the trim. Trimming the head of a region causes the audio in the region to roll in or out to the right of the start point. (The head of the region remains stationary on the Timeline while the tail moves in or out.)

 Locked regions will not move, even if you trim audio before them in Shuffle mode.

- **Trimming with Slip mode.** In Slip mode, other regions in the track will not shift when a region is adjusted with the Trim tool. Any region that gets overlapped when a region is extended with the Trim tool is itself trimmed out in the area of the overlap.

Press and hold the START *key (Windows) or* CONTROL *key (Mac) before you begin trimming in Slip mode to extend a region up to, but not beyond, the border of a neighboring region.*

- **Trimming with Spot mode.** In Spot mode, clicking a region with the Trim tool opens the Spot dialog box, allowing you to specify the start time or end time to use for trimming the region.
- **Trimming with Grid mode.** In Grid mode, the Trim tool moves incrementally, snapping to Grid lines as the region is lengthened or shortened. Any region that gets overlapped when a region is extended with the Trim tool is itself trimmed out in the area of the overlap.

The Trim Region Command

The Trim Region command in the Edit menu allows you trim a region to the boundaries of a selection or to trim (clear) all audio in a region to the left or right of the insertion point.

To use the Trim Region command based on a selection within a region, do the following:

1. Select the portion of a region you want to retain.

Audio selected for trimming

2. Choose EDIT > TRIM REGION > TO SELECTION. The portion of the region outside of the selection will be deleted.

Selection after trimming

The Shuffle mode affects the Trim Region operation in the same way that it affects the operation of the Trim tool; the trimmed audio moves on the Timeline so that the region head retains its position, and any regions after the trimmed region move by the amount of the trim.

 You can also press CTRL+T *(Windows) or* COMMAND+T *(Mac) to trim a region to a selection.*

To use the Trim Region command to clear audio preceding or following the insertion point, do the following:

1. Position the insertion point within a region where you want the region to start or end.
2. Choose EDIT > TRIM REGION > START TO INSERTION or EDIT >TRIM REGION > END TO INSERTION to trim all audio before the insertion point or after the insertion point, respectively.

Using the Nudge Function

Pro Tools allows you to set an increment for adjusting the placement of regions and selections in small, precise amounts using the keyboard. The increment amount, or *Nudge value*, is set much like the Grid size. Nudging a region is similar to moving a region in Grid mode, in that the region is moved incrementally by predefined units.

You can use the Nudge function in any of the four editing modes, although it's most commonly used in Slip, Shuffle, and Grid modes. Nudging will always move the selected region or regions without moving adjacent regions, regardless of Edit mode.

Configuring the Nudge Value

The Nudge value can be based on frames, time code, bar and beat values, a time measurement (in milliseconds), or a specified number of samples, depending on the Time Scale selected.

To configure the Nudge value, do the following:

1. Click the NUDGE VALUE pop-up selector in the toolbar area of the Edit window.

Nudge value pop-up selector

2. From the Nudge value pop-up menu, choose the desired Time Scale. The menu will close after you make a selection.

Selecting a Time Scale for the Nudge

3. Click the NUDGE VALUE pop-up selector again to choose a corresponding Nudge size; the options available will vary depending on the Time Scale selected in Step 2.

Selecting a Nudge size

The Follow Main Time Scale option at the bottom of the Nudge value pop-up menu enables the Nudge value to change automatically whenever the Main Time Scale is changed, adopting the last used value for that Time Scale.

To maintain the Nudge in a Time Scale that is different from your Main Time Scale, deselect this option.

Nudging Regions

To nudge a single region or multiple regions, do the following:

1. Verify that the Nudge Time Scale and size have been set as desired. (See the preceding "Configuring the Nudge Value" section.)
2. With the GRABBER tool, select the region or regions you want to nudge.
3. On the numeric keypad, press the PLUS key [+] to move the region(s) later in the track or the MINUS key [–] to move the region(s) earlier in the track. The regions will move incrementally by the Nudge value.

 If you are using a laptop computer that does not have a numeric keypad, you can use the Function key (marked Fn) and the corresponding +/– keys to nudge regions.

 You can manually enter a Nudge value by typing it directly into the Nudge display.

Nudging Selections

In addition to nudging regions, you can also nudge selections that do not contain entire regions using the Plus [+] and Minus [–] keys on the numeric keypad. You can even nudge the start and end times of a selection independently.

To nudge the start time of a selection, press ALT (Windows) or OPTION (Mac) and one of the following:

- The PLUS key [+] to nudge the selection start later using the current Nudge value
- The MINUS key [–] to nudge the selection start earlier using the current Nudge value

To nudge the end time of a selection, press CTRL (Windows) or COMMAND (Mac) and one of the following:

- The PLUS key [+] to nudge the selection end later using the current Nudge value
- The MINUS key [–] to nudge the selection end earlier using the current Nudge value

---

ADD THE SHIFT KEY TO FREELY NUDGE ANY SELECTION

When a selection start or end touches a region boundary, nudging that start or end will trim the underlying region. Similarly, nudging with one or more entire regions selected will move the selected region(s). By holding Shift while nudging, you can nudge the selection without affecting the underlying region(s).

Creating Fade Effects

A *fade* is a steady volume ramp up or ramp down that Pro Tools can create on any region boundary you desire. Fades have many different applications, from smoothing out an edit, to creating seamless region overlaps, to building volume fade-ins and fade-outs for music and sound effects. This section covers the process of creating simple fade-ins, fades-outs, and crossfades for a variety of useful applications.

Fade-Ins and Fade-Outs

Fade-in and fade-out effects can be created at the beginning or ending of any audio region, respectively, using a selection that touches or crosses the region boundary.

Following are some basic guidelines for creating fades:

- Make your selection to match the desired fade; the length of the fade is determined by the selection length.
- Make a selection that touches or crosses an open region boundary (i.e., a boundary that is not adjacent to another region); boundaries between adjacent regions can be faded only with a crossfade (see the "Crossfades" section that follows).
- To create a fade-in, touch or cross the beginning region boundary; to create a fade-out, touch or cross an ending region boundary.
- Fade-ins always begin at the head boundary, and fade-outs always end at the tail boundary. Extending a selection into a blank area beyond a region's boundaries will not change the fade length.
- Fades are calculated in RAM prior to being rendered to disk as a file (stored in the Fades file folder of your session); for the best results, you should ensure that you have enough available RAM from the total allocation assigned to the Pro Tools application.

Keep these guidelines in mind as you prepare your selection for creating a fade.

To create a fade, do the following:

1. Select the beginning or ending of a region. (SHIFT-CLICK additional tracks to create fades on multiple tracks whose regions begin or end simultaneously.)
2. Choose EDIT > FADES > CREATE or press CTRL+F (Windows) or COMMAND+F (Mac). The corresponding Fade-In or Fade-Out dialog box will appear.
3. Choose the desired settings in the dialog box (see the "Fade Settings" section later in this chapter) and click OK. The fade will be generated and rendered in the Track Playlist as a separate region at the head or tail of the source region.

The Fade-In and Fade-Out dialog boxes

Fade-in at the head of a region

Crossfades

Pro Tools allows you to create crossfades between any two adjacent audio subset regions. *Crossfading* is essentially the process of overlapping two audio sources and fading out the first source while simultaneously fading in the second source. Pro Tools achieves this effect by overlapping the underlying audio on either side of the boundary between the adjacent regions.

To define an area for a crossfade, you must make a selection across the end of an outgoing region's file and the beginning of an incoming region's file, and both regions must have sufficient audio in their underlying audio files to extend across the length of the selection.

To create a crossfade between two adjacent regions, do the following:

1. Make a selection across the boundary between the regions.

Area for crossfade selected in the Edit window

2. Choose EDIT > FADES > CREATE or press CTRL+F (Windows) or COMMAND+F (Mac). The Fades dialog box will open.

The Fades dialog box displaying a crossfade (mono track shown)

3. Choose the desired settings in the Fades dialog box (see the "Fade Settings" section that follows) and click **OK**. If sufficient underlying audio is available, the crossfade will be generated and rendered in the Track Playlist as a separate region between the source regions.

Crossfade rendered between regions

 You can audition and view the resulting crossfade before generating it by clicking the corresponding icons on the left edge of the Fades dialog box.

If either or both source regions lack sufficient underlying audio to generate a crossfade based on the selection boundaries, a warning will display after you click **OK** in the Fades dialog box to alert you that the attempted crossfade is invalid.

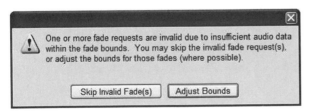

Invalid fade warning

Clicking the ADJUST BOUNDS button in this warning box will adjust the placement and length of the fade to fit the available audio from the incoming or outgoing region. If insufficient audio is available to overlap the regions at all, no fade will be created.

Fade Settings

The Fades dialog box displays the fade-in shape in red and the fade-out shape in blue. Either shape can be changed by choosing from the seven presets in the Shape drop-down selectors or by choosing one of the two editable fade shapes using the radio buttons. The shape of each curve determines how the amplitude of a region changes during the course of the fade.

Undoing Your Work

Often, your editing tasks will involve performing a series of related steps to achieve a desired effect. Along the way, you might find that you want to go back to an earlier point, either to start over or to do a before-and-after comparison of the composition. Fortunately, Pro Tools provides rich undo options that give you the flexibility you need to work without worry.

Using Multi-Level Undo

Multi-level undo operations make it possible to revert to earlier stages of work during the editing process. This in turn enables you to experiment more freely, with the confidence of knowing that you can return to an earlier point if you are not satisfied with the results.

Pro Tools provides up to 32 levels of edit undo. All commands that are undoable are stored sequentially in a queue for undo/redo purposes. However, certain commands cause changes that are not undoable, and any of these events will clear the undo queue.

Some common actions that *cannot* be undone include the following:

- Deleting tracks
- Closing a session and/or quitting Pro Tools
- Clearing audio from the Region List
- Destructive recording

The Pro Tools default settings provide the maximum of 32 levels of undo operation. If available memory for your system is running low, you can lower this setting to free up memory used by the undo queue. (Large undo queues require more RAM and can affect system performance if you have insufficient RAM.)

To change the number of levels of undo, follow these steps:

1. Choose SETUP > PREFERENCES and then click the EDITING tab.

2. At the bottom of the dialog box, enter the desired undo setting between 1 and 32 and click **OK**.

Levels of undo, as set in the Editing Preferences tab

Undoable actions are stored sequentially in the queue, with the most recent action at the front of the queue. Actions must be undone in reverse order; you cannot undo an individual action out of sequence.

To access the Undo command, choose **EDIT > UNDO** or press **CTRL+Z** (Windows) or **COMMAND+Z** (Mac). The Undo command in the Edit menu lists the action to be undone along with the command name.

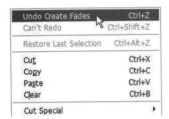

The Undo command, showing the action that will be undone

To perform multiple undo operations, repeat the above process as needed, up to the limit set on the Editing Preferences page.

If you undo an action that you want to keep, you can reinstate the action using the Redo command. To access the Redo command, choose **EDIT > REDO** or press **CTRL+SHIFT+Z** (Windows) or **COMMAND+SHIFT+Z** (Mac). Like the Undo command, the Redo command lists the action that it will affect.

Undo History

The Undo History window displays the undo queue, showing up to the last 32 actions that can be undone. You can use this window to view the recent actions taken and the sequence of those actions, as well as any actions recently undone. The Undo History window allows you to instantly return to any previous state from the actions listed. The Undo History can also show the creation time of each action, enabling you to revert to the state a session held at a particular time.

To show the Undo History window, choose **Window > Undo History**. The Undo History window shows undoable operations that have been performed in bold and operations that have already been undone in italics.

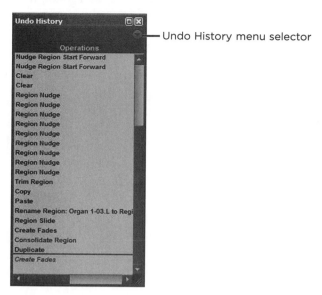

The Undo History window

The following actions can be performed using the Undo History window:

- **Multiple simultaneous undos.** To undo multiple operations in the Undo History window, click on the last bold operation that you want to undo in the list. The selected operation and all operations performed after it will be undone; the undone operations will display in italics.

- **Multiple simultaneous redos.** To redo multiple operations in the Undo History window, click the latest italicized operation that you want to redo in the list. The selected operation and all operations that precede it will be redone; the redone operations will again display in bold.

- **Undo all.** To undo all the operations in the undo queue, click the **Undo History Menu** selector and choose **Undo All** from the pop-up menu.

- **Redo all.** To redo all the operations in the redo queue, click the **Undo History Menu** selector and choose **Redo All**.

- **Clear the queue.** To clear the undo queue, click the **Undo History Menu** selector and choose **Clear Undo Queue**. When you select this option, a dialog box opens, verifying the action; click **Yes** to complete the command.

When the number of operations in the Undo History exceeds 32 or the limit set in the Edit Preferences, the operations at the top of the list are removed. The operation next in line to be pushed out of the queue is shown in red.

Restore Last Selection

Pro Tools provides a separate command that enables you to restore your last Edit or Timeline selection in the event that you lose the selection or find that you need to reuse a selection you had made previously.

To restore the last selection, choose **Edit > Restore Last Selection** or press **Ctrl+Alt+Z** (Windows) or **Command+Option+Z** (Mac).

Revert to Saved

If you need to undo changes that are not available in the Undo History, you can use the Revert to Saved command to restore the last saved version of your session. Reverting to the last saved version has the same effect as closing the session without saving changes and then reopening it.

To revert to the last saved version of your session, do the following:

1. Choose FILE > REVERT TO SAVED. A dialog box will prompt you to verify that you want to revert the session.

2. Click REVERT to continue.

Chapter 9

Basic Mixing Techniques

This chapter covers basic mixing techniques and processes as they are performed in a Pro Tools environment. It includes discussions of mixer terminology, Mix window configuration (including configuring inserts, sends, and returns), basic automation, and real-time plug-ins.

Objectives

After you complete this chapter, you will be able to:

- Configure inserts and send-and-return paths to add signal processing to your tracks
- Configure the Sends view in the Mix window to display a single send across all tracks
- Record and edit basic automation for your mix
- Add plug-ins to your tracks for internal effects processing and sound shaping

Introduction

In this chapter, we focus on using Pro Tools' mix functions to route signals, set levels, and add effects when creating a session mix and preparing for mixdown. For the purposes of this course, we will limit our focus to standard stereo mixing. Other mixing options, such as mixing for surround sound, are covered in advanced courses.

Basic Mixer Terminology

The fundamental job of any audio mixer is to route incoming and outgoing audio via the mixer's inputs and outputs. Additional signal routing and processing can be achieved using the mixer's inserts and send and return functions. These terms are defined in the following sections as they apply to general audio mixing; specific Pro Tools applications of these concepts are described in "The Pro Tools Mix Window" section later in this chapter.

Inputs

The term *input* refers to an audio signal traveling into an audio hardware device, such as a mixer or an audio interface.

The inputs available from within the Mix window in the Pro Tools software vary depending on the Pro Tools system and hardware interface you are using.

Outputs

The term *output* refers to an audio signal traveling out of an audio hardware device, such as a mixer or an audio interface.

The outputs available from within the Mix window in Pro Tools also vary depending on the Pro Tools system and hardware interface you are using.

Inserts

Most mixers have a feature known as a *channel insert*. A channel insert is an audio patch point that allows either a plug-in insert or a hardware signal processor to be inserted directly into the signal path of the audio channel.

Pro Tools provides 10 insert positions per track, allowing you to process a track's signal through multiple software plug-ins and/or external effects loops in series.

Sends and Returns

The term *send* refers to a signal path carrying a mix output of one or more Audio tracks routed for parallel processing. The send may route to an external receiving device, such as an external reverb or digital delay, or to an internal processor, such as a software plug-in. Sends can be *pre-fader*, meaning the send level is independent of the channel's fader level, or *post-fader*, meaning the send level is affected by the channel's fader level. Pro Tools allows you to set sends to pre- or post-fader, as needed.

When using a send for external processing, the sent signal is received on the input of an external device, some type of effect is added to the signal, and then the signal is returned to the original sending device through an *auxiliary input* or *auxiliary return*. When using a send for internal processing, effects are added by a plug-in applied to the send signal; the processed signal is added to the mix through an auxiliary input channel.

The return inputs provide level and pan controls, allowing precise control over how the reintroduced signal combines with other audio in the system.

The Pro Tools Mix Window

Many of Pro Tools' mixing operations and functions are performed using the Mix window. The Mix window in Pro Tools is similar to a standard mixing console. If you are acquainted with mixing console functions, the Pro Tools Mix window will be familiar territory. This window offers a variety of display options, many of which can also be customized.

The Mix window can be displayed or hidden as needed. To toggle the Mix window display on or off, choose WINDOW > MIX. If the Mix window is already open but is inactive (such as when it is hidden behind another window), this command will make it active, bringing it to the front of the display.

 Press CTRL+= *(Windows) or* COMMAND+= *(Mac) to toggle between the Mix and Edit windows.*

Mix window controls

Configuring the Mix Window

The Mix window includes several component parts, a number of which can be selectively turned on and off as needed. Among the parts of the Mix window that you will use to create a session mix are Track Volume Faders, Pan controls, I/O selectors, and Insert and Send selectors.

 The Input and Output selectors (I/O selectors) include Audio Input Path selectors and Audio Output Path selectors, as well as MIDI Input selectors and MIDI Output selectors (MIDI and Instrument tracks only).

To create a session mix, you will set the Volume Faders and Pan controls for each track to achieve an appropriate blend of audio levels and the desired positioning of sounds within the stereo field. You can make changes in real time during playback/mixdown either by manually adjusting the controls or by using automation. (See the "Basic Automation" section later in this chapter.)

The Input selectors and Output selectors are used to route signals to and from your tracks. Often, the primary I/O routing for your mix will already be set as needed, based on the routing you used during recording and editing operations. However, your mix might call for new or different input and output settings for certain tracks; use these selectors to configure your I/O as needed. See the following "Input and Output Selectors" section for more detail.

Mixing also often involves using inserts and sends to add various types of signal processing to the audio on a session's tracks. Use the Insert and Send selectors in the Mix window to achieve these operations. See the "Inserts and Sends Views" section later in this chapter for more detail.

Input and Output Selectors

The Mix window always displays the main Input and Output selectors for each track in the session. Though much of your signal routing might have been set up during the recording and editing stages of your project, it is always a good idea to double-check the I/O settings when you begin mixing.

Input Paths

For tracks that are playing back material from their own Edit Playlist, no input routing is necessary. Tracks that are receiving input from other sources will need to have their inputs set accordingly.

When modifying or setting up tracks for mixing, pay particular attention to the Audio Input Path selector settings for the following types of tracks:

- Auxiliary Input tracks
- Instrument tracks
- Audio tracks used for internal mixdown or bounce destinations

For Auxiliary Input tracks and Instrument tracks, the Audio Input Path selector is often used to route audio from an available input source connection on the system. For internal mixdown on Audio tracks, the Input Path selector is often used to route audio from an internal bus. (See Chapter 10, "Finishing Your Work," for more information on setting up an internal mixdown.)

The following diagram shows how the Audio Input Path selector for an Auxiliary Input track corresponds to the input connectors of an Mbox 2 used to route live input from a synthesizer.

Common signal flow using an Auxiliary Input track for live input with an Mbox 2

Output Paths

Pro Tools gives you the flexibility to route the output of each track to any output channel or bus. For the purposes of creating a stereo mix, however, you will generally select the main stereo outputs of your audio interface.

To set up your mix, verify that the Audio Output Path selectors for the tracks in your session are set to the main outputs of your audio interface, as appropriate, so that the audio from each track is included in the stereo mix. Exceptions would include the following:

- Tracks that you don't want to include in the mix
- MIDI tracks feeding an outboard device
- Tracks sent to a bus to create a sub-mix

If needed, use the Audio Output Path selector to remove a track from the stereo mix and/or to select any of the other available outputs. The following diagram shows how the Audio Output Path selector on an Audio track corresponds to the output connectors of an Mbox 2.

Signal Path
(to Mbox 2)

LEFT

RIGHT

Signal flow from an Auxiliary Input track to stereo (left and right) monitor outputs on an Mbox 2

Inserts and Sends Views

The Mix window has independent view areas for the track inserts and the track sends. These view areas can each be toggled on or off in the Mix window.

- **Inserts view.** The two Inserts view areas (Inserts A–E and Inserts F–J) allow you to access and view the 10 track Insert selectors. (Five are displayed in each view area.)

Insert selectors
(A–E or F–J)

Inserts view area

- **Sends view.** The two Sends view areas (Sends A–E and Sends F–J) allow you to access and view the 10 track Send selectors. (Five are displayed in each view area.)

Send selectors
(A–E or F–J)

Sends view area

To toggle the display of an Insert or Sends view area in the Mix window, choose VIEW > MIX WINDOW VIEWS and click an option in the submenu to select or deselect it.

Toggling the Inserts F–J view area from the Mix Window submenu

The two Sends view areas can be further customized to display their sends in one of two ways.

- **Assignments.** Shows the status of all five track Send selectors simultaneously. Each send that has been assigned will display the send assignment.

Sends view in Assignments display mode

- **Single Send.** Shows only one Send selector at a time across all tracks. On any tracks that have that send assigned, the Sends view will display the assignment and send level controls. In Single Send display mode, each Sends view area can be set to display any one of its five Send selectors.

Sends View in Single Send display mode (Send B displayed)

To toggle between Send Assignments view and Single Send view, choose VIEW > SENDS A-E or VIEW > SENDS F-J and select the desired display mode from the submenu. The corresponding Sends view will be displayed using the chosen mode.

Selecting Single Send display mode for Send B

 The Inserts and Sends view areas are available in both the Mix and Edit windows and can be shown or hidden independently in each window.

Configuring Inserts

With an Inserts view area displayed in the Mix window, you can insert a processor on any track. To add an insert processor, click on the Insert selector and choose a plug-in option or an I/O option from the pop-up menu. Plug-ins provide software-based signal processing, while I/O routing lets you use an external hardware device.

Plug-In Insert

Plug-in inserts can route audio through a software add-on from within the channel strip in the Mix window.

Choose a plug-in insert to add a software signal processor, such as the 1-band EQ III plug-in, directly into the signal path of the channel.

Hardware I/O Insert

Hardware I/O inserts can route audio through an external device connected to parallel inputs and outputs of an audio interface. This option requires an audio interface with available hardware inputs and outputs for line-level signals, such as a 003 family interface.

 Hardware inserts are covered in the Pro Tools 110 course.

Audio Playback →

← Plug-in Output

Signal flow through a plug-in insert (EQ III shown)

Configuring Sends and Returns

Sends are used to route a track's signal to a secondary path for parallel processing (internal or external) without interrupting the signal flow through the originating track. To add the processed signal back into the mix, it is usually returned via an Auxiliary Input.

To route a send to an external device, choose INTERFACE from the Send selector and select the appropriate output(s) on your audio interface. Connect these outputs to the external device and return the processed signal from the device to available inputs on your audio interface. This signal is the return, which then must be routed to the Audio Input of an Auxiliary Input track.

To route a send to an internal processor, such as a plug-in on an Auxiliary Input, choose BUS from the Send selector and select the appropriate bus for routing the signal. Busses can also be used to create sub-mixes that are returned via an Auxiliary Input.

Basic Automation

For a very simple mix, you can probably set your Track Volume Faders, Pan Sliders, and other controls and leave them unchanged from the start of the mix to the end. Most mixes are more complex, though, and require dynamic changes during the course of playback. Pro Tools allows you to record and edit these changes, automating various controls on your tracks. The automatable controls include volume, pan, mute, and real-time plug-in controls, depending on the track type.

Tracks in Pro Tools use automation modes to determine how automation is used on the track. You can set the automation mode for each track independently using a pop-up menu. The following sections discuss three of these modes, Write, Read, and Off, to illustrate the basic automation functions that Pro Tools offers.

Recording Automation (Write Mode)

By setting automation on a track to Write mode, you can record the changes you make to the controls on the track in real time. The basic steps for recording automation in Write mode are as follows:

1. Enable the automation type that you want to record, such as volume or pan, as follows:

    a. Choose **WINDOW > AUTOMATION**. The Automation window will open.

    b. Verify that the automation type is write-enabled (armed) for the session. Many automatable controls are armed by default.

    c. If needed, click on an automation type to toggle its state (armed versus suspended).

Toggling an automation type in the Automation Enable window

 The buttons in the Automation Enable window toggle between red to indicate enabled *automation types and dark gray to indicate* suspended *automation types.*

2. Put the track in automation writing mode by choosing **WRITE** from the Automation Mode selector.

Automation Mode selector in the Edit window and Mix window

Selecting Write mode from the Automation Mode selector pop-up menu

3. Begin playback to start automation recording, and adjust controls as needed. Pro Tools will record all adjustments performed on enabled controls.

If you are not satisfied with the automation, you can repeat these steps to write new automation over the previous data.

Viewing and Editing Breakpoint Automation

Each Pro Tools track contains a single automation playlist for each automatable parameter. The automation playlist can be displayed in the Edit window, providing a convenient way to view the recorded automation changes over time. While visible, the automation playlist can also be edited and refined using Edit tools, such as the Grabber.

To display the automation playlist, do the following:

1. Click on the TRACK VIEW SELECTOR in the Edit window.

Track View selector

2. Select the automation playlist that you want to display from the TRACK VIEW pop-up menu. The automation graph line will be displayed, superimposed on the track audio or MIDI data.

Showing the Volume automation Track view

Pro Tools also allows you to view automation playlists by clicking on the SHOW/HIDE AUTOMATION LANES button (triangle) at the head of a track. The Volume automation lane will be displayed beneath the parent track. Additional automation lanes can be displayed by clicking the plus sign (+) at the head of the Volume automation lane.

Showing Volume automation in an automation lane

You can edit an automation playlist by adding, moving, or deleting breakpoints using the Grabber tool. To edit a playlist with the Grabber tool, do any of the following:

- Click on the automation graph line to add a breakpoint.
- Click and drag an existing breakpoint to adjust its position.
- ALT-CLICK (Windows) or OPTION-CLICK (Mac) on an existing breakpoint to remove it.

Editing the Volume playlist using the Grabber tool

Automation playlists can also be edited using other Edit tools. Additional information on using and editing automation is provided in advanced courses.

Playing Back Automation (Read Mode)

The default automation mode for a track is Read mode. In this mode, the automation playlist is used to play the automation data that has been recorded or written for a track. Automation is not recorded in Read mode, but the automation playlist can be edited with the Edit tools.

To return to Read mode when a different mode has been activated, click the AUTOMATON MODE SELECTOR and choose READ.

 Use Read mode to play back automation without running the risk of recording over any of it.

Turning Automation Off

The Off mode turns off automation for all automatable parameters on the track, such as the following:

- Volume
- Pan
- Mute

- Send volume, pan, and mute
- Plug-in controls
- MIDI volume, pan, and mute

In Off mode, automation is not recorded during playback, and existing automation data for all parameters is ignored. To turn automation off, click the AUTOMATION MODE SELECTOR and choose OFF.

Real-Time Plug-Ins

As you learned in earlier chapters, plug-ins can be used to add functionality to a Pro Tools session, such as a metronome click or a virtual instrument. Plug-ins are independent software programs that function as add-ons to Pro Tools. Plug-ins exist for a multitude of sound-processing applications—from synthesis to effects processing to sonic modeling of hardware processors, amplifiers, and microphones.

Pro Tools provides two main categories of plug-ins:

- Real-time processing, provided by RTAS and TDM plug-ins
- File-based processing (non-real-time), provided by AudioSuite plug-ins

 Details on using AudioSuite plug-ins are provided in the Pro Tools 110 course.

The following sections explain the basic concepts behind real-time plug-ins.

Real-Time Plug-In Features

Real-time plug-ins are available as track inserts in Pro Tools. When you add a real-time plug-in to a track, it processes the audio or MIDI data non-destructively and in real time—you instantly hear its effect on the track while playing back audio.

As discussed in Chapter 1, Pro Tools supports two formats of real-time plug-ins: *TDM* and *RTAS*. The difference between the formats lies in how your system provides processing power for the plug-in. Both types of plug-ins function as track inserts, are applied to audio during playback, and process audio non-destructively in real time.

TDM Plug-Ins (Pro Tools|HD Systems Only)

TDM plug-ins are designed for use on Pro Tools|HD systems with TDM hardware and rely on the processing power of Digidesign DSP cards.

RTAS Plug-Ins (All Pro Tools Systems)

Real-Time AudioSuite, or RTAS, plug-ins rely on the processing power of the host computer. The more powerful your computer, the greater the number and variety of RTAS plug-ins that you can use simultaneously. You can increase the number of RTAS plug-ins your system can support by increasing the Hardware Buffer Size and CPU Usage Limit. See Chapter 2 for details on adjusting these parameters.

Real-Time Plug-In Formats

Plug-ins can be used in mono, multi-mono, or multi-channel formats. (For the purposes of this book, discussion of multi-channel formats will be limited to stereo configurations.) The plug-in format(s) available depend on the plug-in selected and the format of the track (mono or stereo). You should generally use multi-channel plug-ins for stereo tracks, if possible; if no multi-channel version is available, use a multi-mono version.

- **Mono plug-ins.** Plug-ins in this format are designed for use on mono tracks. Some mono plug-ins can generate stereo output from a mono channel.
- **Multi-mono plug-ins.** Plug-ins in this format can be used on stereo tracks or multi-channel surround tracks. Multi-mono plug-ins analyze and process each channel independently. Controls for all channels are linked by default so that adjustments are made to all channels in tandem. The controls can be unlinked for specialized purposes, allowing you to adjust channels independently.
- **Multi-channel plug-ins.** Plug-ins in this format are designed for use on stereo or multi-channel surround tracks. Controls for all channels are always linked together in multi-channel plug-ins.

Plug-Ins Provided with Pro Tools

Pro Tools comes bundled with a variety of additional software packages that extend its functionality. Among the extras bundled with Pro Tools are the DigiRack plug-ins listed in Appendix A and the Creative Collection plug-ins listed in Appendix B. Among these, you will find dynamics processors, EQs, reverbs, delays, flangers, choruses, and a variety of other special effects.

Two commonly used general-purpose Pro Tools plug-ins are the DigiRack EQ III plug-in and the DigiRack Dynamics III plug-in. These plug-ins support both TDM and RTAS formats for real-time, non-destructive processing.

DigiRack EQ III

The DigiRack EQ III is an equalizer plug-in for adjusting the frequency spectrum of audio material in Pro Tools. This plug-in can be added to a track in a 1-band, 4-band, or 7-band parametric EQ configuration. The plug-in includes selectable shelving filters and settings as well as separate high-pass, low-pass, and variable Q notch filters.

EQ III is available as a mono or multi-mono plug-in. (Stereo and multi-channel tracks are supported through multi-mono operation.)

To add the EQ III plug-in to a Pro Tools track, do one of the following:

- For a mono track, click on an INSERT SELECTOR and choose PLUG-IN > EQ > 1-BAND EQ 3 (MONO) (or choose the 4- or 7-Band EQ 3, as appropriate). The DigiRack EQ III plug-in window will open.

- For a stereo track, click on an INSERT SELECTOR and choose MULTI-MONO PLUG-IN > EQ > 1-BAND EQ 3 (MONO) (or choose the 4- or 7-Band EQ 3, as appropriate). The multi-mono DigiRack EQ III plug-in window will open.

The DigiRack EQ III 7-band equalizer plug-in window (mono shown)

DigiRack Dynamics III

The Dynamics III plug-in provides a suite of dynamics processing plug-ins, including a Compressor/ Limiter, an Expander/Gate, and a De-Esser. Dynamics III also includes an interactive dynamics display graph for ease of use, speed, and accuracy.

The Compressor/Limiter and Expander/Gate plug-ins are available in mono, stereo, and multi-channel surround formats; the De-Esser plug-in is available in mono and stereo formats only.

The Compressor/Limiter plug-in can be used to control dynamic levels, using standard attack, release, threshold, and ratio controls. The Expander/Gate plug-in can be added to a track to eliminate unwanted background noise by fine-tuning the ratio, attack, hold, release, and range. The De-Esser can be used to reduce sibilants, using frequency and range controls.

To add a Dynamics III plug-in to a Pro Tools track, do one of the following:

- For a mono track, click on an **INSERT SELECTOR** and choose **PLUG-IN > DYNAMICS > COMPRESSOR/LIMITER DYN 3 (MONO)** (or choose the De-Esser or Expander/Gate Dyn 3, as appropriate). The selected DigiRack Dynamics III plug-in window will open.

- For a stereo track, click on an **INSERT SELECTOR** and choose **PLUG-IN > MULTI-CHANNEL PLUG-IN > DYNAMICS > COMPRESSOR/LIMITER DYN 3 (STEREO)** (or choose the De-Esser or Expander/Gate Dyn 3, as appropriate). The selected DigiRack Dynamics III plug-in window will open.

The DigiRack Compressor/Limiter Dynamics III plug-in window (mono shown)

Chapter 10

Finishing Your Work

This chapter covers processes that you can use to create copies of your work in various formats. It describes how to create a session backup, how to mix down tracks for use within or outside of Pro Tools, and how to create an audio CD of your completed mix.

Objectives

After you complete this chapter, you will be able to:

- Understand the purpose of the Save Copy In command and recognize situations in which you should use it
- Create a copy of your session for use on a different Pro Tools system
- Create a mixdown of tracks in your session by bouncing to tracks or bouncing to disk
- Select appropriate options for your bounced files when bouncing to disk
- Create an audio CD of your bounced files to share your results with others

Introduction

After completing any significant recording, editing, or mixing work, it is wise to safeguard your work by creating a backup copy. You might also need to convert your session for subsequent work on another system or bounce your tracks to share your results as a completed mix. The sections in this chapter provide details on the processes you can use to create a finished copy of your work at any milestone point in your project's lifecycle.

Backing Up Your Session

Creating backups of your sessions is critical for archival and disaster recovery purposes. Because Pro Tools sessions are stored electronically, you typically will have no physical media housing your work other than a hard drive. As a result, it is possible to accidentally lose your work by deleting or overwriting files, having a file become corrupt, contracting a virus, or having a drive fail.

To protect yourself against these problems, it is a good idea to create regular session backups. Some of the best protection measures include creating multiple copies of your files, using a separate drive for backup copies, and storing backup copies offsite to protect against disasters such as fire or flood. The more valuable your sessions, the more robust your backup plans should be. At a minimum, you should create a backup session upon completing any work that would be difficult or time-consuming to re-create, especially if the recording has significant value or importance to you or your clients.

Saving a Session Copy

To create a session backup, you can save a copy of your session and all related files using the Save Copy In command. Unlike the Save As command, which creates a copy of the Pro Tools session file only, the Save Copy In command can be used to save all files used in the session, allowing you to create a self-contained duplicate session folder in a separate location, such as on another drive.

The Save Copy In command saves a copy of your current session without closing the original session, meaning that as you continue to work, any subsequent changes are saved in the original and do not affect the copy.

 One key difference between the Save As command and the Save Copy In command is its effect on the open session. After a Save As operation, the open session will be the renamed copy *that you created. By contrast, after a Save Copy In operation, the* original session *will remain open, not the copy.*

When using the Save Copy In command, you have a number of options available that allow you to convert and consolidate session information as you are saving. Some of the more useful applications of the Save Copy In command are as follows:

- It allows you to back up an entire Pro Tools session and all of its associated files without leaving the original session.
- It allows multiple versions of a session to be saved at various stages of a project. Later, these versions can be used as a basis of comparison or to easily revert to an earlier stage of the project.
- It allows sessions to be saved using a different resolution (16-bit or 24-bit), sample rate (up to the maximum rate supported by your system), and/or file format (AIFF or WAV) from the original. This allows complete flexibility and compatibility with other Pro Tools systems.

- It allows all session audio files, fade files, video files, and plug-in settings to be copied into a single folder.
- It allows a current Pro Tools session to be saved as an earlier version so that it can be opened on older Pro Tools systems.

To use this saving option, do the following:

1. Choose FILE > SAVE COPY IN. A special Save dialog box will open, allowing you to specify format options for the session copy.

The Save Session Copy dialog box

2. In the Session Format drop-down menu, choose from among the available format options as needed to maintain compatibility with an earlier Pro Tools version.

Selecting an earlier Pro Tools version

3. In the Session Parameters section of the dialog box, choose a desired audio file type, sample rate, and bit depth. These parameters default to the settings of your current session and can be changed as needed.

 If you choose the Pro Tools 5.1 -> 6.9 Session option in Step 2 and either the AIFF or WAV file format in Step 3, the Enforce PC/Mac Compatibility check box will become available. Enabling this option ensures that the session and its associated files will be compatible with supported Mac and Windows Pro Tools systems.

4. To limit the character set to a single language, select the LIMIT CHARACTER SET option. A pop-up menu will appear, allowing you to select the desired language encoding.

5. In the Items to Copy section of the dialog box, enable additional options as desired:

Optional items that can be copied with the session

- **All Audio Files.** If you are changing the original sample rate or bit depth of the session, this option will be selected automatically; otherwise, you can choose whether to copy all associated audio files for the session using this option.

- **All Non-WAV Audio Files.** If your session contains more than one file type, you can choose to copy only non-native files in the session. For example, if your session file format is set to WAV files, but your session also includes some imported AIFF files, you can choose to copy the AIFF files by checking the box. If All Audio Files is selected, this check box will be selected and grayed out.

- **Don't Copy Fade Files.** Fade files will not be copied if no audio files are copied (the check box will be grayed out); if All Audio Files is selected, fade files can be excluded by selecting this check box.

- **Don't Copy Rendered Elastic Files.** Rendered Elastic Audio files will not be copied if no audio files are copied (the option will be grayed out). If All Audio Files is selected, rendered Elastic Audio files can be excluded by selecting this check box.

- **Session Plug-In Settings Folder.** This option copies the session's Plug-In Settings folder, if present, to the new session location.

- **Root Plug-In Settings Folder.** This option copies the contents of the root-level Plug-In Settings folder to a folder in the new session named Place in Root Settings Folder. These files will need to be moved to the root-level Plug-In Settings folder on the destination system.

 The location options for plug-in settings files are discussed in advanced Pro Tools courses.

- **Movie/Video Files.** This option copies movie or video files (if present in the session) to the new session location.

6. Click SAVE when you are finished selecting all of the options you want. The new session and optional files will be saved into the directory location you selected.

Sharing a Session between Systems

After completing your editing work on a session, you might want to save and convert your session data for use on a different Pro Tools system. The Save Copy In command can be used to ensure the compatibility of your session. See the preceding "Saving a Session Copy" section.

Creating a Stereo Mixdown

Mixing down is the process of recording the output from multiple tracks to a stereo or multi-channel format. This process is also often referred to as *bouncing*, which can be done for the entire mix or to combine selected tracks to free up resources or reduce track count. Mixdown is often the last phase of music production, but in Pro Tools mixdown can be done any time you want to bounce tracks or create a completed mix for use outside of your session.

The most common mixdown technique in Pro Tools is to bounce to a stereo mix. You can record your mix to Audio tracks within your session or create an external recording using the Bounce to Disk command. Once you have created a stereo mix, you can play back the results outside of Pro Tools and share your composition with others by burning the file onto a CD.

 Pro Tools with Complete Production Toolkit 2 and Pro Tools HD also provide multi-channel mixdown and bouncing options for use in surround-sound applications.

Considerations for Bouncing Audio

Most digital audio workstations provide functions for mixing down or bouncing tracks; however, not all systems approach the process the same way. When performing a bounce with Pro Tools, it is important to recognize that the bounce will be performed in real time and will capture all audible information in your mix just as you hear it during playback.

The following principles apply to bouncing in Pro Tools:

- **Pro Tools bounces all audible tracks in real time.** When you play back your session, all tracks that you hear are included in the bounce. Any tracks that are muted will not be included. If you have soloed any tracks or regions, only those soloed elements will be present in the bounce.

- **Pro Tools bounces tracks based on the output path.** All source tracks for the bounce must be assigned to the same output path. Any audio not assigned to that common output path will not be represented in the bounce file.

- **Pro Tools does not require extra voices to bounce to disk.** You can use all available voices in your system when using the Bounce to Disk command, without requiring extra voiced tracks for recording the bounced file.

- **The bounced file will be a "flattened" version of your session.** Inserts, sends, and external effects are applied permanently to the bounced tracks, so make sure that you set levels carefully before bouncing tracks. Listen closely to ensure that everything sounds as it should. Pay close attention to levels, being sure to avoid clipping.

- **Pro Tools bounces tracks based on Timeline selections.** If you have made a selection on the Timeline (or on a track with Timeline and Edit selections linked), Pro Tools will bounce all audible tracks for the length of the selection only. If no selection is present in any track, Pro Tools will bounce the audible tracks in your session from the start of the session or from the playback cursor position to the end of the longest track in the session.

- **Bounced material is automatically time-stamped.** You can drag a bounced file into a track and place it at the same location as the original material using Spot mode.

Bouncing to Tracks

To create a stereo mixdown (or a submix) within Pro Tools, you can record any or all of your session tracks to an available stereo Audio track. This technique lets you add live input to the mix, adjusting volume, pan, mute, and other controls in real time during the mixdown process. Recording to tracks requires that you have an available voiced track for each channel that you will be recording. For a stereo mix using Pro Tools 9, this simply means that you will need a stereo Audio track or two mono Audio tracks available.

 Bouncing tracks in a large session using Pro Tools HD might require that you consider voice allocation. Voicing considerations are covered in advanced courses.

The typical process for creating a stereo mixdown within a session is to combine the audio output of selected tracks using an internal bus and to record the resulting mix onto a separate stereo Audio track.

To create a stereo mixdown using this method, do the following:

1. Create a stereo mix from the source tracks as described in Chapter 9, using appropriate settings for volume, panning, inserts, sends, plug-ins, and automation.

2. Set the output for each track you want to include to the same unused stereo bus. These tracks will be the source playback tracks for the bus bounce.

Outputs set to bus 3–4 (stereo)

3. Create a stereo Audio track and record-enable the track. This track will be the destination track for the bus bounce.

4. Set the inputs for the stereo track to correspond to the stereo output bus you selected in Step 2, and set the output for the track to your main output path (typically analog outputs 1–2).

— Track input, set to the bounce bus
— Track output, set to the main output path

Stereo Audio track set up for an internal bounce

5. Do one of the following:
   - Make a selection (to manually set the start and end times for the bounce).
   - Place the playback cursor at the beginning of the session or at the desired start point.
6. In the Transport window, click the RECORD button followed by the PLAY button to begin recording the bounce.
7. During recording, perform any desired "live" mixing, such as Volume Fader adjustments and panning changes.
8. Allow recording to continue until playback stops automatically (if recording from a selection) or until you reach the desired end point. To stop the recording manually, press the STOP button in the Transport window or press the SPACE BAR.

 After the recording is complete, you should see the waveform for your combined source tracks on the destination tracks. If no waveform is present, check the settings for your source outputs and record inputs and verify that the faders are set to an audible level.

9. Disarm the record-enabled track and rename the recorded region, if desired.

Once you have combined multiple tracks into a single stereo track, you can continue with more recording or editing, using the stereo track in place of any original tracks to free up resources. You can also use the stereo track as part of a Bounce to Disk operation to create a completed audio mix.

Bouncing to Disk

The Bounce to Disk command allows you to mix your entire session directly to a hard drive in the same way a mixdown would occur with a traditional studio setup. This can be useful when you want to work with the mixed recording outside of Pro Tools, such as when you are posting song files to the Internet or burning them to CD. The Bounce to Disk function also provides more robust control than you have when bouncing to tracks, enabling you to set the bit depth, file format, and sample rate for the resulting bounced file.

The Bounce to Disk command combines the outputs of all currently audible tracks routed to a common output or output pair to create a new audio file on a selected hard drive or other supported volume. The newly bounced file can be automatically imported into the session at the completion of the bounce, if desired.

To bounce all currently audible tracks, do the following:

1. Adjust track output levels and finalize an automated mix. Any inserts or effects settings that are active on your tracks will be permanently written to the bounced audio files.

2. Make sure that all of the tracks you want to include in the bounce are audible. If you want to create a sub-mix of tracks, solo only those tracks. Conversely, if you want to mix down all tracks in your session, make sure no tracks are soloed or muted.

3. Assign the output of each track you want to include in your bounce to the same output pair by clicking the AUDIO OUTPUT PATH SELECTOR and choosing the corresponding output from the pop-up menu.

Selecting an output pair

4. Choose FILE > BOUNCE TO > DISK. The Bounce dialog box will appear.

The Bounce dialog box

5. Select the output pair that you used in Step 3 from the BOUNCE SOURCE drop-down list.

6. Choose the desired file type for your bounce file from the FILE TYPE pop-up menu. Available options include the following:

- **WAV.** This is the default file format for Windows- and Mac-based Pro Tools systems and is supported by many other Windows and Mac applications.

- **AIFF.** This file format is primarily used on Mac systems. Use the AIFF format if you plan to import the bounced audio into other Mac applications.

- **MP3.** This file format is used for streaming audio on the Internet, personal computers, and portable devices. Use this file format when you want to play back bounced files using MP3-compatible applications and devices.

- **QuickTime.** This is a file format for multimedia developed by Apple. Use the QuickTime format if you plan to use your audio in multimedia applications that support QuickTime, such as Adobe Premiere, Final Cut Pro, or Macromedia Director.

- **Windows Media (Windows systems only).** Microsoft's Windows Media Audio-9 file format is used for creating high-quality digital media files for streaming and download-and-play applications on PCs, set-top boxes, and portable devices. The WMA-9 file format supports 16- and 24-bit audio files, sample rates up to 96 kHz, multi-channel audio from stereo through 7.1 surround, lossless encoding, and file sizes that are roughly one-half the size of an equivalent MP3 file.

- **MXF.** MXF (*Material Exchange Format*) is a media file format that includes both video and audio files and is designed for the interchange of audio-visual material with associated data and metadata. This option requires Enforce Avid Compatibility to be selected (checked).

7. Choose the MULTIPLE MONO or STEREO INTERLEAVED file format for your stereo bounce from the FORMAT pop-up menu.

Selecting a format for the bounced file

- **Multiple Mono.** This option creates split stereo files from the stereo bus path. Mono files will be created for the left and right channels, with .L and .R suffixes appended to the file names, respectively. Use this file format if you want to import the bounced audio back into a Pro Tools session without conversion. This option is not available for use with MP3 or Windows Media file types.

 The Multiple Mono format can also be used for multi-channel mixes. Multi-channel mixdown is covered in advanced courses.

- **Stereo Interleaved.** Choose this option to create a single interleaved stereo file from the stereo bus path. This file format is directly compatible with most applications that process stereo files for commercial use, including all Apple software applications and Roxio's Toast software application.

 A third option, the Mono (Summed) format, provides a single audio file that is a summed mono mix of the bus path. Choose this option if you need to create a composite mix of mono tracks. All panning information will be disregarded.

8. Choose the desired bit depth for the bounced file(s) from the BIT DEPTH pop-up menu. You can choose 8-, 16-, or 24-bit resolution.

- **8-bit.** Use this option to minimize file size for recordings that do not require rich dynamic resolution. Eight-bit files are often used in multimedia applications.

  If the audio you are working with is relatively simple, such as a voice-over, you can use the Pro Tools Squeezer feature to optimize results when you convert to 8-bit. Squeezer improves dynamics by preprocessing the audio before converting it. However, Squeezer does not work well with all material and should be tested on your audio before you convert an entire session with it.

- **16-bit.** This is the standard resolution for compact discs. Use this option if you plan to burn your bounce to CD without further processing.

- **24-bit.** This setting provides the highest dynamic resolution. Use this option when you want to create a bounce that retains full resolution, such as a final mix that is ready to master.

9. Choose the desired sample rate for the bounce files from the SAMPLE RATE pop-up menu. Higher sampling rates will provide better audio fidelity but will also increase the size of the resulting file(s).

The standard sample rate for compact discs is 44.1 kHz; the standard rate for professional and DVD video is 48 kHz. Selecting a multiple of the standard sample rate for the destination media will simplify the final sample rate conversion (44.1, 88.2, or 176.4 kHz for CD audio; 48, 96, or 192 kHz for DVD audio).

If you plan to burn your bounced audio directly to CD without further processing, choose 44.1 kHz as the sample rate for the bounce.

10. If the sample rate for your bounce differs from your session's sample rate, the Conversion Quality pop-up list will become available. Select the Conversion Quality setting based on the project needs. Higher settings require longer rendering times. The default choice (Good) is adequate for general-purpose bounces.

The Conversion Quality pop-up list

11. Choose from the two conversion options, if applicable.

- **Convert During Bounce.** This option converts file type, sample rate, and bit depth during the bounce process. This option generally takes less time, but it might not maintain plug-in automation accuracy. This option is best for bounces that do not involve plug-in automation.

- **Convert After Bounce.** This option converts file type, sample rate, and bit depth after bouncing is complete. This option is more time-consuming than Convert During Bounce, but it offers the highest level of plug-in automation accuracy possible.

12. To automatically import the newly bounced files into the Region List of your session, select the IMPORT AFTER BOUNCE option.

The Import After Bounce option is available only if the target bit depth and sample rate for the bounce file match the bit depth and sample rate of your session.

13. After confirming your settings, click the BOUNCE button. A Save dialog box will prompt you to name the new audio file and will allow you to navigate to the desired location to store the file.

The Save Bounce As dialog box

14. Select a destination for the new audio file, enter a name, and click SAVE. The audio will play back as Pro Tools processes your bounce, and a countdown window will appear, displaying the time remaining for your bounce to complete.

The Bounce to Disk countdown window

 You will not hear the bounce file play back in real time if you are not monitoring the bounce source.

 If you did not select the Import After Bounce option, you can import the bounced files to your session later using the Import Audio command.

Burning Songs to CD

Both PCs and Macs enable you to create audio CDs from your bounced mix using software included with your computer or software purchased from a third-party developer. You can copy one or more bounced files to create tracks on either compact disc–recordable (CD-R) or compact disc–rewritable (CD-RW) media.

This section provides an overview of the typical processes of burning audio CDs on Windows and Mac operating systems. The exact steps may vary, depending on the operating system and software you use.

 CD-R discs provide a universal format that can be played on most CD players; CD-RW discs can typically be played only by using a CD-ROM drive.

When creating an audio CD using CD-R or CD-RW media, you must copy all tracks at the same time. You cannot add subsequent tracks after you have burned the disc. (CD-RW discs allow you to erase the disc and start over, however.)

Creating a CD Using Windows Media Player

On Windows systems, you can create (burn) an audio CD using Windows Media Player. The Player converts and copies tracks to the compact disc and burns the audio CD according to the Red Book audio format.

To create a CD, you must have a CD recorder (burner) installed or attached to your computer and a blank CD to which you can copy tracks.

Supported File Types

Windows Media Player can use any of the following file types to create an audio CD:

- .wma (Windows Media Audio) files
- .mp3 files
- .wav files

During the CD creation process, Windows Media Player automatically converts the files to .cda format for use on the CD.

Burning a CD

To burn your bounced audio to a CD on a Windows system, do the following:

1. Insert a blank CD-R or CD-RW in your CD-ROM drive. A dialog box will open, prompting you for the action you want to take.

Windows dialog box for blank CDs

2. Choose BURN AN AUDIO CD USING WINDOWS MEDIA PLAYER. Windows Media Player will open.

3. Click on BLANK DISC on the left side of the Windows Media Player window.

4. Open the Windows folder containing your bounced audio files and drag them to the Burn List in Windows Media Player (right side panel).

5. Click the START BURN button at the top of the Burn List. The selected tracks will be converted and burned to the disc, and the CD will eject when finished.

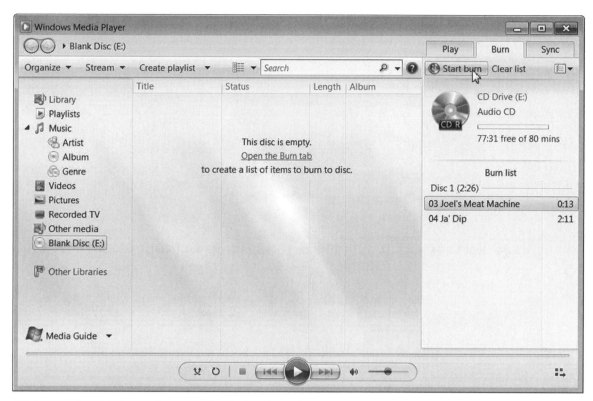

Clicking on the Start Burn button to begin burning a CD

Creating a CD Using iTunes

Apple's iTunes software allows you to create audio CDs on both Windows and Mac computers. To create an audio CD from iTunes, your computer must have the iTunes software and a CD recorder (burner) installed or attached.

 If iTunes is not already installed on your system, you can download a copy from the Apple website at www.apple.com/itunes.

By default, iTunes burns CDs in a universal format that can be used on Windows or Mac computers and in any standard CD player.

To burn an audio CD of your bounced files using iTunes, do the following:

1. Insert a blank CD into the optical drive of your computer. A dialog box will open, prompting you for the action you want to take.

Windows dialog box for blank CDs

2. Select **CREATE A CD USING ITUNES** (Windows) or select **OPEN ITUNES** from the Action drop-down list and click **OK** (Mac). iTunes will launch, and a second dialog box will open, providing directions for burning items on the CD.

Directions for burning a CD from iTunes

3. Review the directions and click **OK**.

4. If your files are not already in iTunes, do one of the following:
   - From within iTunes, choose **FILE > ADD FILE TO LIBRARY**. Navigate to and select the files you wish to import, selecting them one at a time and clicking **OPEN**.
   - From Windows or the Mac Finder, open the folder containing your bounced audio files and drag the files you want to include into iTunes.

5. With the files added to your iTunes Music library, create a new playlist and drag the files from the Music library into the playlist.

6. Name the playlist for easy identification.

7. When you are ready, select the playlist and choose FILE > BURN PLAYLIST TO DISC from the iTunes menus. A Burn Settings dialog box will open.

Burn Settings dialog box

8. In the Burn Settings dialog box, ensure that AUDIO CD is listed for the Disc Format setting. You can also modify the Gap Between Songs setting when burning multiple files to specify the amount of silence to include between tracks.

9. When you are ready, click the BURN button. The files in the playlist will be burned to the disc.

When burning is complete, you can eject the CD to share your recording with friends, band mates, and others.

 The process for burning a CD can vary depending on the version of iTunes you are using. See the iTunes documentation for further details.

PART III

Hands-On Projects

Components

Overview

Part III of this course includes two projects that allow you to work with pre-recorded sessions to experiment with Audio, MIDI, and Video files. Throughout this part, you will apply many of the concepts that you learned in Parts I and II of this book. The goal of the projects is to illustrate the concepts discussed earlier in the book using straightforward, practical workflows. The projects also include examples of more advanced functionality to broaden your understanding of Pro Tools in the music and post-production environments.

Overview

Project Introduction and Setup

The following pages describe the two hands-on projects included in this course and provide setup instructions for the work you will be doing. Included is a description of Pro Tools system requirements and instructions for installing the media files from the DVD for use in the projects.

Getting to Know the Projects

The projects that you will complete are real-world sessions provided in incomplete form. This part of the coursework includes two projects, one from a music production workflow and one from a video post-production workflow. While these projects remain focused on the core set of Pro Tools functions described in the first two parts of the book, you will find that the workflows occasionally introduce concepts that have not been covered. (These concepts are discussed in later courses.)

Project 1

Project 1, the Music Hands-On Project, is a one-minute segment of a song by Ballet Mechanique. The session consists of 10 tracks in rough form. To complete this project, you will add Audio and Instrument tracks, add drums using the Xpand!^{2} and Boom plug-ins, import audio and MIDI, and add loops and effects processing to polish the mix.

Project 2

Project 2, the Post Hands-On Project, is a 45-second commercial spot for Glad Trash Bags consisting of 20 tracks in rough form. To complete this project, you will import video footage as a QuickTime movie, import additional music and sound effects files, make various improvements and enhancements to the audio, replace the music bed, and add effects processing to polish the mix.

Pro Tools System Requirements

To complete these projects, you will need a qualified audio interface and compatible Pro Tools software installed. The projects are designed for Pro Tools 9.0. Many parts of the projects can be completed using earlier Pro Tools versions with slight modifications in various steps; however, to complete the projects as written, you will need current software. Some menu commands, preference options, dialog boxes, and user interface features may vary on older systems.

Installing Project Session Files

Before you begin work on the projects, you will need to install the project files on an available hard drive. The project files are provided on the DVD and include session templates, audio files, MIDI files, and other media files that you will need to complete the projects.

System Requirements for Project Sessions

The projects are designed to be completed using Pro Tools 9 software with a qualified Avid audio interface. Users running Pro Tools 9 software using built-in audio on Mac computers (Core Audio) or third-party audio interfaces that support Core Audio (Mac) or ASIO (Windows) drivers may also be able to complete the projects; however, the projects have not been tested with these configurations. The projects can also be completed using any current Pro Tools|HD or Pro Tools|HD Native system with Pro Tools HD 9.x software.

See Chapter 1 for a description of qualified interfaces or check the Avid website for qualified products (www.avid.com/compatibility).

You will need space available on your destination drive for the session files and related media. If possible, select a hard drive that is separate from your system drive to use as the destination for the session files.

The minimum recommended disk space for completing both projects is 1 GB:

- 250 MB for the Music project session files
- 500 MB for the Post project session files
- 250 MB available for recording and additional processing

To check the available space on your selected drive, do the following:

- In Windows, click on the START icon in the lower left and select COMPUTER to view information about the available drives.
- On a Mac, click on the selected drive icon from the desktop and choose FILE > GET INFO to display the Information window for the drive.

Installation Instructions for Session Files

To install the project session files and related media, copy the materials from the DVD to your selected hard drive:

1. Insert the DVD and open it to view the included files and folders.
2. Open the HANDS-ON PROJECTS folder.
3. Copy the MUSIC HANDS-ON PROJECT and the POST HANDS-ON PROJECT folders from the DVD to your selected hard drive.
4. Close the DVD window when copying is completed.

Project 1

Music Hands-On Project

In this project, you will complete a one-minute song snippet. To complete this project, you will add Audio and Instrument tracks, add drums using the Xpand!^{2} and Boom plug-ins, import audio and MIDI, and add loops and effects processing to polish the mix.

The media files for this project are provided courtesy of Eric Kuehnl of Ballet Mechanique:

> WRITTEN BY: Eric Kuehnl and Zack Vieira
>
> PERFORMED AND PRODUCED BY: Ballet Mechanique ©2008

 The audio files provided for this project are strictly for use to complete the exercises contained herein. No rights are granted to use the files, or any portion thereof, in any commercial or non-commercial production or performance.

Powering Up

To get started on this project, you will need to power up your system. It is important to power up properly to avoid problems that could possibly damage your equipment.

When using audio equipment, you should power up components in the order that the audio signal flows through them. The general process for powering up a Pro Tools 9.0 system is as follows (see your system documentation for powering up a Pro Tools|HD system):

1. Power up external hard drives, if used.
2. Verify connections and power up audio/MIDI interfaces.
3. Start the computer.
4. Power up your monitoring system, if applicable.
5. Launch Pro Tools.

Refer to Chapter 2 for more details on powering up your system.

Opening the Music Project

In this section of the hands-on project, you will open the project and prepare your session for the work you will be doing.

The session you will use for this project was saved in a special format called a *session template*. When you open the session template, Pro Tools will create a new session based on the template, leaving the original template file unchanged. All existing tracks and audio files used in the template file will be duplicated in your new session.

Locate and Open the Session Template

Pro Tools provides a number of ways to open a session or session template. You can navigate to the session folder in your computer's Explorer or Finder window and double-click on the session or template file to open it. You can also locate and open the session or template file from the Workspace browser.

Locate and open the Music session template:

1. From the desktop, navigate to your copy of the session template using an Explorer window (Windows) or a Finder window (Mac). The template file is named *Music Project PT9.ptt*.

   Or

   Locate the session template using the Workspace browser:

   a. Choose WINDOW > WORKSPACE.

   b. Click the FIND icon (magnifying glass) to activate a search.

   c. Type **Music Project PT9** in the Name field.

   d. Select SESSION FILE TEMPLATE from the Kind pop-up menu.

   e. Click the SEARCH button. After a few moments the session template will display in the lower area of the Workspace browser.

2. Double-click on the template file to open it.

3. In the resulting New Session dialog box, select the defaults for the audio file type (.wav), bit depth (24 bit), and sample rate (44.1 kHz) and click **OK**.

New Session dialog box for the Music project

4. Select a save location for the new session, rename the session if desired (for example, add a dash and your initials at the end of the file name), and click **SAVE**.

Save dialog box for the Music project

Refer to Chapter 3 for additional information on locating and opening sessions.

Orient the Session Windows

When the session opens, you will see the Edit window displayed on your screen. You will use this window for much of the arranging and editing you do in this project. You will also use the Mix window, the Transport window, and the Score Editor window. As you work, you may need to reposition and resize the windows to maximize your efficiency.

You can use the following steps to create a basic starting point, or you can position and size the windows as you go.

Set a starting position and size for the windows:

1. If you used the Workspace browser to open the session, bring it to the front and close it. (Choose **WINDOW > WORKSPACE** or press **ALT+;** (Windows) or **OPTION+;** (Mac) to view the Workspace browser; then repeat the action to close the window.)

2. Open both the Mix window (**WINDOW > MIX**) and the Transport window (**WINDOW > TRANSPORT**).

3. Press **CTRL+=** (Windows) or **COMMAND+=** (Mac) to toggle to the Edit window and bring it to the front.

4. Choose **WINDOW > ARRANGE > CASCADE** to arrange the Mix and Edit windows in a cascading fashion. (Alternatively, you can maximize each window as you open them for full-screen views.)

5. Position the Transport window where it will least interfere with your work. Try the top or bottom of the screen.

The 10 tracks in the session are displayed horizontally (left to right) in the Mix window and vertically (top to bottom) in the Edit window. From time to time, you might need to scroll each window and/or reposition the Transport window to view and work with a particular track.

Session windows oriented for the start of the project

Set the Preferences

This project requires certain preference settings. Before continuing, you will need to verify the Zoom Toggle Preference settings for your session. You will also need to ensure that the preference for Timeline Insertion/Play Start Marker Follows Playback is off. Although you can change this setting in the Preferences dialog box, Pro Tools also makes it available via a button in the Edit window.

Some of the Preferences settings on older systems may vary. Users on systems prior to Pro Tools 8.0 should use those settings that are applicable.

Check Preferences settings:

1. Choose SETUP > PREFERENCES. The Preferences dialog box will open.
2. Click on the EDITING tab.
3. In the ZOOM TOGGLE section of the Editing tab, select the following settings:
   - Verify that both VERTICAL MIDI ZOOM and HORIZONTAL ZOOM are set to Selection.
   - Verify that REMOVE RANGE SELECTION AFTER ZOOMING IN is unchecked.
   - Set TRACK HEIGHT to Jumbo.
   - Set TRACK VIEW to Waveform/Notes.
   - Verify that ZOOM TOGGLE FOLLOWS EDIT SELECTION is unchecked.

Preference settings under the Editing tab

4. Click **OK** to close the Preferences dialog box.

Check other settings:

- Verify that the INSERTION FOLLOWS PLAYBACK button is off (unlit) in the Edit window toolbar.

Insertion Follows Playback button in the Edit window

Connect Monitoring Devices

If you have a monitoring system connected to the left and right outputs of your audio interface, you will use that to listen to the session playback. If you do not have a monitoring system, you can listen to the session playback using headphones on a compatible interface. If your interface has an available headphone jack, plug in your headphones and test the playback level.

Creating New Tracks

In this section of the project, you will create the new tracks needed for the session. Additional details on the commands and processes used in this section can be found in Chapter 3.

Create and Name Tracks

You will need to create two new tracks for the session. Both tracks will play back MIDI information using virtual instruments. When creating tracks, you will select the track type and format, based on how each track will be used. In this case, the tracks will be used for stereo virtual instruments, so you will create two stereo Instrument tracks.

Create new Instrument tracks:

1. If needed, activate the Edit window by clicking on it or choosing WINDOW > EDIT.
2. Choose TRACK > NEW. The New Tracks dialog box will open, displaying Mono, Audio Track, and Samples as default selections from left to right.
3. Type the number **2** into the number field. This will create two tracks.
4. Click on the TRACK FORMAT pop-up menu and choose STEREO.
5. Click on the TRACK TYPE pop-up menu and choose INSTRUMENT TRACK.
6. Click CREATE. The new tracks will be added to the session.

Creating the new tracks for your session

Name and reposition your new tracks:

1. Double-click on the nameplate of the first Instrument track (Inst 1) to open the Track Name dialog box.
2. Type **DRUMS** in the Name the Track field.
3. Add comments to help identify the track function, such as "Instrument – Xpand![2]."

Naming the Drums track

4. Click the **NEXT** button. You will see Inst 2 displayed.
5. Type **BOOM** in the Name the Track field and add comments, such as "Instrument – Boom."
6. Click **OK**. The tracks will display with their new names.
7. With both tracks still selected, click on the nameplate of the Drums track and drag the tracks to the top of the Tracks display area in the Edit window (above the Groove-E track).

New tracks positioned at the top of the Edit window

Save Your Session

After making any significant changes to a session, it is a good idea to save. Doing so will minimize any rework that you have to do in the event that something disrupts your progress (such as a power outage).

Save your work:

1. Choose **FILE > SAVE** to save your progress up to this point.

Working with MIDI Data

For this section of the project, you will add the Xpand!^{2} and Boom virtual instrument plug-ins to your Instrument tracks, add a MIDI region from the Region List, and create MIDI data using a variety of Edit tools.

Add a Virtual Instrument

In the previous section, you created an Instrument track and named it Drums. Now, you will add a virtual instrument to this track using the Xpand!^{2} plug-in. This will allow the Instrument track to play back audio based on MIDI data.

Insert Xpand!^{2} onto the Drums track:

1. Choose **WINDOW > MIX** or press **CTRL+=** (Windows) or **COMMAND+=** (Mac) to bring the Mix window forward and make it active.

2. In the Mix window, click on **INSERT SELECTOR A** on the Drums track.

Insert selector A on the Drums track (Mix window)

3. Choose **MULTICHANNEL PLUG-IN > INSTRUMENT > XPAND2 (STEREO)** from the pop-up list. The Xpand!^{2} plug-in window will appear on screen.

4. Click on the **LIBRARIAN MENU** and choose **26 DRUMS > +02 POP KIT**.

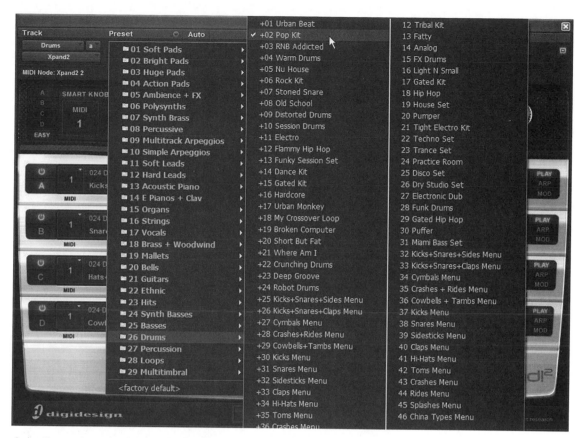

Selecting a drum kit for the Xpand!² plug-in

5. Click on the **CLOSE** button in the upper-right corner (Windows) or upper-left corner (Mac) of the Xpand!² window to close the plug-in window.

Drag in a MIDI Region

The session's Region List includes a MIDI region containing a previously recorded MIDI drum performance for this song. You will now bring it onto the Drums track.

Drag the DrumKit region onto the Drums track:

1. Toggle back to the Edit window by choosing **WINDOW > EDIT** or pressing **CTRL+=** (Windows) or **COMMAND+=** (Mac).

2. With the **GRABBER** tool, select the DrumKit region in the Region List.

3. Drag the DrumKit region from the Region List onto the Drums track. Position the region to start at the beginning of the session (1|1|000).

4. Solo the Drums track by clicking on the track's **SOLO** button (labeled "S") in the Edit window under the track name.

You can also toggle Solo mode on and off for any track containing the Edit cursor by pressing **SHIFT+S** *on the computer's QWERTY keyboard.*

5. Press the SPACE BAR to audition the MIDI drums. Press the SPACE BAR a second time to stop playback.

6. If necessary, adjust the region placement to ensure that it begins at 1|1|000.

7. Unsolo the Drums track.

Add another Virtual Instrument

In the previous section, you added an Xpand!² virtual instrument plug-in to the Drums track. Now, you will add a Boom virtual instrument plug-in to the Boom track.

Insert Boom onto the Boom track:

1. Choose WINDOW > MIX or press CTRL+= (Windows) or COMMAND+= (Mac) to again activate the Mix window.

2. Click on INSERT SELECTOR A on the Boom track.

3. Choose MULTICHANNEL PLUG-IN > INSTRUMENT > BOOM (STEREO) from the pop-up list. The Boom plug-in window will appear on screen.

The Boom instrument plug-in

4. Click on the LIBRARIAN MENU and choose 086-100 > STANDART BEAT 090.

5. Click on the CLOSE button in the upper-right corner (Windows) or upper-left corner (Mac) of the Boom window to close the plug-in window.

Create a MIDI Region

Pro Tools provides a variety of ways to create MIDI data. In this section, you will use the Pencil tool to trigger playback of the Boom virtual instrument.

Draw MIDI data to control pattern playback of Boom:

1. Press **CTRL+=** (Windows) or **COMMAND+=** (Mac) to toggle back to the Edit window.

2. Click on the **TRACK VIEW SELECTOR** of the Boom track and choose **NOTES** from the pop-up menu.

Clicking on the Track View selector and selecting Notes view

3. With the **PENCIL** tool, draw a note beginning at 13|1|000 and extending to 36|1|000. You may need to trim the note to get the perfect length.

 MIDI notes in the range of C3 through D#4 each trigger a different pattern in Boom. Click and hold the note to audition the current pattern; drag the note up or down to select a different pattern.

4. Press the **SPACE BAR** to audition the Boom drum pattern with your session. Press the **SPACE BAR** a second time to stop playback. If needed, adjust the note position to change the pattern and audition again until you're happy with the playback.

Edit MIDI Performance

Next, you need to edit the SynthBass track to help it stand out more. To do this, you will edit the velocities of the MIDI events on SynthBass track. Because this track contains a single region repeated multiple times, you can use a Pro Tools feature called *mirrored MIDI editing* to make the change. Any changes made to the one MIDI region will be reflected in all of the other instances of the region.

View the MIDI velocity stalks on the SynthBass track:

1. Locate the SynthBass track in the Edit window.
2. With the **GRABBER** tool, select the first SynthBass region on the track.
3. Press **E** on your keyboard to activate Zoom Toggle. The selection will expand, filling the available space in the window, and the track will change to Notes view.
4. Click on the **TRACK VIEW SELECTOR** for the SynthBass track and choose **VELOCITY** from the pop-up menu. (Alternatively, you can display the Velocity controller lane for the track by clicking the Show/Hide Lanes button [triangle] at the head of the track.)

Track View selector on the SynthBass track

The Velocity view displays velocity stalks associated with each MIDI note, representing the velocity value for that note. (The longer the stalk, the higher the velocity value.)

Edit the velocities for the first region:

1. Enable Loop Playback mode by choosing **OPTIONS > LOOP PLAYBACK**.
2. Press the **SPACE BAR** to play back the selection and allow it to continue playing throughout this section.
3. Click the **MIRRORED MIDI EDITING** button at the top of the Edit window to enable mirrored MIDI editing. The button will turn blue when active.

Click the Mirrored MIDI Editing button to enable it.

4. With the **GRABBER** tool, click any open area of the track to deselect all of the notes in the region.
5. With the **GRABBER** tool still active, click on the diamond at the top of the second velocity stalk so that it becomes selected. The diamond will turn white, and the corresponding note will become highlighted.
6. Press and hold the **SHIFT** key while clicking on alternating velocity stalks so that every other velocity stalk is selected.

7. With alternating stalks selected, click any selected velocity stalk and drag it upward. This will increase the velocity of all highlighted notes, allowing the synth bass to cut through the mix.

Raising velocity stalks of selected notes

8. When you are satisfied with the result, stop playback.
9. Press **E** on your keyboard to return the session to its previous view and click the MIRRORED MIDI EDITING button a second time to disable mirrored MIDI editing.

Notice that the velocity changes that you made are reflected in subsequent occurrences of the SynthBass region.

Save Work in Progress

You have now completed your work with MIDI data. You should take this opportunity to save your work in progress.

Save your work:

1. Choose FILE > SAVE to save your progress up to this point.

Working with Audio Data

In the next section of the project, you will use a variety of techniques to manipulate audio regions.

Import an Audio File to a Track

As you've already seen, the Workspace browser is a great resource for locating, opening, and importing all sorts of media files. For this part of the project, you will use the Workspace browser to import an audio file containing an electronic loop for the song.

Locate the Groove-E audio file with the Workspace browser:

1. Choose WINDOW > WORKSPACE to open the Workspace browser.

 You can also press ALT+; (Windows) or OPTION+; (Mac) to toggle the Workspace browser open and closed.

2. Click the FIND button (magnifying glass), if it's not already active, to reveal the search fields or click RESET to clear the previous search.

3. Type **Groove-E** in the Name field.

4. Select AUDIO FILE from the Kind pop-up menu.

Selecting the file type from the Kind pop-up menu

5. Click SEARCH. After a moment, the Groove-E file will appear in the lower pane of the Workspace browser.

Drag the audio file to the Groove-E Audio track:

1. Reposition the Workspace browser, if necessary, so you can see both the Groove-E track in the Edit window and the Groove-E audio file in the Workspace browser.

2. Drag the GROOVE-E audio file from the Workspace browser onto the Groove-E track in the Edit window.

3. Use the GRABBER tool to drag the Groove-E file to start at 13|1|000.

 Use the Bars|Beats Ruler as a reference while positioning the Groove-E file.

4. Close the Workspace browser to reduce on-screen clutter.

Use Region Looping

Now that you've imported the audio file, it's time to clean it up and loop it.

Clean up the audio file using the Trim tool:

1. Solo the Groove-E track.

2. With the TRIMMER tool, trim the end of the region to 17|1|000. This will make the region exactly four bars long.

3. With the GRABBER tool, select the region.

4. With Loop Playback enabled, press the SPACE BAR to audition the region and ensure that it loops smoothly.

5. Press the SPACE BAR again to stop playback and take the track out of Solo mode.

Loop the region:

1. With the Groove-E region still selected, choose **REGION > LOOP**. The Region Looping dialog box will appear on screen.

2. Select the **LOOP LENGTH** option and type **24|0|000** in the corresponding field to extend the loop to 24 bars.

The Region Looping dialog box

3. Click **OK**.

The region will now display a looped arrow at the bottom, indicating that it is a looped region. It has been extended out to 24 bars in length.

Import a Region Group to a Track

For this part of the project, we'll return to the Workspace browser to import a region group. A region group can be thought of as simply a collection of individual regions grouped together to look and act as a single, larger region.

Locate the SynthPads region group with the Workspace browser:

1. Choose **WINDOW > WORKSPACE** to open the Workspace browser.

2. Click the **FIND** button (magnifying glass) if it's not already active or click **RESET** to clear the previous search.

3. Type **SynthPads** in the Name field.

4. Select **REGION GROUP FILE** from the Kind pop-up menu.

5. Click **SEARCH**. After a moment, the SynthPads region group file will appear in the lower pane of the Workspace browser.

Drag the region group to the Pad 1 and Pad 2 Audio tracks:

1. Reposition the Workspace browser, if necessary, so you can see both the Pad 1 and Pad 2 tracks in the Edit window and the SynthPads region group in the Workspace browser.

2. Drag the SynthPads file from the Workspace browser onto the Pad tracks in the Edit window.

3. Use the **GRABBER** tool to drag the SynthPads file to the session start.

If the Missing Files dialog box appears, select the check box for **REGENERATE MISSING FADES WITHOUT SEARCHING** *and click* **OK**.

4. Close the Workspace browser to reduce on-screen clutter.

Insert Time

For this part of the project, we're going to add a four-bar intro to the song.

Select the location to insert time at the beginning of the song:

1. Press **ENTER** (Windows) or **RETURN** (Mac) to set the Edit Selection Start to 1|1|000.

2. In the Edit Selection Length field at the top of the Edit window, enter **4|0|000**:
   - Click in the first field to activate it and type **4**. The remaining fields will zero out.
   - Press **ENTER** (Windows) or **RETURN** (Mac) to confirm the entry.

Entering the Edit Selection Length values

You now have a four-bar selection spanning from bar 1 to bar 5.

Use the Insert Time operation to add the selected amount of time:

1. Choose **EVENT > TIME OPERATIONS > INSERT TIME**. The Time Operations window will appear on screen.

2. Verify that the Start, End, and Length times are correct. The values should be the following:
   - **START:** 1|1|000
   - **END:** 5|1|000
   - **LENGTH:** 4|0|000

The Time Operations window

3. Click **APPLY**. Four bars will be inserted into the session.

4. Close the Time Operations window.

Edit the SynthLead track:

1. If necessary, scroll the Edit window so that the SynthLead track is visible on screen.

2. Click the **SPOT** button in the upper-left corner of the Edit window to activate Spot mode.

3. While holding down **ALT** (Windows) or **OPTION** (Mac), use the **GRABBER** tool to click in the BigRiff_02 region at the end of the track. The Spot Dialog box will open.

4. Set the Time Scale to BARS:BEATS.

5. In the Start field, type **1|1|000** and click **OK**. A copy of the region will move to the beginning of the session.

The Spot dialog box

6. Click the GRID button to reactivate Grid mode.

Listen to the edit:

1. Press ENTER (Windows) or RETURN (Mac) to go to the beginning of the session.
2. Press the SPACE BAR to begin playback.

You should now hear a four-bar intro featuring only the SynthLead track.

Save Work in Progress

You have now imported the additional audio files and completed the editing tasks needed for the session. You should take this opportunity to save your work.

Save your work:

1. Choose FILE > SAVE to save your progress up to this point.

Mixing in Pro Tools

Now that the editing is complete, you will use some of the mixing features in Pro Tools to add real-time processing to the project and blend the sound elements together. You will complete this work using the Mix window.

Add EQ

The bass guitar track has a little too much low end, making it difficult to blend with the drums and synth bass. To fix the problem, you will use the DigiRack EQ III plug-in to roll off some of the low end.

Insert the 1-Band EQ III plug-in on the E-Bass track:

1. Choose **WINDOW > MIX** or press **CTRL+=** (Windows) or **COMMAND+=** (Mac) to activate the Mix window.

2. Click on **INSERT SELECTOR B** of the E-Bass track and choose **PLUG-IN > EQ > EQ 3 1-BAND (MONO)** from the pop-up menu. The 1-Band EQ III plug-in window will appear.

3. In the 1-Band EQ III plug-in window, select the **HIGH-PASS** filter type.

Using the High-Pass filter in the EQ III plug-in window

Adjust the EQ to roll off the low end:

1. Solo the E-Bass track by clicking on the **SOLO (S)** button just above the Volume Fader in the Mix window.

2. Open the Memory Locations window (**WINDOW > MEMORY LOCATIONS**) and click on **VERSE 1** to place the insertion point at the beginning of the first verse.

 If needed, you can resize the Memory Locations window by clicking on any window border and dragging with the double-headed arrow.

3. Press the **SPACE BAR** to initiate playback.

4. In the 1-Band EQ III plug-in window, drag the gray ball to the left or right until you hear the desired reduction in low frequencies when playing back (try around 80 to 120 Hz).

5. Unsolo the E-Bass track and press the **SPACE BAR** to stop playback.

6. Close the EQ III plug-in window to reduce on-screen clutter.

Enhance the Guitar

In this part of the project, you will use the Eleven Free plug-in to add guitar amp and speaker cabinet emulation to the Guitar track.

Insert the Eleven Free plug-in on the Guitar track:

1. Click on **INSERT SELECTOR A** of the Guitar track and choose **PLUG-IN > HARMONIC > ELEVEN FREE (MONO)** from the pop-up menu. The Eleven Free plug-in window will appear.

2. In the Eleven Free plug-in window, select the **DC MODERN OVERDRIVE** amp and the **4x12 GREEN 25W** cabinet by clicking on the **AMP TYPE** and **CABINET TYPE** display screens, respectively, and selecting models for each from the pop-up menus.

Selecting an amp type in the Eleven Free plug-in

Adjust the Eleven Free settings:

1. Solo the Guitar track by clicking on the **SOLO (S)** button just above the Volume Fader in the Mix window.

2. Click on **INTRO** in the Memory Locations window to place the insertion point at the beginning of the intro.

3. Press the **SPACE BAR** to initiate playback.

4. In the Eleven Free plug-in window, adjust the **GAIN** setting to achieve a rich, distorted lead sound (try around 10).

5. Adjust the other Eleven Free settings to taste.

6. Unsolo the Guitar track and press the **SPACE BAR** to stop playback.

7. Close the Eleven Free plug-in window and the Memory Locations window to reduce on-screen clutter.

Add Reverb

Next, you will add some reverb to the Guitar track to help it fit into the rest of the mix. This project already includes an Auxiliary track that was previously set up with its input assigned to Bus 1 (Verb) and a D-Verb plug-in configured. Additionally, Send A on the Guitar track has been assigned to Bus 1 (Verb). Therefore, all you will need to do is increase the level of the send on the Guitar track to add reverb to the mix.

Increase the Send A level on the Guitar track:

1. Click on **SEND ASSIGNMENT A** on the Guitar track. The Send A window will appear.

2. Click the **SOLO (S)** button in the Send A window to solo the Guitar track.

The Send A window

3. Press the **SPACE BAR** to begin playback.

4. While listening to the track, raise the level on the Send Fader to introduce reverb. (Try between –10 and –6 dB.)

    The reverb will play back while the Guitar track is soloed because the Reverb track is set to Solo Safe mode. Solo Safe mode is commonly used on Auxiliary tracks to prevent them from being muted when another track is soloed.

 *You can place a track in Solo Safe mode by **CTRL-CLICKING** (Windows) or **COMMAND-CLICKING** (Mac) on the Solo button in the Edit or Mix window.*

 More information on Solo Safe mode can be found in the Pro Tools 110 course.

5. When you are satisfied with the results, press the **SPACE BAR** to stop playback.

6. Press the **SOLO (S)** button to take the track out of Solo mode and then close the Send A window.

Save Work in Progress

Before continuing with work on your session mix, you should take this opportunity to save your work.

Save your work:

1. Choose **FILE > SAVE** to save your progress up to this point.

Mix the Project

The project is now ready for mixing to blend all of the tracks together. You will use the Volume Faders and Pan Sliders to create a stereo mix.

Getting Started

To get started, you will determine the contribution of each track to the overall mix by soloing each track individually. Tracks such as the Verb track only process audio that passes through them and cannot be isolated by soloing. Such tracks can be muted and unmuted to identify their contribution to the mix.

Balance the main tracks:

1. Click the RETURN TO ZERO button in the Transport window to place the insertion point at the beginning of the Timeline.

Transport window

2. Press the SPACE BAR to begin playback.
3. Solo each Audio and Instrument track for a few moments by clicking the Solo button above the Volume Fader in the Mix window.

   a. Consider how the track contributes to the overall mix and make adjustments as needed using the Volume Fader.

   b. When you are satisfied with the results, take the track out of Solo mode and move on to the next track.

4. Use the PAN knobs on the mono tracks to give some stereo separation to your mix. Offset panning to the left or right, using your discretion, to help distinguish each track in the mix.
5. When you are finished, press the SPACE BAR again to stop playback.

Adjust the effects tracks:

1. Press the SPACE BAR to begin playback.
2. Toggle MUTE on and off for the Verb track to determine the track's contribution to the mix.
3. Make adjustments to the effects track levels as desired.
4. When you are finished, press the SPACE BAR again to stop playback.

Completing the Mix

Complete this portion of the project using your discretion, experimenting until you are happy with the results.

Save Work in Progress

You have now created a complete mix for your project. You should take this opportunity to save your work.

Save your work:

1. Choose FILE > SAVE to save your progress up to this point.

Finishing Your Work

For this part of the project, you will use the Score Editor to print a score for the SynthBass track. You will then create a stereo bounce of your session mix. Lastly, you will archive your work. This process will allow you to create a backup of your work without consuming excess disk space with unnecessary files.

Print the Score

It is often useful to create a score of a finished session. This might be used as a reference for live performance of the song. It could also be sent for copyright submission or to a publisher for licensing.

Open the Score Editor and modify the score setup:

1. Press ENTER (Windows) or RETURN (Mac) to ensure that the insertion point is located at the beginning of the Timeline.
2. Choose WINDOW > SCORE EDITOR to open the Score Editor window.

Score Editor window

3. Right-click in the Score Editor and select SCORE SETUP or choose FILE > SCORE SETUP to open the Score Setup window.

4. In the Score Setup window, enter a title for the composition in the Title field and enter your name in the Composer field.

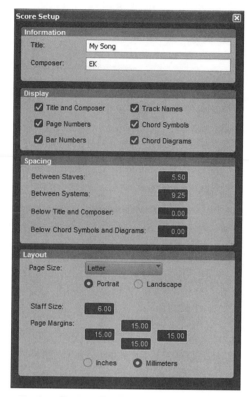

Score Setup window

5. Close the Score Setup window.

Determine which tracks will be included in the score:

1. If it is not already visible, display the Track List by clicking the Show/Hide Track List button at the bottom left of the Score Editor.

2. Show or hide tracks as desired by clicking on the TRACK SHOW/HIDE icon to the left of each track name in the Track List. The icon will turn light gray to indicate a hidden track.

   For this project, hide the Drums and Boom tracks, so that only the SynthBass track is shown in the Score Editor.

Track List after hiding the Drums and Boom tracks

Configure the staff and print the score:

1. Right-click in the Score Editor and select NOTATION DISPLAY TRACK SETTINGS from the pop-up menu or double-click on a CLEF symbol on the SynthBass track. The Notation Display Track Settings dialog box will open.

2. With the track set to SynthBass, click on the CLEF pop-up menu and change it from Grand Staff to Bass Clef.

Setting the clef for the SynthBass track

3. Close the dialog box.

4. Right-click in the Score Editor again and choose PRINT SCORE or choose FILE > PRINT SCORE. The Print dialog box will open.

5. Configure the Print dialog settings as desired and click PRINT to print the score.

6. When you are finished, close the Score Editor window.

Add Maxim

Next, you will add a Maxim plug-in to the master fader. Maxim is a type of plug-in commonly referred to as an *ultra-maximizer*. The purpose of this type of plug-in is to maximize the overall level of the mix, while simultaneously limiting peaks to prevent clipping. The end result is a mix that sounds louder while preserving the overall quality of the mix.

 Maxim performs "look-ahead" analysis, anticipating peaks in audio material and preserving attack transients during reduction. This makes Maxim more transparent and maintains the character of the original audio signal without clipping or distortion.

Insert the Maxim plug-in on the master fader:

1. In the Mix window, click on INSERT SELECTOR A of the Master 1 track and choose MULTICHANNEL PLUG-IN > DYNAMICS > MAXIM (STEREO). The Maxim plug-in window will appear.

2. In the Maxim plug-in window, be sure that DITHER is disabled (unlit). (You will insert a separate dither plug-in later.)

The Maxim plug-in window

Adjust the Maxim settings to make the mix louder:

1. Open the Memory Locations window (WINDOW > MEMORY LOCATIONS) and click on CHORUS 1 to place the insertion point at the beginning of the chorus.

2. Press the SPACE BAR to initiate playback.

3. In the Maxim plug-in window, set the CEILING slider to –0.1 dB. (The parameter value is displayed at the bottom of the slider.) This sets the maximum allowable level for the limiting function of Maxim.

4. While listening to the mix, adjust the THRESHOLD slider to achieve the desired volume. Adjusting the slider down actually increases the volume. A good starting point is around –3.0 dB.

5. When you're happy with the overall level of the mix, press the SPACE BAR to stop playback.

6. Close the Maxim window and the Memory Locations window to reduce on-screen clutter.

Add Dither

Next, you will make an external bounce of the finished project. The purpose of the bounce is to produce a CD-quality stereo audio file that you can burn to an audio CD. For this, you will need to create a 16-bit audio file from your 24-bit session. To do so, you will need to add dither to the master fader. Dithering helps preserve the quality of audio during bit reduction, preventing quantization errors and LSB clipping.

 As a rule of thumb, you should always add dither when bouncing to a lower bit depth.

Add dither to the master fader:

1. In the Mix window, click on **INSERT SELECTOR B** of the Master 1 track and choose **MULTICHANNEL PLUG-IN > DITHER > POWR DITHER (STEREO)**. The POWr Dither plug-in window will appear on screen.

2. Choose the following settings in the POWr Dither plug-in window:

   - 16 bit
   - Noise Shaping Type 3

The POWr Dither plug-in

3. Close the POWr Dither plug-in window.

Dither will now be added to your mix during playback.

Bounce the Song

For this part of the project, you will use the Bounce to Disk command to make a stereo file from your session.

Make a 16-bit stereo bounce of your session:

1. Choose **WINDOW > EDIT** or press **CTRL+=** (Windows) or **COMMAND+=** (Mac) to activate the Edit window.

2. With the **SELECTOR** tool, click anywhere in the session.

3. Press **ENTER** (Windows) or **RETURN** (Mac) to place the insertion point at the start of the session.

4. Press **CTRL+SHIFT+ENTER** (Windows) or **OPTION+SHIFT+RETURN** (Mac) to make a selection extending to the end of the session.

5. Choose **FILE > BOUNCE TO > DISK**. The Bounce dialog box will appear on screen.

6. Select the following settings in the Bounce dialog box:

   - **FILE TYPE:** WAV
   - **FORMAT:** Stereo Interleaved
   - **BIT DEPTH:** 16 bit
   - **SAMPLE RATE:** 44.1 kHz
   - **CONVERT AFTER BOUNCE:** Selected

7. Click **BOUNCE**. The Save Bounce As dialog box will appear on screen.

8. Select a location for the audio file and enter a name for the bounce.

9. Click **SAVE**. You will hear playback begin as Pro Tools creates a 16-bit stereo mix of your session.

Settings for the Bounce dialog box

Archive Your Work

Now that your project is complete, you will need to back it up for storage. On a real-world project, you might also need to deliver the session to the client. Because many files are associated with a session, something could get lost if the archival process isn't completed properly. Fortunately, Pro Tools can help ensure that you keep the files you need and remove the files you do not.

 The archival process will permanently remove any audio that is not currently being used in the session. This could limit your creative possibilities, should you need to revise some aspect of the session in the future. Perform this process only after *the project is complete.*

Remove Unused Material

To save disk space, you will first remove any audio files and regions that are no longer being used by the session. To remove unused audio files and regions, complete the following steps:

1. Click on the **REGION LIST POP-UP** menu and choose **SELECT > UNUSED**. All of the regions that are not included on a Track Playlist will be selected.

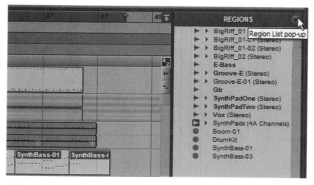

Click the Region List pop-up menu to select unused regions.

2. Click on the REGION LIST POP-UP menu a second time and choose CLEAR. The Clear Regions dialog box will appear on screen.

3. Click REMOVE in the Clear Regions dialog box to remove the regions from your session. The audio files will be removed from the session without being deleted from the drive. If you later find that you need an audio file that has been removed, you can re-import it into your session.

Collect Session Files in a New Location

To save a copy of your session and all associated files, do the following:

1. Choose FILE > SAVE COPY IN. The Save Session Copy dialog box will appear on screen.

2. In the ITEMS TO COPY area, place a check next to ALL AUDIO FILES.

3. Click the OK button. A Save dialog box will appear.

4. Choose a directory to store the session copy and name the copy of the session. For backup and archive purposes, it is best to save to a drive other than the one used for the current session.

5. Click the SAVE button. Pro Tools will begin processing the save, copying the session file along with all of the audio files into the directory you chose.

6. Choose FILE > CLOSE SESSION to close the original session. If you are prompted to save, choose OK or SAVE to save your changes in the original session. (It will be saved with the unused material removed.)

Compact Your Session

You have one more step to complete your archive: compacting. Most regions in a session reference only a part of a larger audio recording. Because the copied session is now complete, it is safe to compact the session. Compacting is the process of removing the audio from a file that is not used by any region. Hence, only the used portions of the audio files remain, reducing the amount of disk space being consumed.

To compact your project's audio files, do the following:

1. From the File menu, choose OPEN SESSION.

2. Navigate to the copy of your project that you created in the previous section; select the session file and click OPEN. A dialog box may appear, indicating that the original disk allocation cannot be used; click NO to avoid saving a report.

3. When the session opens, click on the REGION LIST POP-UP menu and choose SELECT > ALL. All of the regions in the Region List will be selected.

4. Click on the REGION LIST POP-UP menu a second time and choose COMPACT. The Compact dialog box will appear on screen with a description of the compacting process.

5. Click COMPACT to compact the audio files. Pro Tools will begin modifying the files.

6. When you are finished, save your work by choosing FILE > SAVE and close your session by choosing FILE > CLOSE SESSION.

This concludes the Music Hands-On Project.

Project 2

Post Hands-On Project

In this project, you will work with a 45-second commercial spot consisting of 20 tracks in rough form. To complete the project, you will import video footage as a QuickTime movie, import additional music and sound effects files, make various improvements and enhancements to the audio, and add effects processing to polish the mix.

The media files for this project are provided courtesy of Robert Campbell at One Union Recording:

- **CHIEF CREATIVE OFFICER:** Lisa Bennett
- **DIRECTOR OF PRODUCTION:** Frank Brooks
- **CREATIVE DIRECTOR:** Mike Andrews
- **COPYWRITER:** Brett Landry
- **ART DIRECTOR:** Dave Cuccinello
- **PRODUCER:** Bryan Holt
- **CLIENT:** Glad Trash Bags

 The audio and video files provided for this project are to be used only to complete the exercises contained herein. No rights are granted to use the files, or any portion thereof, in any commercial or non-commercial production or video.

Powering Up

To get started on this project, you will need to power up your system. It is important to power up properly to avoid problems that could possibly damage your equipment.

When using audio equipment, you should power up components in the order that the audio signal flows through them. The general process for powering up a Pro Tools system is as follows (see your system documentation for powering up a Pro Tools|HD system):

1. Power up external hard drives, if used.
2. Verify connections and power up audio/MIDI interfaces.
3. Start the computer.
4. Power up your monitoring system, if applicable.
5. Launch Pro Tools.

Refer to Chapter 2 for more details on powering up your system.

Opening the Post Project

In this section of the hands-on project, you will open the Post project and prepare your session for the work you will be doing.

The session you will use for this project was saved in a special format called a *session template*. When you open the session template, Pro Tools will create a new session based on the template, leaving the original template file unchanged. All existing tracks and audio files used in the template file will be duplicated in your new session.

Locate and Open the Session

Pro Tools provides a number of ways to open a session or session template. You can navigate to the session folder in your Explorer or Finder window and double-click on the session or template file to open it. You can also locate and open the session or template file from the Workspace browser.

Locate and open the Post session template:

1. From the desktop, navigate to your copy of the session using an Explorer window (Windows) or a Finder window (Mac).

   Or

   Locate the session using the Workspace browser:

   a. Choose WINDOW > WORKSPACE.

   b. Click the FIND icon (magnifying glass) to activate a search.

   c. Type **Post Project PT9** in the Name field.

   d. Select SESSION FILE TEMPLATE from the Kind pop-up menu.

   e. Click the SEARCH button. After a few moments the session will display in the lower (green and white) area of the Workspace browser.

2. Double-click on the template file to open it.

3. In the resulting New Session dialog box, accept the default settings for file type (.wav), bit depth (24 bits), and sample rate (48 kHz) and click **OK**.

New Session dialog box for the Post project

4. Select a save location for the new session, rename the session if desired (for example, add a dash and your initials at the end of the file name), and click **SAVE**.

Refer to Chapter 3 for additional information on locating and opening sessions.

Orient the Session Windows

When the session opens, you will see the Edit window displayed on your screen. You will use the Edit window for much of the recording and editing you do in this project. You will also be using the Mix window throughout the project. As you work, you will want to reposition and resize the windows to maximize your efficiency.

You can use the following steps at this point to create a basic starting point, or you can position and size the windows as you go.

Set a starting position and size for the windows:

1. Choose **WINDOW > MIX** to open the Mix window.

2. Press **CTRL+=** (Windows) or **COMMAND+=** (Mac) to toggle to the Edit window and bring it to the front.

3. Choose **WINDOW > ARRANGE > CASCADE** to arrange the Mix and Edit windows in a cascading fashion. (Alternatively, you can maximize each window for full-screen views.)

The 20 tracks in the session are displayed horizontally (left to right) in the Mix window and vertically (top to bottom) in the Edit window. From time to time, you might need to scroll each window and/or reposition the open windows to view and work with a particular track.

Session windows oriented for the start of the project

Set the Preferences

For this project, you will need to configure certain preference settings that affect the placement of the insertion point/selection during operation. Before continuing, make sure the following preferences are set accordingly.

 Some of the Preferences settings on older systems may vary. Users on systems prior to Pro Tools 8.0 should use those settings that are applicable.

Check preferences settings:

1. Choose SETUP > PREFERENCES. The Preferences window will open.

2. Click on the OPERATION tab.
   - Verify that TIMELINE INSERTION/PLAY START MARKER FOLLOWS PLAYBACK is unchecked.
   - Verify that EDIT INSERTION FOLLOWS SCRUB/SHUTTLE is checked.

3. Click on the EDITING tab.
   - Verify that EDIT SELECTION FOLLOWS REGION LIST SELECTION is checked.

4. In the Zoom Toggle section of the Editing tab, select the following settings:
   - Set both VERTICAL MIDI ZOOM and HORIZONTAL ZOOM to Selection.
   - Verify that REMOVE RANGE SELECTION AFTER ZOOMING IN is unchecked.
   - Set TRACK HEIGHT to Jumbo.
   - Set TRACK VIEW to Waveform / Notes.
   - Verify that ZOOM TOGGLE FOLLOWS EDIT SELECTION is unchecked.
5. Click OK to close the Preferences window.

Preference settings under the Operation tab

Preference settings under the Editing tab

Connect Monitoring Devices

If you have a monitoring system connected to the left and right outputs of your audio interface, you will use that to listen to the session playback. If you do not have a monitoring system, you can listen to the session playback using headphones on compatible audio interfaces. If your interface has an available headphone jack, plug in your headphones and test the playback level.

Creating New Tracks

In this section of the project, you will create a new track needed for the session. Additional details on the commands and processes used in this section can be found in Chapter 3.

Create and Name a Track

For this project, you will need to create one new track that you will use to edit a sound effect. When creating tracks, you should always select the track type and format based on how the tracks will be used. In this case, you will need to edit a stereo sound effect, so a stereo Audio track will be appropriate.

Create a stereo Audio track:

1. Click on the **FX 07** track nameplate toward the bottom of the Edit window to select the track. This will ensure that your new track will appear directly below FX 07, keeping all of the FX tracks together.

 Pro Tools always places new tracks below the lowest selected track in the session. If no tracks are selected, Pro Tools places the new track(s) at the bottom of the session.

2. Choose **TRACK > NEW**. The New Tracks dialog box will open, displaying Mono, Audio Track, and Samples as default selections from left to right.

3. Click on the **TRACK FORMAT** selector and choose **STEREO** from the pop-up menu.

Click the Track Format selector to create a stereo track.

4. Click **CREATE** in the New Tracks dialog box. A new stereo track will be added to the session, beneath the FX 07 track.

5. Double-click on the track name (**AUDIO 1**) to open the Track Name dialog box.

6. Type **FX 08** in the Track Name field and add comments to help identify the track function, such as "Skunk FX."

7. Click **OK**. The track will display with its new name.

Renaming the Audio track

Save Your Session

After making any significant changes to a session, it is a good idea to save your work. That way, if something should disrupt your progress (such as a power outage), you will not have to redo any of your work.

Save your work:

1. Choose FILE > SAVE to save your progress up to this point.

For more information on Save options, see Chapters 3 and 10.

Importing Media

Pro Tools provides many ways to import media into your session. (Refer to Chapter 5 for detailed information regarding importing media.) For this project, you will import a movie and background music using the Import command, and you will import sound effects using the Workspace browser.

Import a Movie

In this section, you will import a QuickTime movie and enhance it with music and sound effects.

Import GiftBasket.mov into your session:

1. Choose FILE > IMPORT > VIDEO. A dialog box will open on screen, prompting you to choose a video file.

2. Navigate to the VIDEO FILES folder (found within the Post Hands-On Project folder that you copied earlier).

Dialog box for importing a video file

3. Select GIFTBASKET.MOV and click OPEN. The Video Import Options dialog box will appear.

4. Uncheck the IMPORT AUDIO FROM FILE option in the dialog box, if it is selected.

5. Select SESSION START in the Location menu and click OK. The movie will be imported into your session and will open in a Video window. A Video track will also display at the top of the Edit window.

The Video window as displayed after importing GiftBasket.mov

 If you find that the Video window consumes too much space on screen, you can resize it. Click and drag near any edge to resize the window.

View the clip (optional):

1. Press ENTER (Windows) or RETURN (Mac) to move the insertion point to the beginning of the Timeline.

2. Press the SPACE BAR to begin playback. The movie clip will play back in time with the audio in the session.

3. When the clip ends, press the SPACE BAR again to stop playback. The insertion point will return to the beginning of the Timeline.

The Video window during playback

Import Files to the Region List

Next, you will need to import some additional music files into your session and place them in the Region List for later use.

Import music audio files to the Region List:

1. Choose **FILE > IMPORT > AUDIO**.

2. In the Import Audio dialog box, navigate to the **NEW MUSIC** folder (found within the Post Hands-On Project folder that you copied earlier).

3. Select the four **NEW MUSIC** files (click on the first, then Shift-click on the last to select them all) and click the **ADD FILES** button (**ADD** button on Mac). The files will be added to the Regions to Import area of the dialog box.

The Import Audio dialog box as it appears after clicking Add Files

4. Click **DONE**. The Audio Import Options dialog box will appear.

5. In the dialog box, select **REGION LIST** for the destination and click **OK**. The regions New Music 1 (Stereo) and New Music 2 (Stereo) will be imported and will display in your Region List.

Upon import, Pro Tools intelligently links the left and right files of each split stereo file together, displaying them as two stereo regions rather than as four individual files. You can reveal the original files by clicking on the disclosure triangles to the left of the region names in the Region List.

Import Files from the Workspace Browser

For this part of the project, you will use the Workspace browser to import a region group containing sound effects. A region group is simply a collection of individual regions grouped together to look and act as a single, larger region.

 Region groups are covered in greater detail in the Pro Tools 110 course.

All of the sound effects have already been edited outside of the current session and grouped together as a single region group. You will need to drag the region group from the Workspace browser onto a stereo Audio track; the region group will automatically be imported into your session.

Locate the region group file called "Skunk Group" with the Workspace browser:

1. Choose **WINDOW > WORKSPACE** to open the Workspace browser. Reposition/resize the windows as necessary so that the Workspace browser is not obscured by the Video window.

 *You can also press **ALT+;** (Windows) or **OPTION+;** (Mac) to toggle the Workspace browser open and closed.*

2. Click the **FIND** button (magnifying glass), if it is not already active, to reveal the search fields or click **RESET** to clear the previous search.

3. Type **Skunk Group** in the **NAME** field.

4. Select **REGION GROUP FILE** from the Kind pop-up menu. Make sure that a check appears next to the disk volume that contains the Post Hands-On Project folder.

5. Click **SEARCH**. After a moment, the Skunk Group file will appear in the lower pane of the Workspace browser.

Drag the region group to the FX 08 stereo Audio track:

1. Reposition the Workspace browser, if necessary, so you can see both the FX 08 track in the Edit window and the Skunk Group file in the Workspace browser.

2. Drag the **SKUNK GROUP** file onto the FX 08 track in the Edit window.

3. If necessary, use the **GRABBER** tool to drag the Skunk Group to the start of the session.

4. Close the Workspace browser to minimize on-screen clutter.

Audition the changes (optional):

1. If necessary, press ENTER (Windows) or RETURN (Mac) to move the insertion point to the beginning of the Timeline.
2. Press the SPACE BAR to begin playback. The movie clip will play back with the existing audio and newly added effects.
3. When the clip ends, press the SPACE BAR again to stop playback. The insertion point will return to the beginning of the Timeline.

Save Work in Progress

Now that you have imported the movie and audio files for the project, you should take the opportunity to save your work.

Save your work:

1. Choose FILE > SAVE to save your progress up to this point.

Editing in Pro Tools

Next, you will do some editing on your project. In the following sections, you will use the Zoomer, Trimmer, and Scrubber tools to modify the project so that it sounds more complete.

Review the Project

Before you begin editing this project, you should familiarize yourself with the progression of the movie. To do so, you can navigate along the Timeline to get a feel for the movie's transitional points.

Because Pro Tools provides a nonlinear editing environment, you can instantly jump to any point on the Timeline at any time. You can use the Selector tool to click at different points within the project and use the Video window to view the action based on the location of the playback cursor.

Experiment with the Selector tool to update the Video window:

- Click on various parts of the Video track with the SELECTOR tool to get a rough idea where the main action transitions fall on the Timeline. Use the SPACE BAR to control playback.
- Experiment with making selections on the Video track and the Audio tracks; try to select a scene from beginning to end and play it back.

 The Video window will always reflect the start time of a Timeline selection. When you are making a selection based on the Video track, you may find it useful to locate the end point first and select backward to the start.

Add Sound Effects

The session is still missing some sound effects. During this part of the project, you will use various editing techniques to add the missing material. Refer to Chapter 6 as needed for details on editing techniques.

Add Wind

The first sound effect that you will add occurs at the point in the movie when the squire walks through the castle. You will need to add the sound of wind to match the action using the Wind02 sound effect in your Region List.

Place the Wind02 region onto the FX 01 track and spot it to the proper location:

1. Identify the FX 01 track on screen and make sure it is visible.

2. Select the **WIND02** region in the Region List (Edit window). If necessary, use the scroll bar to scroll the list until the region is visible.

3. Drag the **WIND02** region from the Region List to any open space on the FX 01 track.

4. Click the **SPOT** button in the upper-left corner of the Edit window to activate Spot mode. (You might have to reposition the Video window first.)

5. With the **GRABBER** tool, click on the region that you just placed on the FX 01 track. The Spot Dialog box will open.

The Spot dialog box

6. If needed, set the Time Scale to **MIN:SECS**.

7. In the Start field, type **0:13.680** (Min:Sec) and click **OK**. The region will move to the start time you typed.

8. Click the **SLIP** button to return to Slip mode.

Audition the sound effect:

1. Activate loop playback by choosing **OPTIONS > LOOP PLAYBACK**. The Play button will display a looping arrow to indicate Loop Playback mode.

2. With the region still selected, press the **SPACE BAR** to play back the sound effect with the picture. During playback, you can solo the FX 01 track by clicking the **S** button under the track name.

*Pro Tools also lets you toggle Solo mode on and off for any track containing the Edit cursor by pressing **SHIFT+S** on the computer's QWERTY keyboard.*

3. When you are finished, press the **SPACE BAR** again to stop playback and click the **S** button, if necessary, to take the track out of Solo mode.

Edit Wind

The wind you've added is a little longer than the scene to which it corresponds. You will use this extra time before and after the scene to create a fade-in and a fade-out effect.

Create a fade-in and a fade-out on the Wind02 region:

1. If it is not already selected, click on the **A...Z** button in the Edit window to enable Commands Keyboard Focus mode. The **A...Z** button is located above the tracks display area on the right. When selected, the button becomes highlighted in yellow.

Clicking the Commands Keyboard Focus button

 Commands Keyboard Focus mode gives you access to many Pro Tools commands at the touch of a single keystroke. Focus keys are covered throughout the Pro Tools training coursework and are summarized in the Pro Tools 310M course.

2. Using the **GRABBER** tool, click the Wind02 region to select it.

3. Press **E** on your keyboard to activate Zoom Toggle. The selected region will expand to fill the available space in the Edit window.

4. With the **SCRUBBER** tool, click and drag near the start of the region.

   Gradually move the mouse back and forth while viewing the Video window. Locate the point where the scene changes to the squire walking. Release the mouse to position the insertion point at this spot.

5. Press **D** on your keyboard to create a fade-in.

6. With the **SCRUBBER** tool, click and drag near the end of the region.

   Gradually move the mouse back and forth while viewing the Video window. Locate the point where the squire approaches the stairs before the scene changes to the king's throne room. Release the mouse to position the insertion point at this spot.

7. Press **G** on your keyboard to create a fade-out.

8. Press **E** on your keyboard to deactivate Zoom Toggle, returning the session to the previous view.

Add Drumstick Drop

The next sound effect you need to add is the Drumstick Drop. For this sound effect, you will need to sync the impact point of the sound effect to the point in the movie at which the drumstick hits the plate. To do this, you will use a Sync Point.

Place the Drumstick Drop sound effect on the FX 05 track and identify a Sync Point:

1. Identify the FX 05 track on screen and make sure it is visible.
2. Locate the DRUMSTICK DROP region in the Region List and drag it onto any open space of the FX 05 track.
3. With the region selected, press **E** on your keyboard to activate Zoom Toggle and zoom in on the region.
4. With the SCRUBBER tool, click and drag across the region until you hear the sound of the drumstick making impact. Release the mouse to position the insertion point as close as possible to the beginning of the impact.
5. Choose REGION > IDENTIFY SYNC POINT. A small triangle will appear in the lower part of the region, under the insertion cursor, signifying a Sync Point at that spot.
6. Press **E** on your keyboard to deactivate Zoom Toggle, returning the session to the previous view.

Having identified a Sync Point in the sound effect region, you will now need to determine the corresponding point in the movie and spot the sound effect to that point.

Spot the Drumstick Drop sound effect to the movie:

1. With the SCRUBBER tool selected, click and drag on the Video track to locate the point when the drumstick hits the plate. The impact should occur somewhere between 0:13.200 and 0:13.500 (Min:Sec). Take note of the exact time location shown in the Main Counter.
2. Click the SPOT button in the Edit window to activate Spot mode.
3. With the GRABBER tool, click on the DRUMSTICK DROP region on the FX 05 track. The Spot Dialog box will appear.
4. In the Sync Point field, type the time that you noted in Step 1. Be sure to use the same Time Scale in this dialog box as displayed in the Main Counter (Min:Sec).
5. Click **OK**. The region's Sync Point will be spotted to the point where the drumstick hits the plate.
6. Click the SLIP button to return to Slip mode.

Audition the sound effect:

1. Using the SELECTOR tool, place the insertion point somewhere around 0:12.000.
2. Press the SPACE BAR to play back the sound effect with the picture.
3. When finished, press the SPACE BAR again to stop playback.
4. Press ENTER (Windows) or RETURN (Mac) to return to the beginning of the Timeline.

Change the Music

Next, you will need to replace the existing music for the project to give the soundtrack a different emotional undertone. To do this, you will select from the music that you imported to the Region List and place the selected music onto the MX New track.

Audition the music in the Region List:

1. Locate the New Music 1 and New Music 2 regions on the Region List. If necessary, scroll the Region List until the New Music regions are visible.

2. ALT-CLICK (Windows) or OPTION-CLICK (Mac) on the NEW MUSIC 1 region in the Region List. The audio region will play back as long as you hold down the mouse button.

3. Release the mouse button to stop the audition.

4. Repeat Steps 2 and 3, auditioning the NEW MUSIC 2 region.

5. After listening to each music region, select the region that you feel is more appropriate for the project. We will refer to this as the Preferred New Music region for descriptive purposes. (You can use either region to complete the project.)

Place the selected region onto the MX New Audio track:

1. Locate the MX Mix track and the MX New track in the Edit window.

2. Using the GRABBER tool, click on the MX_MIX region on the MX Mix track. The region will become highlighted.

3. Hold the START key (Windows) or CONTROL key (Mac) while dragging the PREFERRED NEW MUSIC region from the Region List onto the MX NEW track. The region will appear on the track, aligned to the same start time as the MX_Mix region above it.

 Holding the START key (Windows) or CONTROL key (Mac) while dragging a region from the Region List constrains its placement to begin at the insertion point or the start time of a selection.

4. Mute the MX Mix track by clicking the **M** button under the track name in the Edit window.

5. Press ENTER or RETURN to move the insertion point to the beginning of the Timeline, followed by the SPACE BAR to play back the session with the new music track.

6. At the end of the clip, press the SPACE BAR a second time to stop playback.

Save Work in Progress

You have now completed the editing tasks for your project. You should take this opportunity to save your work.

Save your work:

1. Choose FILE > SAVE to save your progress up to this point.

Mixing in Pro Tools

Now that all of the editing is complete, you will use some of the mixing features in Pro Tools to add some real-time processing and blend all of the sound elements together.

Remove the Hum

The Squire 01 region on the DX 03 track contains a low-frequency hum that you will now need to remove. Using some creative EQ, you can eliminate most of the hum. To do so, you will need to locate and zoom in on the region, insert an EQ plug-in on the track, and selectively adjust the EQ settings.

Locate and zoom in on the Squire 01 region:

1. Click on the SQUIRE 01 region in the Region List to select the region on the Track Playlist. If necessary, scroll the Region List until the region is visible (toward the bottom).

Click on the region in the Region List to select it.

2. Press **E** on your keyboard to activate Zoom Toggle and zoom in. The Squire 01 region will expand to fill the Edit window.

Insert the EQ III 1-Band on the DX 03 track:

1. Choose WINDOW > MIX to activate the Mix window or press CTRL+= (Windows) or COMMAND+= (Mac).

2. Locate the channel strip for the DX 03 track.

3. Click on INSERT SELECTOR A for the track and choose PLUG-IN > EQ > EQ 3 1-BAND (MONO) from the pop-up menu. The EQ III 1-band plug-in window will appear.

The EQ III 1-band plug-in window

Adjust the EQ settings to reduce the hum:

1. Solo the DX 03 track by clicking on the **S** button just above the Volume Fader in the Mix window.
2. Press the SPACE BAR to initiate playback. With Loop Playback enabled, the region will loop until playback is stopped.
3. In the EQ III 1-Band plug-in window, activate a Notch filter in the TYPE section and drag the gray ball in the graphic display to the left until you hear the hum reduced (around 60 Hz).
4. Press the SPACE BAR to stop playback.
5. Close the plug-in window and un-solo the track.
6. Press CTRL+= (Windows) or COMMAND+= (Mac) to toggle to the Edit window and press **E** on your keyboard to return the session to the previous view.

Add Reverb

Next, you will need to add some reverb to the FX 08 track to help it fit into the rest of the mix. This project includes an Auxiliary Input track that has already been configured with the D-Verb plug-in assigned and the track input assigned to Bus 1-2 (Reverb).

Assign a reverb send on the FX 08 track:

1. Press CTRL+= (Windows) or COMMAND+= (Mac) to toggle to the Mix window.
2. Locate the FX 08 channel strip for the Skunk FX.
3. Click on the SEND SELECTOR A for the track and choose BUS > REVERB (STEREO). The Send A window will appear.

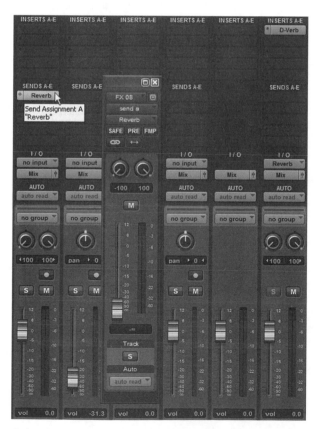

Selecting a send assignment opens the Send window (foreground)

Increase the Send A level on the FX 08 track:

1. Click the SOLO button in the Send A window to solo the FX 08 track.
2. Press CTRL+= (Windows) or COMMAND+= (Mac) to toggle to the Edit window.
3. Using the SELECTOR tool, select the audio near the end of the Skunk Group region group (starting around 0:31.500 and continuing through the end of the region).
4. With Loop Playback enabled, press the SPACE BAR to begin playback.
5. While listening to the track, raise the level on the send fader to introduce the reverb.

    The reverb will play back while the FX 08 track is soloed because the Reverb track is set to Solo Safe mode. Solo Safe is commonly used on Auxiliary tracks to prevent them from being muted when another track is soloed.

 You can place a track in Solo Safe mode by CTRL-CLICKING *(Windows) or* COMMAND-CLICKING *(Mac) on the Solo button in the Edit or Mix window.*

 More information on Solo Safe mode can be found in the Pro Tools 110 course.

6. When you are satisfied with the results, press the SPACE BAR to stop playback.
7. Press the SOLO button to take the track out of solo mode and close the Send A window.

Enhance the Knock

This project includes a knock sweetener effect that sounds a bit dull. You will need to add some delay and EQ to liven up the sound. You will add delay using an AudioSuite plug-in and add EQ using a 7-Band EQ III plug-in insert.

A Note about AudioSuite Plug-Ins

You will be using the DigiRack Delay AudioSuite plug-in to add a delay sound effect. AudioSuite plug-ins behave differently from RTAS in that they are not real-time processors. These plug-ins process and modify audio files on disk, rather than adding the plug-in effect in real time.

 More information on AudioSuite processing can be found in the Pro Tools 110 course.

Zoom in on the Knock Sweetener region on the FX 04 track:

1. Select KNOCK SWEETENER in the Region List to select the region in the Track Playlist.
2. Press E on your keyboard to activate Zoom Toggle. The Knock Sweetener region will expand to fill the Edit window.

Use the DigiRack Delay to process the Knock Sweetener region:

1. Choose AUDIOSUITE > DELAY > DELAY. The DigiRack Delay plug-in window will appear on screen.

2. Verify that USE IN PLAYLIST is highlighted. If it isn't, click to highlight it.

3. Adjust the parameter settings to create a long echo effect. Try the following settings as a starting point:

   - Mix = 25%
   - Delay = 500.00ms
   - Feedback = 40%

DigiRack Delay plug-in

 The Delay plug-in includes separate parameters for the left and right sides. Since you are using it on a mono track, you only need to set the parameters for the left side.

4. To audition the effect, click PREVIEW. During Preview, you may continue to adjust the effect parameters using the sliders, as desired.

5. When you are satisfied with the effect, click PROCESS to process the audio region. A new region will be generated, combining the source audio with the Delay effect and replacing the selected region.

6. Close the Delay plug-in window to reduce on-screen clutter.

Add the EQ III 7-Band to Insert A on the FX 04 track:

1. Using the Inserts column in the Edit window, click on INSERT SELECTOR A for the FX 04 track and choose PLUG-IN > EQ > EQ 3 7-BAND (MONO). The EQ III plug-in window will open.

Clicking Insert Selector A in the Edit window

2. With Loop Playback still active, press the SPACE BAR to start playback. The Knock Sweetener region will repeat until playback is stopped.

3. Experiment by raising and lowering the colored balls in the graphic display of the EQ III plug-in window.

4. When you are satisfied with the results, close the plug-in window and press the SPACE BAR to stop playback.

5. Press E on your keyboard to return the session to the previous view.

Save Work in Progress

You have now created a complete mix for your project. You should take this opportunity to save your work.

Save your work:

1. Choose FILE > SAVE to save your progress up to this point.

Listen to the Automated Mix

This portion of the project allows you to experience some of the power that automation offers by activating the preset automation included in the session.

Throughout this project, you have completed your work with all of the track automation modes set to AUTO OFF. Now you will switch the tracks to AUTO READ mode and play back the session using the previously recorded automation playlists.

 Automation features are covered in detail throughout the courses in the Avid Certified Training Program.

Enable Auto Read automation mode for all tracks:

1. Choose WINDOW > MIX or press CTRL+= (Windows) or COMMAND+= (Mac) to activate the Mix window.

2. ALT-CLICK (Windows) or OPTION-CLICK (Mac) on the AUTOMATION MODE SELECTOR for any track and choose READ. All of the tracks in the session will switch to Read automation mode.

Selecting Read mode from the Automation Mode selector (Mix window)

3. If needed, choose VIEW > NARROW MIX to maximize the number of channel strips being displayed on screen.

Mix window in Narrow Mix view showing all tracks

4. Press ENTER (Windows) or RETURN (Mac) to move to the beginning of the Timeline, followed by the SPACE BAR to play back the session. The Volume Faders and Pan knobs will move automatically to help create a more dynamic mix.

5. When the clip ends, press the SPACE BAR a second time to stop playback.

Finishing Your Work

Now that the project is mixed, you will need to create a bounce of the movie to add your version of the soundtrack to the movie file. This will enable the file to be played in a standard movie player application with the soundtrack you've created so that you can share your work with others.

Lastly, you will need to archive your work. Through the process of creating a project you generate many files, not all of which are needed for the completed session. By archiving your work, you are able to preserve your work without taking up excess disk space due to unnecessary files.

Bounce the Movie

You will use the Bounce to Movie command to add your soundtrack mix to the movie file.

Bounce your mix into the movie file:

1. Choose WINDOW > EDIT or press CTRL+= (Windows) or COMMAND+= (Mac) to activate the Edit window.

2. With the GRABBER tool, click on the GiftBasket region on the Video track to select it.

3. Choose FILE > BOUNCE TO > QUICKTIME MOVIE. The Bounce dialog box will appear on screen.

4. Click BOUNCE. A Save Bounce As dialog box will appear on screen.

5. Select a location for the movie file in the SAVE IN section of the dialog box and enter a name for your file in the FILE NAME field.

6. Click SAVE. You will hear playback begin as Pro Tools creates a QuickTime movie containing your mix and the Video track.

Archive Your Work

Now that your project is complete, you will need to back it up for storage. On a real-world project, you might also need to deliver the session to the client. Because many files are associated with a session, there is a potential that something could get lost if the archival process isn't completed properly. Fortunately, Pro Tools has many features to help ensure that you keep the files you need and remove the files you do not.

In this process, you will complete the following steps:

1. Remove unused audio files and regions that are consuming space on your hard drive.

2. Use the Save Copy In command to "collect" all of the audio and video files and copy them to a new location.

3. Use the Compact Selected command to remove the unused portions of each audio file in the copied session.

 The archival process will permanently remove any audio that is not currently being used in the session. This could limit your creative possibilities, should you need to revise some aspect of the session in the future. Perform this process only after the project is complete.

Remove Unused Material

To remove unused audio files and regions, complete the following steps:

1. Click on the REGION LIST POP-UP menu and choose SELECT > UNUSED. All of the regions that are not included on a Track Playlist will be selected.

Click the Region List pop-up menu to select unused regions.

2. Click on the REGION LIST POP-UP menu a second time and choose CLEAR. The Clear Regions dialog box will appear on screen.

3. Click REMOVE in the Clear Regions dialog box to remove the regions from your session. The audio files will be removed from the session without being deleted from the drive. If you later find that you need an audio file that has been removed, you can re-import it into your session.

Collect Session Files in a New Location

To save a copy of your session and all associated files, do the following:

1. Choose FILE > SAVE COPY IN. The Save Session Copy dialog box will appear on screen.

2. In the ITEMS TO COPY area, select the following:
   - All Audio Files
   - Movie/Video Files

3. Click the OK button. A Save dialog box will appear.

4. Choose a directory to store the session copy and name the copy of the session. If possible, it is best to choose a directory on a drive other than the one used for the current session.

5. Click the SAVE button. Pro Tools will begin processing the save, copying the session file along with all of the audio and video files into the directory you chose.

6. Choose FILE > CLOSE SESSION to close the original session. If you are prompted to save, choose SAVE or OK to save your changes in the original session. (It will be saved with the unused material removed.)

Compact Your Session

You have one more step to complete your archive: compacting. Most regions in a session reference only a part of a larger audio recording. Because the copied session is now complete, it is safe to compact the session. Compacting is the process of removing the audio from a file that is not used by any region. Hence, only the used portions of the audio files remain, reducing the amount of disk space being consumed.

To compact your project's audio files, do the following:

1. From the File menu, choose OPEN SESSION.

2. Navigate to the copy of your project that you created in the previous section; select the session file and click OPEN. A dialog box may appear, indicating that the original disk allocation cannot be used; click NO to avoid saving a report.

3. When the session opens, click on the REGION LIST POP-UP menu and choose SELECT > ALL. All of the regions in the Region List will be selected.

4. Click on the REGION LIST POP-UP menu a second time and choose COMPACT. The Compact dialog box will appear on screen with a description of the compacting process.

5. Click COMPACT to compact the audio files. Pro Tools will begin modifying the files.

6. When finished, save your work by choosing FILE > SAVE and close your session by choosing FILE > CLOSE SESSION.

This concludes the Post Hands-On Project.

PART IV

Course Completion

Components

- Additional Projects

- Course Completion Exam

Overview

Part IV of the Pro Tools 101 course can be completed in an instructor-led environment at an official Pro Tools training center. In this part of the course, you will have the opportunity to work with additional project material, including music sessions by major-label recording artists and post-production sessions for commercial television advertisements and/or movie trailers. Upon completing the coursework, you will be eligible to enroll in the Pro Tools 110 course to continue your Pro Tools training and further your pursuit of Avid Pro Tools certification.

Overview

Information for Course Completion

This section provides information for completing the Pro Tools 101 course through an official Avid Authorized Training Partner. Included are instructions for locating a training center, descriptions of the additional project material that is available, a description of the course assessment exam and completion certificate, and information on the free plug-in promotion currently offered with enrollment in the Pro Tools 110 course.

Locating a Training Center

The Pro Tools 101 course can be completed at any of the 250-plus Avid Authorized Training Partner facilities located in more than 30 countries worldwide. Training centers offering the Pro Tools 101 course include colleges, technical programs, trade schools, high schools, and other institutions. Depending on the school's training format, Pro Tools courses may span days, weeks, or semesters and may or may not be integrated within a broader educational curriculum.

Avid Authorized Training Partner locations have the ability to deliver exams and certification directly, giving students additional enrollment benefits. With locations in countries such as Australia, Canada, China, France, Germany, Ireland, the Netherlands, Spain, Switzerland, the United Kingdom, the United States, and others, official Pro Tools training is available in most major cities worldwide.

A list of available training centers can be found on the Avid website (go to www.avid.com/US/support/training/find-partner). The web-based partner locator can be used to search for training centers by name or by geographic location.

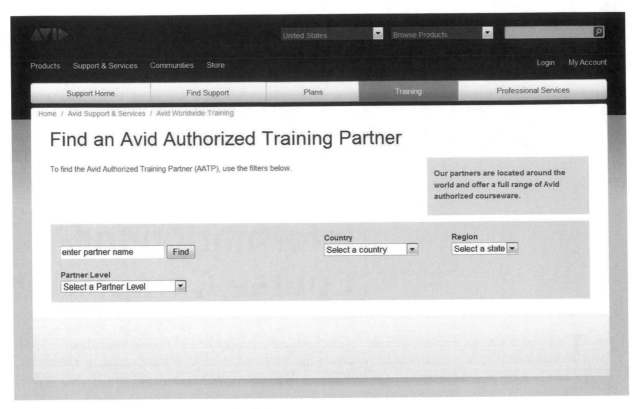

Training partner lookup page on the Avid website

Additional Projects

Additional project materials are available at official training partner facilities. As part of your Pro Tools 101 course completion and other Pro Tools courses that you enroll in, you will have the opportunity to work with many of these projects. (Check with the school for completion requirements and project availability.)

Some of the projects that are commonly available include the following:

- **Black Eyed Peas, "Hey Mama."** This project is a live recording of the band mixed through a VENUE system and recorded as a multi-track session into Pro Tools.
- *The Time Machine.* This project, a movie trailer for the 2002 movie staring Guy Pearce, Samantha Mumba, Jeremy Irons, and Orlando Jones, features video footage from the movie along with dialogue, music, and sound effects. Session and media files provided courtesy of Dreamworks, SKG.
- **Ugly Duckling.** This television commercial for Ugly Duckling Car Rental is an ideal beginning project for students interested in post-production applications for Pro Tools. Session and media files provided courtesy of Greg Kuehn at Peligro Music & Sound Design.

- **Devil's River.** This project created for the Nature Conservancy to promote conservation of the Devil's River land area includes audio backgrounds and some narration along with a QuickTime movie. Students can edit, sync, and mix this project to their own tastes to create a documentary fit for broadcast. Session and media files provided courtesy of Match Frame, San Antonio.
- *NewsRadio.* In this scene from the U.S. sitcom, one of the characters interviews fellow employees about sharing his apartment. The project contains video footage with audio that lends itself to editing and replacing dialogue. Footage produced by Brillstein/Grey Entertainment; session and media files provided courtesy of BGE.
- Session files of releases by popular recording artists, including:
  - Nine Inch Nails, "Only"
  - Paul Oakenfold, "Bleeder"
  - M83, "Don't Save Us from the Flames"
  - 311, "Don't Tread on Me"
  - Chevelle, "Send the Pain Below"
  - Romero/Rich Tozzoli, "La Vida Nueva"
  - Westside Connection, "Gangsta Nation"
  - Ozomatli, *Live at the Fillmore*

Course Assessment Exam

The Pro Tools 101 assessment exam consists of 50 multiple-choice questions. The exam is conducted at Avid Authorized Training Partner facilities upon course completion. Students have a specified time limit to answer all questions. A passing score on the assessment exam entitles you to receive a Certificate of Completion for the course.

Certificate of Completion

Upon successful completion of the coursework and assessment exam, you will receive a Certificate of Completion to formally recognize your accomplishment. The Pro Tools 101 completion certificate signifies that you are prepared to begin the Pro Tools 110 course and continue your progress toward User, Operator, or Expert Certification.

Pro Tools 110 Promotion

After completing the Pro Tools 101 course, you will be eligible to enroll in the next course, Pro Tools 110, at any Avid Authorized Training Partner facility. Avid is currently running a promotional offer that allows you to choose one free plug-in when you enroll and attend the Pro Tools 110 course at any official Avid Authorized Training Partner facility. Upon meeting the promotion requirements, you will receive an activation card with a special Pro Tools 110 Activation Code for a plug-in of your choice from a select list.

PT 110 Activation Card

To obtain a license for your PT 110 plug-in:

1. Visit www.ilok.com to sign up for an iLok.com account.

2. Visit http://secure.digidesign.com/activation/ to input your activation code, select your plug-in choice, and enter your iLok.com user ID. Your iLok.com User ID is the name you create for your iLok.com account. This process will transfer the plug-in license into your iLok.com account.

3. Visit www.ilok.com to transfer the licenses from your iLok.com account to your iLok USB Smart Key.

PT 110 Activation Code:

9340-56405-00 Rev.A

Receive a free plug-in with the Pro Tools 110 course.

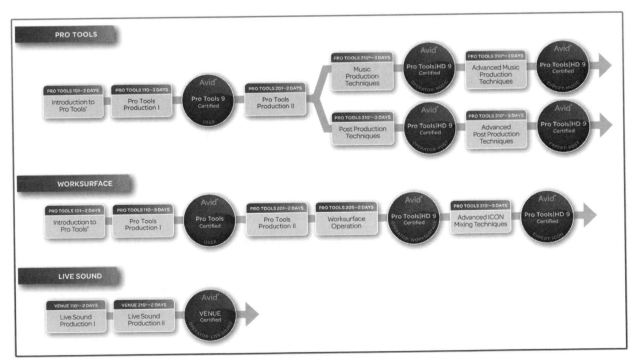

Avid audio coursework and certification options

Appendix A

DigiRack Plug-Ins

The following DigiRack TDM, RTAS, and AudioSuite plug-ins are installed with Pro Tools 9:

- **DigiRack Click** (TDM and RTAS). Creates an audio click during session playback to serve as a metronome-type tempo reference when performing and recording.
- **DigiRack Dither** (TDM and RTAS). Minimizes quantization artifacts when reducing the bit depth of an audio signal.
- **DigiRack D-Verb** (TDM, RTAS, and AudioSuite). Provides studio-quality reverb effects for an audio signal.
- **DigiRack Dynamics III**: Compressor/Limiter, Expander/Gate, De-Esser (TDM, RTAS, and AudioSuite). Provides compression/limiting, expansion/gate, and de-esser processing for level control and gain reduction.
- **DigiRack EQ III**: 7-Band, 2- to 4-Band, 1-Band (TDM, RTAS, and AudioSuite). Provides three formats for equalization, allowing you to choose the number of bands you need to properly EQ each track.
- **DigiRack Mod Delay II** (TDM, RTAS, and AudioSuite). Provides five different plug-ins for delay (echo) effects of various lengths: Short Delay (up to 43 ms), Slap Delay (up to 171 ms), Medium Delay (up to 341 ms), Long Delay (up to 683 ms), and Extra Long Delay (up to 2.73 seconds).
- **DigiRack Pitch** (TDM only). Provides pitch transposition for pitch correction, sound design, and special effects purposes.
- **DigiRack POW-r Dither** (TDM and RTAS). An advanced type of dither providing optimal bit-depth reduction for critical mixdown and mastering tasks.
- **DigiRack ReWire** (RTAS). Provides real-time audio and MIDI streaming between Pro Tools and ReWire client applications, with sample-accurate synchronization and transport control.
- **DigiRack Signal Generator** (TDM, RTAS, and AudioSuite). Produces audio test tones in a variety of frequencies, waveforms, and amplitudes, such as reference signals for calibration.

- **DigiRack Signal Tools**: SurroundScope, PhaseScope (TDM and RTAS). Provides surround metering for multi-channel track types with SurroundScope (Pro Tools HD and Pro Tools with Complete Production Toolkit 2 only) or signal level and phase information for stereo tracks with PhaseScope.
- **DigiRack TimeAdjuster** (TDM and RTAS). Provides compensation for delays due to TDM or RTAS routing; also provides gain compensation (+/– 24 dB) and phase inversion for correcting out-of-phase signals.
- **DigiRack Trim** (TDM and RTAS). Can be used to attenuate an audio signal from –infinity to +6 dB or +12 dB; a multi-mono Trim plug-in provides muting control over individual channels of a multi-channel track.

The following AudioSuite-only DigiRack plug-ins are installed with Pro Tools 9:

- **DigiRack D-Fx** (Chorus, Flanger, Multi-tap Delay, Ping-pong Delay). Adds chorusing (shimmering), flanging (swirling), or delay (echo) effects to a signal, based on the selected plug-in.
- **DigiRack Pitch Shift**. Adjusts the pitch of any source audio file with or without changing its duration.
- **DigiRack Time Compression/Expansion**. Adjusts the duration of selected regions, increasing or decreasing their length without affecting pitch.
- **DigiRack Time Shift**. Provides high-quality time compression and expansion (TCE) algorithms and formant correct pitch shifting.
- **DC Offset Removal**. Removes DC offset (a type of audio artifact) from audio files to prevent pops and clicks in edited material.
- **Duplicate**. Duplicates the selected audio in place, creating a new, continuous audio file.
- **Gain**. Boosts or lowers a selected region's amplitude by a specific amount.
- **Invert**. Reverses the polarity of selected audio.
- **Normalize**. Optimizes the volume level of an audio selection to correct low-amplitude signals or inconsistent volume levels.
- **Reverse**. Replaces audio with a reversed version of the selection to create a reverse envelope effect or backward playback of a selection.

Appendix B

Creative Collection Plug-Ins

The following Creative Collection effects plug-ins are installed with Pro Tools 9:

- **Chorus.** Applies a short modulated delay to give depth and space to the audio signal.
- **Decimator.** Provides bit-crushing, down-sampling, clipping, rectifying, and mangling effects.
- **Distortion.** Colors the audio signal with various types and amounts of distortion.
- **Dynamic Delay.** Provides a delay (echo) that can synchronize to the Pro Tools session tempo and be modulated by an Envelope follower.
- **Enhancer.** Enhances the low and high broadband frequencies of the audio signal.
- **Ensemble.** Applies fluid, shimmering modulation effects to the audio signal.
- **Filter Gate.** Adds aggressive or subtle rhythmic filtering effects to audio signals.
- **Flanger.** Applies a short modulating delay to the audio signal; the Rate control can be synchronized to the Pro Tools session tempo in various rhythmic patterns.
- **Frequency Shifter.** Changes the pitch of the audio signal.
- **FuzzWah.** Colors the audio signal with various types and amounts of distortion and wah filtering.
- **Kill-EQ.** Zaps out the low, mid, or high broadband frequency range from an audio signal for instantaneous "kill switch"–type EQ effects.
- **Multi-Chorus.** Applies a thick, complex Chorus effect to the audio signal, with a user-selectable number of voices (layers).
- **Multi-Tap Delay.** Applies up to six delay lines to the audio signal with selectable rhythmic values, levels, and pan for each.
- **Non-Linear Reverb.** Applies special gated or reversed Reverb effects to the audio signal, creating a synthetic, processed ambience.
- **Phaser.** Applies the classic "whooshy," "squishy" phaser sound to an audio signal; the Rate control can be synchronized to the Pro Tools session tempo in various rhythmic patterns.

- **Reverb.** Applies reverberation to an audio signal to create a sense of room or space.
- **Spring Reverb.** Applies the familiar analog spring reverb sound found in many classic guitar amps and vintage audio gear.
- **Stereo Width.** Creates a wider stereo presence for mono audio signals.
- **Talkbox.** Adds voice-like resonances to audio signals.
- **Vintage Filter.** Applies a modulating, resonant filter to the audio signal.

The following Creative Collection instrument plug-ins are installed with Pro Tools 9:

- **Xpand².** A virtual workstation synthesizer featuring multi-sampled instruments, FM synthesis, wavetable synthesis, and virtual analog synthesis.
- **Boom.** A virtual drum machine featuring a broad range of percussion sounds, paired with a simple, drum-machine-style pattern sequencer.
- **Vacuum.** A virtual analog synthesizer focused on creating rich timbres with a lot of sonic control and employing a new vacuum-tube synthesis method.
- **DB33.** A virtual organ with a focus on re-creating the sounds and controllability of classic tonewheel organs and rotating speaker cabinets.
- **Mini Grand.** A virtual piano instrument with seven different acoustic piano sounds to suit a range of styles.
- **Structure Free.** A sample player that brings the world of Structure-compatible sample libraries to Pro Tools.

Index

A

Absolute Grid mode, 157
adding
dither, 239–240
EQ, 231–232
markers to sessions, 146–151
Maxim plug-ins, 238–239
patches, 120
reverb, 233–234, 259–260
sound effects, 253–256
tracks, 65–68
virtual instruments, 222–223, 224
Add Key Signature button, 123
Add Meter Change button, 121
Add Tempo Change button, 122
adjacent tracks, selecting material on, 136
Advanced Instrument Research (A. I. R.), 10
AES/EBU (Audio Engineering Society/European Broadcast Union), 16–17
After Playback scrolling option, 71
AIFC (Audio Interchange File Compressed), 93
AIFF (Audio Interchange File Format), 63, 93
alias tones, 15
Alt/Option modifier, 46
amplitude, 14–15
measuring, 14–15
resolution, 16
analog audio, 15–16. *See also* **audio; digital audio**
analog-to-digital conversion, 15–16

applying
Edit tools, 45–49
Grabber tool, 165–167
selections, 135–140
Tab keys, 139
Trim tool, 168–169
undo operations, 175–178
Universe view, 130–131
virtual instruments, 113–121
archiving projects, 241–242, 265–266. *See also* **projects**
ASCII characters, incompatibility, 25
audio, 4
analog-to-digital conversion, 15–16
bouncing, 199
files, 29, 84
deleting, 88–89
naming, 86–87
types, 63
formatting, 227–231
importing, 94–100, 227–228
CDs, 99–100
file formats, 92–93
managing, 83–84
recording, 77–89
saving, 231
sessions, 70
storage requirements, 78
tracks, 67. *See also* tracks
Audio Import Options dialog box, 97

S

sample-based operations, MIDI, 106
sample rates, 15
    configuring, 63–64
    importing, 92
    Structure Free, 119–121
Samples Ruler, 54
Sampling Theorem, 15
Save Bounce As dialog box, 205
Save Copy In command, 196
saving
    audio, 231
    mixing, 234
    sessions, 72–73, 196–198, 227, 249
scales, 51–54
Score Editor window, 44
scores
    notation, 4–5. *See also* notation
    printing, 236–238
scrolling
    options, 71, 154
    Universe view, 131
Scrubber tool, 48
SD II (Sound Designer II), 93
selecting
    channels, 120
    output pairs, 202
    track nameplates, 137
selections
    applying, 135–140
    markers, 151
    on multiple tracks, 136–138
    nudging, 171
    out points, 138
    restoring, 177–178
    Timeline, 132–134, 136
    types of, 131–135
selectors
    inputs, 182–186
    outputs, 182–186
Selector tool, 47, 132, 134–135, 136
sends, 180, 186–187
Separate Region command, 163–165
sequencers, MIDI, 104
sessions
    audio, adding, 70
    backups, 30, 196–198
    compacting, 266
    configuring, 62–70

    creating, 61–75
    files, 28–29. *See also* files
    installing projects, 214
    locating, 73–75, 244
    markers, adding, 146–151
    media, importing into, 90–101
    opening, 73–75
    parameters, configuring, 63–64
    saving, 72–73, 227, 249
    sharing, 198
    templates, 63
    views, modifying, 140–146
    windows, orienting, 217–218
setting up projects, 213–214
Setup menu, 35
sharing sessions, 198
shortcuts, formatting, 66
showing. *See also* viewing
    columns, 38
    controls, 39
Shuffle mode, 50, 156, 167
Sibelius Software Ltd., 10, 30
side columns
    Edit windows, 37
    Mix window, 42
signals
    configuring, 82
    MIDI, 4. *See also* MIDI
    routing controls, 41
signatures
    defaults, configuring, 123–124
    rulers, MIDI, 108
sizing
    files, calculating, 78
    Hardware Buffer Size (H/W Buffer Size), 32
    tracks, 140–142
    Universe view, 131
Slip mode, 50, 156, 166
smart keys, 31
Smart Tool, 49
Snap to Grid mode, 51, 157–158
songs
    bouncing, 240–241
    burning to CDs, 205–209
Sound Designer, 6
Sound Designer II (SD II), 7, 93
sound effects, adding, 253–256
S/PDIF (Sony/Philips Digital Interface), 16
split stereo files, 94
Spot Dialog box, 167

License Agreement/Notice of Limited Warranty

By opening the sealed disc container in this book, you agree to the following terms and conditions. If, upon reading the following license agreement and notice of limited warranty, you cannot agree to the terms and conditions set forth, return the unused book with unopened disc to the place where you purchased it for a refund.

License:
The enclosed software is copyrighted by the copyright holder(s) indicated on the software disc. You are licensed to copy the software onto a single computer for use by a single user and to a backup disc. You may not reproduce, make copies, or distribute copies or rent or lease the software in whole or in part, except with written permission of the copyright holder(s). You may transfer the enclosed disc only together with this license, and only if you destroy all other copies of the software and the transferee agrees to the terms of the license. You may not decompile, reverse assemble, or reverse engineer the software.

Notice of Limited Warranty:
The enclosed disc is warranted by Course Technology to be free of physical defects in materials and workmanship for a period of sixty (60) days from end user's purchase of the book/disc combination. During the sixty-day term of the limited warranty, Course Technology will provide a replacement disc upon the return of a defective disc.

Limited Liability:
THE SOLE REMEDY FOR BREACH OF THIS LIMITED WARRANTY SHALL CONSIST ENTIRELY OF REPLACEMENT OF THE DEFECTIVE DISC. IN NO EVENT SHALL COURSE TECHNOLOGY OR THE AUTHOR BE LIABLE FOR ANY OTHER DAMAGES, INCLUDING LOSS OR CORRUPTION OF DATA, CHANGES IN THE FUNCTIONAL CHARACTERISTICS OF THE HARDWARE OR OPERATING SYSTEM, DELETERIOUS INTERACTION WITH OTHER SOFTWARE, OR ANY OTHER SPECIAL, INCIDENTAL, OR CONSEQUENTIAL DAMAGES THAT MAY ARISE, EVEN IF COURSE TECHNOLOGY AND/OR THE AUTHOR HAS PREVIOUSLY BEEN NOTIFIED THAT THE POSSIBILITY OF SUCH DAMAGES EXISTS.

Disclaimer of Warranties:
COURSE TECHNOLOGY AND THE AUTHOR SPECIFICALLY DISCLAIM ANY AND ALL OTHER WARRANTIES, EITHER EXPRESS OR IMPLIED, INCLUDING WARRANTIES OF MERCHANTABILITY, SUITABILITY TO A PARTICULAR TASK OR PURPOSE, OR FREEDOM FROM ERRORS. SOME STATES DO NOT ALLOW FOR EXCLUSION OF IMPLIED WARRANTIES OR LIMITATION OF INCIDENTAL OR CONSEQUENTIAL DAMAGES, SO THESE LIMITATIONS MIGHT NOT APPLY TO YOU.

Other:
This Agreement is governed by the laws of the State of Massachusetts without regard to choice of law principles. The United Convention of Contracts for the International Sale of Goods is specifically disclaimed. This Agreement constitutes the entire agreement between you and Course Technology regarding use of the software.